D1596523

Collective Memory and
the Historical Past

Collective Memory and the Historical Past

Jeffrey Andrew Barash

The University of Chicago Press   CHICAGO & LONDON

The University of Chicago Press, Chicago 60637
The University of Chicago Press, Ltd., London
© 2016 by The University of Chicago
All rights reserved. Published 2016.
Printed in the United States of America

25 24 23 22 21 20 19 18 17 16   1 2 3 4 5

ISBN-13: 978-0-226-39915-7 (cloth)
ISBN-13: 978-0-226-39929-4 (e-book)
DOI: 10.7208/chicago/9780226399294.001.0001

Library of Congress Cataloging-in-Publicaiton Data
Names: Barash, Jeffrey Andrew, author.
Title: Collective memory and the historical past / Jeffrey Andrew Barash.
Description: Chicago ; London : The University of Chicago Press, 2016. |
    Includes bibliographical references and index.
Identifiers: LCCN 2016016553| ISBN 9780226399157 (cloth : alk. paper) |
    ISBN 9780226399294 (e-book)
Subjects: LCSH: Collective memory. | Memory—Social aspects. |
    Collective memory—Philosophy.
Classification: LCC BF378.S65 B366 2016 | DDC 128/.3—dc23 LC record
    available at https://lccn.loc.gov/2016016553

♾ This paper meets the requirements of ANSI/NISO Z39.48-1992
(Permanence of Paper).

For Silvana, who remembers

CONTENTS

ACKNOWLEDGMENTS

This work is the fruit of numerous of years of reflection during which I benefited from the support of several different institutions and from the advice, aid, and encouragement of many friends and colleagues. The late Paul Ricœur, under whose direction I worked at an early stage of my career at the University of Chicago and at the Husserl Archives in Paris, served as a member of the habilitation jury at the Université de Paris X–Nanterre, which examined my work entitled "Memory and Historicity." Our prolonged debates during the years that followed concerning the concept of collective memory were especially important for the elaboration of my present perspective.

I am grateful to the late Reinhart Koselleck, who served as my director at the University of Bielefeld under the auspices of an Alexander von Humboldt Foundation fellowship. The inspiration of his ideas is evident throughout this book, above all in relation to the themes of historicity and historical time.

I would like to thank Professors Lionel Gossman of Princeton University and Doron Mendels of the Hebrew University of Jerusalem, whose inspiration and encouragement were particularly important throughout the years of elaboration of this book. My work greatly benefited from the advice and encouragement of Professors Steven Aschheim, Aleida Assmann, Claudia Bickmann, Marcel Detienne, Dorothee Gelhard, Richard Kearney, John Michael Krois, Vivian Liska, Paul Mendes-Flohr, Jeffrey Olick, Svetlan Lacko Vidulić, and Silvio Yeschua.

I also extend my thanks to the late Paul Jenkins for sharing with me his insight on painting, and to David Brent of the University of Chicago Press for his encouragement and advice. I am grateful for the generous support of two institutions, which permitted me to elaborate this book in its present form: the Alexander von Humboldt Foundation in Bonn, Germany, and the School of Historical Studies of the Institute for Advanced Study in Princeton, where this work was completed. For their generosity and kindness during my stay in Princeton, I extend my special thanks to the Friends of the IAS. Unless otherwise indicated, all translations from foreign-language works are my own.

Introduction:
The Sources of Memory

"What does it mean to remember?" This question might seem commonplace when it is confined to the domain of events recalled in past individual experience; but even in this restricted sense, when memory recollects, for example, a first personal encounter with birth, or with death, the singularity of the remembered image places the deeper possibilities of human understanding in relief.

Beyond the theme of the remembrance of experienced events, my inquiry concerns the philosophical pertinence of the question, "What does it mean to remember?" It focuses not only on the ways in which the traditional answers to this question since the classical investigations of this theme by Plato and by Aristotle have determined specific philosophical orientations but, above all, on the significance and the scope of the question itself. This manner of interpreting memory situates it in relation to a range of human capacities—perception and imagination, volition and intellect—in the determination of Being or "reality." Far from taking memory to be a matter of philosophical abstraction, I argue in what follows that the predominant philosophical arguments regarding the significance and scope of memory owe their persuasive force in given historical periods to the fundamental convictions they convey concerning the sense of human existence and of human interaction in the sociopolitical sphere. Spanning the shifts in the predominant paradigms that have governed the interpretation of memory in the past, a wealth of conceptions of memory has been bequeathed to us by different epochs. Originally examined in traditional forms of metaphysical speculation, the theme of memory was radically reappraised in empiricist reflection on remembered experience as a source of personal identity, as it was fundamentally reoriented in conceptions of reminiscence as an ongoing retrieval of the collective past in the framework of a philosophy of history. In often unexpected ways, past reflection continues to set the semantic and conceptual framework for discussion of memory, even where past orientations have lost their earlier persuasive force. If, however, my analysis of memory in what follows takes as its starting point epoch-making shifts in the predominant paradigms that have governed the interpretation of memory, the evocation of these shifts serves only as a propaedeutic to its central theme: an investigation of the scope and significance of memory as it has emerged in contemporary discourse and contemporary theory. This analysis aims to bring to the fore the central place it has assumed, not only as a faculty among other faculties, serving as an object of cognitive or psychological analysis among individual or group test cases, but as a capacity to retain and communicatively share experience that is a precondition for human interaction.

In its contemporary guise, the question concerning the significance and scope of memory has come to fundamental expression in the current preoccupation with the topic of *collective* memory. *Collective memory*, as it has been termed since the pioneering works of Maurice Halbwachs and Walter Benjamin in the 1920s and 1930s, has indeed become not only a central intellectual focus for a wide variety of disciplines, but a principal concern in contemporary reflection more generally.[1] The present work is inspired by the conviction that the concept of collective memory requires theoretical clarification if it is to be legitimately studied in its own right and distinguished from phenomena in related fields, such as historical analysis or the interpretation of tradition, with which it is often confused. My purpose here is to undertake the work of clarification and to contribute to the theoretical definition of what has become an evasive concept.

As a social practice, collectively retained memory is, of course, as old as human civilization itself, encompassing the rich traditions of oral culture bequeathed since time immemorial. Although I aim to distinguish what I take to be the fluid and fragmentary sphere of collective memory from that of the methodologically elaborated field of history or the codified and institutionally sanctioned practices of tradition, collectively retained memory has at the same time always served as a prerequisite both for historical understanding and for tradition. Be this as it may, the term *collective memory* and the theoretical focus on it as a specific topic of investigation are of relatively recent vintage. The question then arises, "How might we account for the fact that collective memory has attained such widespread attention in our contemporary world?" This question, then, brings us back to our opening query, "What does it mean to remember?" as it is raised in the perspective of our contemporary epoch.

According to the initial presupposition stated at the outset of my analysis, the predominant conceptions or epoch-making paradigms that orient the interpretation of memory bring to expression not only ways of construing it as a faculty of recollection, but something more fundamental: memory engenders the possibility of bringing together past and present in view of the future, and this in turn elicits primary anthropological strivings that, at different historical moments, correspond to the diverse semantic and conceptual presuppositions concerning its significance and its scope. From this standpoint, the understanding of how memory functions in the contemporary world requires that we set in relief the novelty, not of collective memory per se, but of the unprecedented theoretical attention that is currently accorded to its sociopolitical function. The language in which it is couched, and the anthropological aspirations that this language brings to expression, stand out in particular clarity when beheld against the backdrop of previous presuppositions concerning the significance and scope of memory from which our contemporary preoccupation with memory has come to distinguish itself. For this reason, my discussion of the emergence of collective memory as a contemporary topic of investigation takes as its starting point a brief consideration of the principal sources of our historical ways of interpreting memory.

I

Since it is my task to ask the question, "What does it mean to remember" from a philosophical standpoint, I begin by inquiring into the presuppositions that such a standpoint involves. To this end I set in relief the responses of three past philosophical orientations to this question, less for their historical interest than for their seminal role as sources of the presuppositions concerning memory in the Western philosophical tradition. Beyond investigation of the extent to which such presuppositions bequeathed by the past continue to provide the conceptual framework for present understanding, my investigation concerns whether such presuppositions can be legitimately allowed to function *as* presuppositions, establishing the theoretical horizon within which the question of memory itself becomes intelligible.

Certainly, it is not due to its persuasive force in the modern context that we are struck by the first of these orientations: the interpretation of memory originally elaborated in terms of the Platonic theory of *reminiscence*. Indeed, it is perhaps the legacy of thought in what we designate as a post-metaphysical age that the Platonic doctrine of reminiscence, after inspiring centuries of philosophical speculation from Neoplatonism to medieval and Renaissance revivals of Plato, and finding a distant echo in the thought of Leibniz, has all but forfeited its traditional persuasive force.

At the heart of this doctrine stands Plato's interpretation in the *Meno* and *Phaedo* of the metaphysical scope of reminiscence as *anamnesis*. Where sense perception, according to this seminal argument, reveals only ephemeral figments of the senses, reminiscence recalls what *is* eternally, such as the good and the beautiful, to which, as Socrates argues in the *Phaedo*, we refer, as copies to the original, all the objects of sense perception.[2] In virtue of this ontological priority of recollection over sense perception, Socrates advanced the celebrated hypothesis, primarily in the *Meno* and the *Phaedo*, according to which learning is in truth reminiscence.

To appreciate the full ontological scope of this Platonic interpretation of memory, we must not forget the context in which it is presented in the *Phaedo*. At the outset of the dialogue, Phaedo, who witnessed Socrates's death, is asked to recount Socrates's conversation during the last hours of his life. Socrates's thoughts during this momentous day turn toward the theme of reminiscence, since this faculty, in its capacity to recall eternal Being, at the same time gives testimony to the immortality of the soul that reminisces: "If these [eternal] realities exist," as Socrates explains to Simmias, "does it not follow that our souls must exist too even before our birth?"[3]

If the Platonic doctrine of reminiscence as the immortal soul's recollection of the *a priori* source of ultimate truth has lost its persuasive force in the modern context, its main rival has been all the more influential in setting the conceptual framework for understanding memory's scope. At the outset of the modern period, the last great representative of Platonic reminiscence, Leibniz, brought into question the basic presuppositions of this rival position, which he traced to Aristotelian psychology and metaphysics, and which, to his mind, found its radical culmination point in Locke's empiricism, as expressed in *An Essay Concerning Human Understanding*. "There is something solid in what Plato called reminiscence," Leibniz wrote in the preface to his *Nouveaux essais sur l'entendement humain* (New essays on human understanding), referring to the doctrine of the innate ideas, recalled by *anamnesis*, and he then introduced his critique of Lockean empiricism's rejection of innate ideas in the following terms: "Although the author of the *Essay* says a thousand fine things of which I approve, our systems differ very much. His has more relation to Aristotle, and mine to Plato, although we diverge in many things from the doctrines of these two ancients."[4]

In relating Lockean empiricism to Aristotle in this manner, Leibniz recalled the ancient shift in perspective that Aristotle inaugurated in relation to the metaphysics of Plato. In terms of this shift, Aristotle articulated the key presuppositions concerning the scope of memory upon which Locke would later draw. At the same time, Locke's empiricism reached far beyond the confines of the Aristotelian tradition, just as Leibniz freely adapted Plato to his own very different frame of thought.[5] Indeed, Leibniz took account of these differences, as I noted, referring to the "many things" that mark his and Locke's divergence from the doctrines of the ancients. Nonetheless, Leibniz did not elaborate, at least in this regard, on the originality of Locke's theoretical standpoint in relation to the Aristotelian tradition; it is, however, this originality of Locke's that concerns us above all, as it enables us to set in relief for our analysis a second set of traditional assumptions regarding the scope of memory.

Aristotle redefined the scope of reminiscence above all in his short treatise "On Memory and Reminiscence," which is included among the treatises of the *Parva Naturalia*.[6] Whereas in this treatise Aristotle attributed memory not only to humans, but also to the more developed animal species, he limited the faculty of reminiscence to human beings. Memory, according to the Aristotelian theory, is defined as mere retention of past sense images; reminiscence as the consciousness of past images, however, is capable of deliberately employing them to recall ideas that have been forgotten and of associating them in a coherent order. The decisive point is that the faculty of reminiscence, for Aristotle, deploys images that *originate* with sense perception. Reminiscence recalls not *a priori* ideas in the Platonic sense, of which sense objects are considered to be mere fleeting copies, but images *derived* from sense perception. In this way the scope of reminiscence confines itself to the horizon of sense experience. Here reminiscence reveals a decisive affinity to its sister faculty, imagination: both memory and imagination, for Aristotle, are rooted in the perceptual image, of which their representations are simply weaker copies.

Finally, in this Aristotelian perspective even the intellect depends upon sense experience for the objects upon which it works. In a presupposition that Locke would push to its ultimate limit with his notion of the mind as a *tabula rasa*, Aristotle proposed the famous dictum according to which nothing is in the intellect which has not first been in the senses.

One readily understands why the decisive question for Leibniz, in his defense of innate ideas and the Platonic doctrine of reminiscence against what he sees as the Aristotelian inspiration of Locke, is

> whether the soul in itself is entirely empty, like the tablet on which nothing has been written (*tabula rasa*) according to Aristotle and the author of the *Essay*, and whether all that is traced thereon comes solely from the senses and experience; or whether the soul contains originally the principles of several notions and doctrines which external objects merely awaken on occasions, as I believe, with Plato, and even with the schoolmen, and with all those who take in this sense the passage of St. Paul ("Romans," 2, 15), where he remarks that the law of God is written in the heart.[7]

As I hinted, Leibniz's comparison of Locke to Aristotle did not do justice to the originality of Locke's innovation. And this originality comes to light above all where Locke radicalized the Aristotelian doctrine by extending it in a way that Aristotle had not anticipated. Like Aristotle, Locke placed in question the autonomy the Platonic tradition had accorded to reminiscence; for Locke, as for Aristotle, the images deployed by memory/reminiscence are,[8] like those of imagination, weaker copies of perceptual images. Locke, however, completely revised the Aristotelian doctrine, since he situated not only memory and imagination, but also *intellect* within the confines of sense experience.

If, for Aristotle, intellect (*Nous*), like reminiscence and imagination, operated on objects furnished by the senses, this did not mean that its grasp was limited to the mutable aspect of objects presented in sense experience. As we read in book 3 of *De Anima*, the active intellect distinguishes itself from both reminiscence and imagination by its capacity to make intelligible the eternal structure of Being underlying both sense objects and the soul itself.[9] Thus, Aristotle's limitation of the scope of reminiscence, which depended not on eternal ideas but on sense perception, did not bring into question the identity of the rational soul in its capacity to delve into ultimate metaphysical principles underlying the mutable perspective of experience.

Leibniz's distress over Lockean empiricism, as becomes clear in the arguments presented in his *Nouveaux essais sur l'entendement humain*, stemmed above all from the radical new vision of the self presented in Locke's *Essay*. In Locke's perspective, the self emerges against a horizon of profound opacity, for the transparency and fixity of its identity as a creature capable of attaining definitive metaphysical understanding of its own substantial being and that of its world dissolve. This novel conclusion follows directly from Locke's stipulation not only that intellect, or "understanding," operates on objects presented by the senses, but that *all* it can know is confined within the sphere of sense experience. For this very reason, understanding could not penetrate, any more than memory or imagination, beyond the horizon of sense experience to comprehension of the ultimate metaphysical structure of reality. Not only Being, comprising the substance underlying external objects, but even that substance constituting the metaphysical identity of the soul itself remained beyond the purview of the finite human intellect.

It is here that we reach the decisive point: once self-understanding is conceived in terms of personal experience of the self, rather than of intellectual insight into the substantial principle of the soul, memory itself changes its scope. As Locke recalls in the famous chapter 27 in the second book of *An Essay Concerning Human Understanding*, entitled "On Identity and Diversity," besides my physical identity, only personal identity is given to me in my experience of myself. But what then is personal identity? Personal identity refers for Locke to my perception of myself over time. Personal identity, in other words, is nothing other than the traces of the different moments of perception of myself that memory retains. With the evaporation of any traditional claim to metaphysical knowledge of the self as substance, only memory remains to assure the ongoing coherence of personal identity. In Locke's own eloquent terms,

> To find wherein personal identity consists, we must consider what *person* stands for;—which, I think, is a thinking intelligent being, that has reason and reflection, and can consider itself as itself, as the same thinking thing, in different times and places; which it does only by that consciousness which is inseparable from thinking, and, as it seems to me, essential to it: it being impossible for any one to perceive without perceiving that he does perceive. When we see, hear, smell, taste, feel, meditate, or will anything, we know that we do so. Thus it is always as to our present sensations and perceptions: and by this every one is to himself that which he calls self:—it not being considered, in this case, whether the same self be continued in the same or divers substances.
>
> [. . .] and as far as this consciousness can be extended backwards to any past action or thought, so far reaches the identity of that person.[10]

It would be difficult to exaggerate the importance of the Lockean model of the self whose identity, insofar as it reaches beyond the mere physical sameness of the body, rests on present consciousness nourished by the memory of personal experience. It would reach beyond the context of our present investigation to deal with the enormous impact of this model on later philosophical and psychological orientations up through the twentieth century. Suffice it to note that even such original twentieth-century works as Bergson's *Matière et mémoire* (Matter and memory), which explicitly attempted to overcome the Lockean conception of memory, remained prisoner to his fundamental premise. Bergson's theory of memory, indeed, brought into question the Lockean presupposition bequeathed by the Aristotelian heritage, according to which the images of memory, like those of the imagination, are but weaker residues of perceptual representations, for he distinguished imagination from what he took to be the fundamental form of memory that he termed "pure memory" (*la mémoire pure*). Pure memory denotes the virtual state of the past, the reservoir of possible past experiences that do not persist in the form of images but depend on imagery to bring them to awareness in a given present. Pure memory is a prefigurative "nebulosity" from which images are crystallized in later representations.[11] For Bergson, the images through which pure memory of past experience is made present are singular representations. They correspond to what Bergson termed the "memory image" (*mémoire image*), which he distinguished from all habitually remembered, mechanical performances (*mémoire habitude*). "Habit memory" concerns acts enabled by learned skills, such as the capacity to spontaneously type on a keyboard, to play a musical instrument, or ride a bicycle, whereas image memory recalls a singular image that never repeats itself in exactly the same form. Habit memory, in other words "repeats," whereas the recollection of the singular past "imagines."[12] Of these two types of memory, Bergson stipulated that only the ability to recall the singular image, as it brings pure memory into present awareness, can be called memory in a genuine sense. It is the authentic form of memory, for habit memory is less memory itself than a "clarification through memory" of habitual activity.[13] But here is the important point: although the original form of memory as "pure memory" is essentially distinguished from imagination, the ability to retrieve the remembered past in any given present nevertheless depends on recollection through images. The memory image is drawn from the representations of past *personal* experience, and here Bergson tacitly reasserts the Lockean assumption that memory pertains to the representations of past experience in the sphere of personal identity.

In what way, however, might one break out of the limited scope of the personal sphere and conceive of memory in more comprehensive terms? The ongoing persuasiveness of the Lockean model in our age tempts us to ask how an alternative theory might be envisioned.

I I

This leads us to a third orientation—one that bursts beyond the confines of the personal self, shifting emphasis from the recollection of personal experience to a broader notion of collective remembrance that, in its historical movement, gives sustenance to personal identity. We recall in passing Hegel's *Phänomenologie des Geistes* (Phenomenology of the spirit) for its restitution to memory (*Erinnerung*) of its absolute privilege. From this vantage point, remembrance designates the historicity of the Spirit. It describes the coherent movement of the Spirit as an interiorization (*Er-Innerung*)[14] that maintains itself amid its shifts, retrievals, and successive reconfigurations. In the course of this movement, the object of remembrance, far from originating in the immutable Platonic dimension of Being, is itself re-elaborated in the movement of interiorization. At the same time, the autonomy accorded to remembrance radically distinguishes it from the sense images deployed by sense perception or by the imagination. Far from constituting the original source of remembrance, the sense image—the "representation" (*Vorstellung*)—designates only a preliminary aspect of the Spirit's object, elaborated in the course of its movement. Without retrieving Platonic reminiscence, Hegelian recollection, as interiorization and remembrance of the Spirit's movement, thus recovers its absolute priority over the sense imagery of perception and imagination.[15]

Hegel's identification of recollection with Spirit introduced an epoch-making interpretation of memory in its specifically collective scope. Indeed, with Hegel's reflection, we can pinpoint the genesis in the modern period of a principle strand of reflection on remembrance in the collective sphere that was closely tied to conceptions of memory as a *historical* elaboration through which collectivities attain self-understanding over time. Nourished by a contemporary situation of dislocation and upheaval on a European scale in the aftermath of the French Revolution and the profound discontinuity wrought by the overthrow of the *ancien régime*, and by the widespread challenge to the traditional authority of the Christian religion, Hegel's philosophy endowed memory in the collective sphere with the capacity to take up and re-elaborate the disparate aspects of past experience, whereby discontinuous and seemingly incommensurable moments of the past are encompassed within the unified movement of the whole. In thus setting recollection at the level of historical becoming, memory was made the organ of continuity of the Spirit in its successive historical configurations spanning the course of generations. The remembrance of collective experience and historical comprehension of the past were brought together in the absolute reflection of the Spirit, for which the essential significance of the past—as "remembered" past—is not only continually available to awareness in a given present, but is placed in the more comprehensive perspective attained by virtue of its forward movement. In the "Night of Self-consciousness," as Hegel wrote in the *Phänomenologie des Geistes*, "where its former Being has disappeared," it is nonetheless raised in memory (*Er-Innerung*) to a higher substantial form.[16]

The *absolute* basis of Hegel's initial interpretation of recollection in the historical realm, incorporated in his later attempts to construct an all-encompassing philosophy of history, lost its persuasive force during the decades following his death in 1831. Yet the conviction that Hegel brought into the forefront of philosophical analysis, according to which human beings, who define themselves through their activity in a meaningful process of history, *are* essentially historical by virtue of their retention and re-elaboration of past collective experience, inspired a variety of conceptions of the interaction and development of national groups and of civilizations. Independently of any question of Hegel's "influence" on posterity, different orientations embraced the idea that memory retains the disparate moments of the historical past and serves as the basis of a process of development of the identity of human groups in the elaboration of the immanent meaning of history. "Memory creates the chain of Tradition," as Hegel interpreted the collective reach of memory, citing a thought originally formulated by Herder.[17] Memory, in the perspective of the *Phänomenologie des Geistes*, which draws together the diverse threads of historical movement of the self-consciousness of the Spirit, also attests its capacity to surmount and surpass upheavals through which the unquestioned authority of tradition in one epoch is brought into question in the epoch that follows. In the wake of Hegel's legacy, memory was interpreted as the organ of continuity, not only for personal identity or that of small groups, or even of vast nations, but of the history of humanity as a whole. Yet if memory's scope is extended to the collective sphere, it remains entirely subordinate to models of historical becoming through which past experience may be made available to the present and is lent new significance by virtue of its relation to the coherence of history as an overarching process.

Ernst Renan credited Hegel with having provided the philosophy of history with its profoundest expression, conceiving it as the "history of a being which develops through its inner force, creating itself and attaining by degrees its full self-possession."[18] At the same time, without explicit reference to the Hegelian legacy, Renan extended the idea of memory in the collective sphere in a more specifically political direction, interpreting it both as the source of the identity and historical continuity of national groups. A national group, as he interpreted it in his celebrated address "Qu'est-ce qu'une Nation?" (What is a nation?) is a "spiritual principle"; for this reason, neither a common language, a community of interests, a shared geographical position, nor a common racial ancestry is sufficient to account for its continuity, but only a "rich heritage of recollections" and the will to extend this heritage into the future. Be this as it may, in the interest of national unity, Renan also underlined what he took to be the importance for the members of a nation of the ability to forget sources of conflict that divided them in the past.[19]

Toward the end of the nineteenth century, and in a variety of contexts, the rise of a series of theoretical positions that can loosely be grouped under the heading of "historism," advanced parallel interpretations of memory in the collective sphere that bore an unmistakable affinity with Hegel's understanding of *Erinnerung* in the *Phänomenologie des Geistes*. Thinkers like Johann Gustav Droysen, Wilhelm Dilthey, and Bendetto Croce, who each followed Hegel's lead in renouncing the assumptions of traditional metaphysics that postulated a fixed human essence capable of grasping immutable truth, at the same time questioned Hegel's presupposition that an absolute metaphysical grasp of historical becoming might emerge in the course of history itself. In a more limited anthropological perspective, each of them elaborated on the insight that memory serves as a principle of social cohesion and of human historical identity in opposition to the empiricist orientation, which, on the basis of personal memory and personal identity, constructed an atomized social framework. Beyond being a storehouse of sensuous images, memory served as a spiritual principle conferring continuity on the historical movement of peoples through time. A brief consideration of the three seminal examples of Johann Gustav Droysen, Wilhelm Dilthey, and Benedetto Croce will help clarify their conceptions of memory in the sphere of historical becoming. It provides the strongest argument in a late nineteenth- and early twentieth-century context in favor of the long reach of memory as a capacity to lend cohesion to the diversity of historical epochs and thereby to illuminate the depths of the historical past. In this manner each of these thinkers both paid tribute to the Hegelian source of mnemonic theory and, at the same time, from their different perspectives, revealed the fragility of this source of interpretation of the significance and scope of memory in the collective sphere.

In his work on the principles of historical understanding, *Historik*, Johann

Gustav Droysen made of memory in the collective sphere a principal element of historical interpretation. Memory is the organ of continuity between past and present, which presupposes the development of the present out of re-membered past forms of human life. Retrieval of the past in memory both acknowledges and assures its continuity with the present, through which the present recognizes itself to be a mediated result of historical becoming.[20] But memory goes beyond this act of mediation in the temporal realm, for it is also in memory, according to this conception, that the impermanence of the fluctuating realm of experience is overcome. As Droysen wrote, "Only when remembered (*er-innert*) do events of the past, to the extent that and in the way in which the knowing spirit possesses them, lose their transiency. Only when known are they endowed with certitude."[21]

In his theory of history and of historical knowledge, Wilhelm Dilthey related memory in the collective sphere to the central historical capacity to "relive" the past (*Nacherleben*), which concerned not only the possibility of reconstituting it from outside, as a mere concatenation of events, but in its in-ner, living significance.[22] Conceived in this sense, remembrance (*Erinnerung*) was not simply a faculty for recollecting images of past experience, nor even for reconfiguring the course of an individual life or the existence of contem-porary groups; like Droysen, Dilthey interpreted memory to be a capacity for bringing the historical past to life in the present and thus for mediating between the individual and contemporary groups and the historical past. In this capacity to remember the past in the present, memory is the source of the cohesion (*Zusammenhang*) of history itself in the diversity of its moments.[23]

Finally, Bendetto Croce also raised memory in its collective scope to the level of historical understanding. Analogous to the way in which an individual distinguishes remembered occurrences from fantasy images, so memory, as it is expanded into the collective sphere, draws on the fund of remembered experiences of humanity that have been established on the basis of credible evidence. According to his work *Aesthetic as a Science of Expression and Gen-eral Linguistic* (1902), history is what both "the individual and humanity re-member of their past."[24]

In the wake of Hegel's *Phänomenologie des Geistes*, Droysen, Dilthey, and Croce each presupposed an essential distance of the past from the present that can be bridged only through the retrieval in historical memory of what can no longer be experienced in its original form. Nonetheless, against He-gel's grand metaphysical synthesis, the anthropological standpoint embraced by each of these thinkers presupposed the finite perspective of every epoch of history, including the present, and this finitude imposes extensive limits on the synthetic capacity of memory in its efforts toward historical understanding. Indeed, the irreducible singularity of each historical perspective, involving given linguistic forms of expression and given value systems, makes impossible a grasp of the meaning of history as a total process. As an essentially anthropological capacity, remembrance takes on the character of a meta-personal and super-individual principle of historical cohesion and continuity that nonetheless renounces the intellectual constructs and systematic claims with which it has traditionally been associated.

In the framework of our attempt to clarify the significance and scope of memory in the collective sphere, this critical premise renders any application of the term *memory* to the historical world highly problematic. In view of the modifications that modes of understanding and values undergo over the course of generations, in what sense might the concept of *remembrance* be legitimately applied to a grasp of the historical past? If in its original sense *memory* attests the continuity of the personal self over time and the ongoing relation of the self to an experiential world, how might we be said to "remember" an historical past that has never been experienced, but which is inferred on the basis of narratives and other traces that the past has bequeathed? In using the term *remembrance* to refer not only to testimony drawn from the experience of living generations, but to what has been left by the historical past, each of these thinkers postulated the possibility of grasping its inner sense—its cohesion, or *Zusammenhang*, in the vocabulary of Droysen and of Dilthey—in spite of the differences in sensibility and in understanding that separate our world from the one we seek to comprehend. Dilthey indeed acknowledged the impossibility of retrieving the "experience" (*Erlebnis*) of those who lived in the historical past, which to him signified the modes of experience of past epochs and their worldviews, yet he was confident that continuity could be established through the "revivification" (*Nacherleben*) of the past in recollection. The possibility of experiencing the intense religiosity, as he stipulated, that inspired Luther and his contemporaries, is "very limited" for those living in a later, more secularized period, but we are nonetheless able to "revivify" their initial experience and grasp its significance in its continuity with our present world. The establishment of such continuity with the past, as Dilthey explained, always presupposes the possibility of recreating it in memory.[25]

In similar fashion, Croce addressed the skeptical doubt concerning the historian's capacity to retrieve the truth of the past, and he admonished that the certitude of history is of a different order than that required by the analytic and demonstrative criteria of the natural sciences, for the criteria of historical understanding lie in "memory and authority."[26] In elaborating on this point in his later work, *Theory and History of Historiography* (1917), Croce empha-sized that each present has a selective view of the past since, as he noted, "To forget one aspect of history and to remember another one is nothing but the rhythm of the life of the spirit." Each epoch chooses to remember in relation to its present preoccupations. Nonetheless, the forgetfulness that this involves does not invalidate the claim of historical understanding to retrieve the mean-ing of the past, for what is neglected in one epoch may be revived at a later time. This ongoing possibility of remembrance attests that in spite of changes and discontinuities, history forms a cohesive process in which "the spirit bears with it all its history, which coincides with itself."[27]

Like his older contemporary Dilthey, Croce thus evinced confidence in the capacity of historical understanding to penetrate the inner sense of the histor-ical past as retained in memory. This confidence paradoxically recalls an as-sumption harking back to the origins of the philosophical tradition: in spite of the critical outlook they shared, and their professed rejection of all traditional metaphysics, their ready assumption that *memory* attests a spiritual unity and continuity withstanding the flux of the empirical realm subtly introduces an enduring Platonic motif into their general conceptions of the historical world. The quest for permanence and stability of truth and of theoretical norms be-yond the essential historicity of human life, depending on an ongoing capacity to retain the essential experience of the past in memory, thereby harked back to the first source of mnemonic theory in Western intellectual traditions as they themselves entered their twilight hour.[28] In the work of Dilthey or Croce, this Platonic motif remained implicit and was never acknowledged as such. In Droysen's *Historik*, however, written several decades before the works of Dilthey and Croce I have cited, this motif came explicitly to the fore. In this work, Droysen's reference to Plato's theory of reminiscence places in a wholly original light the problematic aspect of the assumption characteristic of these proponents of nineteenth- and early twentieth-century historism concerning memory as the source of historical cohesion.

As a scholar of antiquity and a translator of Greek literature, Droysen gave this Platonic motif direct expression in his allusions to historical remem-brance as "*anamnesis.*" In this guise, he interpreted memory to be the capac-ity to bring the past into presence and, through an act of will, to affirm its meaning for the future. This unity in time made of the past the mirror of a superior significance, through which the historian's reminiscence gleaned the eternal sources of the movement of the human spirit over time.[29]

In other sections of *Historik*, however, Droysen's analysis of memory did not strictly conform to this theoretical model. In his vivid portrayal of human historical events, his analysis often confined itself to the finite realm of historical flux, and in such instances he presented a different estimation of the historical reach of memory. In departing from his general theoretical framework, Droysen interpreted memory less as a reminiscence of eternally significant forms than as a capacity to recollect collectively experienced actions and events, which he distinguished from historical representation. The discrepancy that he portrayed between collective memory and comprehension of the historical past brings to light an interpretation of the significance and scope of collective memory that anticipates a decisive methodological paradigm of the twentieth century.

At one point in *Historik*, Droysen drew a distinction between orally transmitted memories retained by living generations that, following their disappearance, may later be forgotten, and written historical accounts in which remembered events are transmitted to posterity. Where events arouse only a mediocre interest, historical accounts often record details that a group retains in memory in piecemeal form. Droysen presented as an example the short-lived attempt during the Revolution of 1848 to achieve democratic reform in Germany through the Frankfurt Parliament, of which he himself had been an elected representative. It met with no success, as he recalled, and was soon aborted. Due to the failure of this initial attempt at political reform, it aroused little long-term interest, and most of the intricate details surrounding its proceedings were quickly forgotten. The recollections and other traces of this event were transmitted only in piecemeal form to posterity. Conversely, the immediate engagement of wide sectors of the German population in the violent French revolutionary wars in Germany kept alive the collectively shared memories of these events which, among German families, were orally transmitted to younger generations well into the 1830s and 1840s. These oral accounts, however, were of particular interest due to the very different picture they presented of the great Revolution, above all in comparison to the literary reconstructions of French apologists such as Thiers or Lamartine. And Droysen concluded, "But with the third and fourth generations, the warm and vivacious plenitude of what has been handed down gradually dies out; the written legacy, where it exists, in its fixed and definitive organization and form, the *fable convenue*, rises to predominance."[30]

Droysen's distinction here between the lived experience recalled by collective memory and historical representation is noteworthy. In drawing an essential distinction between collectively retained memory, transmitted through oral accounts, and written historical representation, Droysen suggested that memory may provide a vibrant perspective that, due to the historian's singular point of view or her distance from events, historical accounts may overlook. This distinction, indeed, and the emphasis he placed on the factual basis of living memory, implicitly brings into question the presumed primacy of historical understanding in relation to memory in the collective sphere. Most important, Droysen's depiction of collectively retained and orally transmitted experiences that are effaced following the demise of the generations that bore them in living memory, places implicitly in evidence the limits of his own theoretical tendency to identify historical understanding with the capacity through memory to penetrate the inner significance of the past. Indeed, in his example, the memory collectively retained by living generations displays a certain incommensurability with the more indirect forms of recollection upon which historical representation draws. Here we find grounds for a reappraisal of the general assumption of the philosophy of history that historical reconstruction, through the synthetic activity of present *memory*, deploys its capacity to retrieve the essential meaning of the historical past. This lingering assumption that I have identified with the third source of traditional theories of memory would lose its persuasive force only in light of the profound experience of historical discontinuity during later decades, above all in the aftermath of the World War.

III

If Nietzsche's philosophy has often been associated with a turning point in Western thought that signaled the emergence of a radical new form of questioning of its traditional expressions, this questioning also involved predominant earlier assumptions concerning the significance and scope of memory. Nietzsche's radical challenge to contemporary conceptions of memory and of historical modes of thought was roughly contemporaneous with Droysen's theoretical elaboration of historical method and prior to the high point of historist reflection in the decades before World War I. If Nietzsche's critique included the Platonic metaphysics of memory and the empiricist conception of memory in the field of personal identity, he directed his attack above all against the Hegelian conception of memory as the organ of historical cohesion.

The impact of Nietzsche's challenge to previous interpretations of memory and of historical understanding aimed at what he took to be unquestioned contemporary assumptions concerning the *significance* of remembrance in the collective sphere, and it was here that he engaged the brunt of his attack against modern conceptions of recollection of the past as a source of group cohesion and collective identity. The challenge he elaborated in the second

of his *Unzeitgemässe Betrachtungen* (Untimely meditations) sought to undermine the central role the modern world accorded to collective remembrance
of the past, which, in the form of historical reflection, served to orient modern
thought as a whole.

In Nietzsche's perspective, the essential role the modern world accords
to what he termed the "historical sense," which came to its foremost expression in Hegel's philosophy, presupposed the spontaneous meaningfulness of
history as a *process*. This conception of the historical process approaches the
past as if it were a fixed acquisition to which "memory opens all of its doors"
and which it retains like so many "indigestible stones."[31] In accord with this
assumption, the modern historical sense, which identifies the meaning of the
past with its objective position in the context of the whole, takes for granted
the continuity between past and present, and thus the intelligibility of the past
in light of the present. Here however, modern historical understanding, in
presupposing a self-sustaining continuity between past and present, adopts
an essentially unhistorical premise: directly here, as Nietzsche wrote, "Despite all their historical study, they do not at all understand how unhistori-
cally they think and act."[32] Notwithstanding its claim to scientific rigor, the
legacy of this Hegelian idea of history as a self-sustaining process introduced
nothing less than a new mythology that had cast its spell over contemporary
intellectual life.[33] The mythology of the modern historical sense overlooks the
fact that the essential meaning of the past may remain hidden to modern eyes;
the past reveals itself to be a "pronouncement of the oracle" (*Orakelspruch*)
that creative vision alone may divine.[34] Far from a product of the historical
sense, creative vision belongs only to the builders of the present who are able
to mobilize understanding of the past in view of the future. This is the genuine purpose of historical insight. By contrast, the illusory persuasion that the
present is a cumulative product of the past historical process, and that its essential meaning is available to historical remembrance, is anything but a benign presumption, for it inhibits creative action in the present and engenders
passivity; in this situation, the weight of historical memory, which modernity
entertains the illusion of being able to master, represents a particular danger
to the coherence of modern identity. And Nietzsche's antidote to the burden
of historical memory is particularly illuminating for our discussion: he advocated nothing less than the imaginative act of artistic recreation, liberated
from all subservience to factual data and, above all, from the life-inhibiting
force of a hyperactive modern memory. In this vein Nietzsche wrote in *Vom
Nutzen und Nachteil der Historie für das Leben* (On the use and abuse of history for life): "Only when historiography tolerates being transformed into art,

and thus becomes a pure artistic creation, can it maintain or perhaps even arouse instincts. Such historiography would, however, completely contradict the analytic and unartistic traits of our time, according to which such transformation would represent a falsification."[35] Due to what he took to be the oppressive character of memory conveyed in the guise of modern historical consciousness, Nietzsche devaluated it in favor of the creative activity of the imagination.

At later points in my analysis, I return to Nietzsche's critique of the modern historical sense and, in light of this critique, to his conception of the remembered past as a potential burden that only imaginative re-creation might overcome. It is of importance to note at this point that Nietzsche, even as he attacked the Hegelian legacy in underlining the problematic side of the remembered past and of historical knowledge, nonetheless shared a tacit presupposition *with* Hegel and with the predominant currents of nineteenth-century historical reflection that followed in Hegel's wake: he readily accepted the idea of an analogy between memory in the collective sphere and *historical understanding*.[36]

Without abandoning this idea of historical understanding as a form of group memory, Nietzsche reoriented this motif in his later thought; following this change, his understanding of memory in the collective sphere underwent a noteworthy modification. From the period of his work *Human, All Too Human* until the *Genealogy of Morals*, Nietzsche became increasingly receptive to biological theories of adaptation and evolution, and his conception of memory was strongly marked by this new point of view. His focus on memory concerned less its place in conscious awareness, whether in the personal or group sphere, or as it animates the modern "historical sense," than its subterranean workings underlying human historical development. In company with contemporary biologists such as Wilhelm Roux, with whose works he was familiar, or Ewald Hering, he speculated in numerous later writings and fragments that all organisms are endowed with "memory" and that human societies, in particular, depend on biologically inherited memory traces that account for their organization and development.[37] Parallel to an influential current of contemporary intellectuals in Europe, Nietzsche began to speculate about the role of what he took to be an "organic memory" shared among human groups.[38] According to his interpretation, organic memory comes to expression in basic group dispositions and habits that are incorporated, through a process of adaptation and selection over long periods of time, into their biological structure and are subsequently transmitted to future generations. In Nietzsche's perspective, which reworked contemporary biological theories in light of his specific philosophical orientation, organic memory is not a fixed property but changes as groups adapt to new circumstances calling for novel forms of social organization. From this standpoint, habitual attitudes, after generations of social practice, are inscribed in memory as bodily dispositions that favor adaptation not only to the natural but also to the social environment. As they are gradually selected, they configure as "organic memory" the biological structure of human groups. This channeling of group attitudes and activity in accordance with long-term habits and dispositions that social regulations and constraints impose is the principal source of the historical movement of human civilizations. As Nietzsche concisely formulated this viewpoint in the late work *Jenseits von Gut und Böse* (Beyond good and evil*)*: "It is in no way possible that a person should *not* incorporate the traits and the past life of his or her parents, however much appearances may indicate otherwise. This is the problem of race (*Rasse*)."[39]

In *Zur Genealogie der Moral* (The genealogy of morals), Nietzsche further elaborated the biological undergirding of this theory of memory. Memory, instilled by what Nietzsche termed "mnemotechnics" among human groups, serves to impress dispositions on the body and, in particular, on the nervous system. Recollections spanning generations, inspired for example by the terror of witnessing violent reprisals and cruel punishment, are particularly potent. This memory, according to Nietzsche's celebrated theory, can account for the almost mechanical regularity of behavior and, above all, for the ability to "make and keep promises," through which it becomes possible to "profit from the advantages of society." "With the help of this kind of memory," as Nietzsche continues, "one finally came 'to reason.'"[40]

In relation to Nietzsche's early works, which focused on the burdensome character of the modern historical sense and denounced as illusory the modern claim to retrieve the essential meaning of the past in its continuity with the present, the biological focus of Nietzsche's later writings situated the topic of memory in a fully different sphere. In this later period Nietzsche maintained his earlier skepticism in regard to modern ideas of historical continuity, not because he doubted the existence of a unified historical development, but because modern methods of historical understanding were, to his mind, incapable of uncovering its real basis. In Nietzsche's later work, socially conditioned dispositions that had been biologically selected over time were seen as providing an appropriate "genealogical" account of the cohesion and historical development of human collectivities. The continuity he questioned at the level of a spiritual unity drawing on conscious recollection of the past was displaced to the unconscious level of sociologically molded organic memory that linked together the long epochs of human history. However sharply he re-jected the orientation inaugurated by Hegel, and however clearly his method contrasted with subsequent historist models that had appropriated and re-fashioned Hegel's idealist assumptions, Nietzsche's later thought adopted on a fully different basis an analogous presupposition concerning the long-term continuity of history as a process. In inverting the speculative premises that inspired the Hegelian idealist legacy, Nietzsche assumed that memory in the collective sphere, through natural evolution and the mechanisms of social se-lection, bridges the gap between the heterogeneous epochs of human history. Like Hegel and the proponents of historism, but on a radically different basis, Nietzsche thus postulated that "remembrance" in the collective sphere pro-vides a principal of cohesion spanning the epochs of human history.

IV

Much of the recent literature dealing with collective memory has highlighted the significance of psychological and psychoanalytic research stemming from the work of Sigmund Freud and his school. As a medical doctor with a tech-nical interest in the relation between organic and psychological processes, Freud was familiar, at an early point in his career, with the theories of organic memory formulated by Ewald Hering, whom he knew personally, and with the works of popularizers of these theories, such as Samuel Butler.[41] His early works touched only occasionally upon this theme, which he considered to be highly speculative, and the central role he accorded to memory in early writings like the *Studies on Hysteria* or the *Interpretation of Dreams* dwelt on it from an essentially psychological perspective. As he acknowledged in writ-ings before the 1920s, he aimed to distinguish psychoanalytic method from all forms of biological speculation.[42]

According to the celebrated psychological theory that formed the basis of his lifelong efforts, all human relations are founded on the dynamics of the individual's early experiences in the nuclear family, in which unconscious wishes and the mechanisms of repression of these wishes are constitutive of the general pattern of human development. Since the sexual and aggressive drives at the basis of these wishes, like the mechanisms of the superego calling for their repression, are taken to be universal to all human individuals, they come to expression both in individuals and in all forms of group existence. The interaction of unconscious desire and its repression tacitly molds the psychology of the self and conditions everyday behavior in ways that, if they escape awareness, commonly underlie psychological symptoms and neuroses to which they may lead. Here Freud's hypotheses concerning the universality of such phenomena as the Oedipus or the castration complexes as key components in the genesis of human psychic life have raised a long-standing debate concerning the claims of psychoanalytic theory as a whole.

Freud's interest in repressed experience and in the unconscious memory of the childhood past and its traumatic episodes led him to his epoch-making theory concerning the perdurability of latent forms of memory and the pathological hold they may exert on conscious life. It mattered little in this respect that fragmented memories arising from repressed experiences of the childhood past were refashioned in relation to symbols and fantasies that were either imaginary or had little direct relation to the initial experience that occasioned them. In their association with fantasies and symbols drawn from later elaborations, such memory fragments, or "screen memories," (*Deckerinnerungen*) were seen to be of decisive significance as clues to the specific psychic energies that exercise their power over a given patient.[43] In the perspective of Freud's theory, the fragmentary memories derived from earliest childhood are subject to distortion and continuous subsequent revision in relation to the elementary unconscious drives and the repression that patterns them, which accounts for their specific form and the possibility of their pathological effects. The therapeutic aim of Freud and his followers has emphasized the role of working through such repressed unconscious memories with the intention of liberating individuals from their obsessive grip. Here the therapist focuses on memories that come to expression in the form of symptoms, revealing present sources of anxiety, tension, and illness. As a central part of the dynamics of this process, repressed memories need to be taken beyond their symptomatic expression as repressed experience and consciously worked through. "Remembering, Repeating, Working Through" is indeed the title that Freud gave to his famous paper on this subject which, in recent years, has aroused particular interest in philosophy and the human sciences.[44]

Freud was above all convinced that such repressed unconscious impulses did not only concern individual patients, since for him frustration and trauma were decisive factors that also characterize larger human groups. In the context of his early works, Freud had already drawn suggestive parallels between the individual and collective spheres in his depiction of the dream-work. As he noted in *The Interpretation of Dreams*, the symbolic expressions that come to awareness in the dream content, as the effects of psychic mechanisms designed to dissimulate unacceptable unconscious wishes, correspond to analogous phenomena in the political sphere. According to this theory, the dream-work that hides the unacceptable content of repressed desires through symbolization and related psychic mechanisms runs parallel to the work of the political writer who, through similar tactics, aims to conceal the explicit content of a political message before the watchful eyes of the government censor.[45]

In the period beginning with World War I, Freud increasingly turned his attention to this parallel between the individual and group experience at its different levels, above all in the framework of vast collectivities. It is here that he began to elaborate his theory of mass psychology (*Massenpsychologie*) as a branch of psychoanalytic investigation that aimed to place in evidence not only individual but collective pathologies. Of central importance to Freud's conception of shared latent memory is the conviction that group identities, as they orient personal experience and the memories that nourish it, may be accounted for in terms of specific drives that come to expression at all levels of human interaction. In his theory of mass psychology, Freud proposed that the dynamics of vast groups and mass movements are essentially extensions of individual and family relations that do not fundamentally differ from them.[46] Thus, the theory of psychological drives and anxieties at work in the individual psyche serves as the basis for the general theory of repressed memory, which is extended to interpretations of the significance and scope of memory in the collective sphere. Freud accounted for the specific differences between individual functions and the dynamics of vast groups above all in underlining the assumption that group identification and conformity arises from a libidinal attachment to the leader and to the group as a whole that requires a weakening of the sense of individuality and autonomy.[47]

In subsequent years, Freud increasingly sought to understand the genesis of individual psychic dynamics in relation to the long-term development of human civilization. It is in works developed in this period, from *Beyond the Pleasure Principle* (1920) to *The Future of an Illusion* (1927), that Freud elaborated what might be termed a specific theory of collective memory as the fragmentary retention of dimly recalled and fully re-elaborated remembrances of the early prehistoric traumas of human civilization. Here Freud sought to trace contemporary religious and sociocultural phenomena to their genesis in primal family relations. As in the dream-work and in the recovery of fragmented memories of the distant past in individual awareness, sociocultural and religious experience similarly bring to expression recollections of an archaic collective past in which primeval traumas recall the fulfillment of unconscious drives, which, as they are subjected to the mechanisms of sublimation or repression, are subsequently elaborated in the form of symbols. In *The Future of an Illusion*, Freud advanced the famous hypothesis that the monotheistic religions, as central features in the historical articulation of sociocultural life, found their counterpart in vague reminiscences of the archaic killing of the primal father, who was subsequently resurrected as a divinity. On this basis, Freud believed that "the store of religious ideas includes not only wish-fulfillments but important historical recollections."[48]

It is in this framework, too, that Freud increasingly sought to account for individual and collective experience in terms of an organic basis for the transmission among generations of the archaic memory traces that account for the psychic patterning of human awareness. Already in the period of World War I, the quest to understand the genetic sources of the psychic forms of individual and collective life brought Freud back to the hypothesis of a possible organic basis for long-term psychic tendencies, the idea, as he expressed it, that "all of our provisional ideas in psychology will presumably someday be based on an organic substructure."[49] In subsequent years, this conviction became an ever-more central feature of Freud's psychoanalytic theory of culture. In his last work indeed, *Moses and Monotheism*, he described this presupposition as an "unavoidable audacity" (*unvermeidliche Kühnheit*).[50] Here collective memory, conceived as the genetically inherited traces of an archaic past that work unconsciously in re-elaborated symbols and patterns of interaction, accounts for the sociocultural and religious forms of contemporary civilization and for the individual and collective pathologies that arise within it. Freud concisely summarized his hypothesis in the final part of *Moses and Monotheism* in the following terms:

> The behavior of neurotic children towards their parents in the Oedipus and castration complex abounds in [. . .] reactions, which seem unjustified in the individual case and only become intelligible phylogenetically— by their connection with the experience of earlier generations. [. . .] The archaic heritage of human beings comprises not only dispositions but also subject-matter—memory-traces of the experience of former generations. [. . .] If we assume the survival of these memory-traces in the archaic heritage, we have bridged the gulf between individual and group psychology: we can deal with peoples as we do with an individual neurotic.[51]

In the framework of our current investigation of the sources and contemporary significance of theoretical interpretations of collective memory, it matters little whether a psychological conception of memory identifies its primary function with an essentially psychic dynamic engendered by archaic traumas that continue to operate independently of the conscious awareness of individuals and groups, or whether, in addition, it depends upon a phylogenetic or organic component for its transmission. In all of its forms, as we have seen, the conception of unconscious, inherited memory plays a general anthropological role at the different levels of human interaction, from the psychological dynamics among individuals in the nuclear family to the psychic mechanisms at work in the interaction of vast groups over time. On the basis of this conception, Freud postulated essential lines of *continuity* in human psychic dispositions spanning the millennia since the beginning of human civilization. In line with this hypothesis, unconscious memory, as it transmits the traces of primeval family trauma throughout subsequent human history, assumes a trans-historical role. This presupposition concerning the synthetic capacity of collective memory, bridging the diverse epochs of human history, tacitly shares a presupposition with earlier paradigms governing the post-Hegelian conceptions of memory that I have considered thus far: like these conceptions, whether in idealist or biological form, it posits "memory" as the organ of continuity between past and present, linking together the brief life spans of contemporaneous generations in a given epoch with human history as a whole.

The limits of Freud's methodology come to light, however, as soon as we shift our attention from the psychoanalytic conception of the trans-historical function of unconscious memory in assuring continuity between past and present, to focus on the *discontinuities* that have been an essential feature of the modern period. Freud himself was quite indifferent to the theme of radical discontinuity introduced by the advent of mass society and the conditions of twentieth-century existence. Beginning with his work on mass psychology, he interpreted the emergence of mass society less as a novel development marking an essential departure from the past than as a recrudescence in modern guise of latent reminiscences of archaic relations among the primitive horde.[52] In repressed or sublimated form, such reminiscences provided the unconscious sources underlying the dynamics of modern mass interrelations.

Nevertheless, Freud was able to formulate his hypothesis concerning this line of continuity between primitive family relations and modern mass societies only by discounting aspects of historical change that did not correspond to his model. Radical discontinuity ushered in by the advent of mass modes of coexistence, does not, however, simply provoke a *repetition* of the past in an updated form; far from being a by-product of the dynamics of individual and small-group relations, it brings into view a sphere that bears no analogy to such relations. Large-scale discontinuity leaves in its wake a disparity between the singular texture of the past in view of the present, a fundamental distinction between what is collectively retained among contemporaneous generations and the historical past lying beyond all living memory. It is this singularity in contextual structure, marked by the forms of symbolic interaction that predominate in it, that distinguishes the unique contours of a given past from those of historical periods that are different from it and resists reduction to uniform models of trans-historical continuity. No attempt to reconstitute the historical past in terms of general, all-encompassing conceptions, such as memory traces and the psychic mechanisms they arouse, can possibly hope to fathom the singular texture that most essentially characterizes it. Here collective capacities of apprehension and of remembrance encounter limits that no speculative attempt at psychological reconstruction, however audacious, might hope to overstep.

In view of the phenomenon of historical discontinuity—which, contrary to the continuities imposed by psychic constructs, places in evidence contextual singularity—the phenomenon of *latency* itself takes on a different guise. If Freud's theory had the merit of pointing out the role of latent memory lying beyond the sphere of both individual and group awareness, and of the imaginary elaborations to which it is subject where it crosses the threshold of consciousness, this insight by no means authorizes the further presupposition according to which psychological forms of latency are necessarily the *primary* forms through which memory may be interpreted. On a collective level, the phenomenon of latency is not solely the product of mechanisms of psychological repression and sublimation analogous to those at work in the individual psyche; latency concerns still more directly those aspects of the past that elude such reductive forms of reconstruction since, in the wake of changes in contextual horizon, they gradually forfeit their ready intelligibility for later periods. Amid successive shifts in the modes of collective coexistence, given forms of symbolic interaction lose their currency and become opaque in relation to a subsequent group perspective. If, on the collective level, latency may indeed result from forgetting or repression, it must first and foremost be attributed to another source: the lacunae left by shifting contextual horizons and by metamorphoses in the singular nuances of symbolic interaction that lend them significance. Here the topic of latency opens the way to interpretation of the *passive* strata of collective memory which, even after they have faded from active group awareness, leave traces that retain an implicit meaning in the forgotten recesses of the past. Within the deep layers of symbolic signification, passivity subsists in the form of dispositions that are spontaneously re-elaborated in the singular contexts of successive later generations. I postpone further consideration of this theme, however, until the second part of this work, where I interpret it in relation to the temporal articulations of collective memory.

V

In my attempt thus far to interpret the significance and scope of collective memory, I have identified the gradual emergence in the post-Hegelian world of a conception of it that, in extending it beyond the sphere of personal identity, limits it to *anthropological* activity in a sociopolitical framework. As a vehicle of popular culture, memory in the collective sphere had, of course, traditionally showed a remarkable vitality during past eras. The broad expressions of collective remembrance, originally rooted in an oral legacy in predominantly rural societies that were transmitted from generation to generation, were at the source of traditions that are today topics of literary and historical interpretation. As recorded and conveyed, such narratives, especially in popular form, could only be of marginal concern for the predominant metaphysical and theological persuasions elaborated in the centuries between the Platonic and Aristotelian origins of the Western philosophical tradition, and their medieval Christian ramifications and, in the centuries following the Renaissance and the Reformation, the gradual rise of a predominantly secular culture. This is significant less for any distinction it might indicate between "higher" and "lower" forms of traditional cultural life, than for the way it accounts for the emergence of conditions of contemporary visibility of collective memory as a central theme of theoretical investigation. The conception of collective memory that, in a broad latitude of possibilities, has emerged in contemporary discourse, and that I seek to delimit more closely, hardly preoccupied traditional metaphysics and theology, since the anthropological foundations of memory were absorbed within ideational configurations primarily focused on what was taken to be their atemporal and extra-human source; at a later point, as their anthropological scope came more directly into focus, they were subsumed under speculative models, whether ideal or natural, of what was taken to be the movement of history as a whole. The cohesion of history as a universal process preserved in human memory was conceived either in accord with a spiritual principle of accumulated and communicated knowledge or in terms of natural mechanisms governing organic memory and its transmission from generation to generation. All of these conceptions shared the unquestioned presupposition concerning the trans-historical function of memory in the collective sphere.

Besides the rise to predominance of conceptions of the essentially anthropological scope of memory in the collective sphere, the focus on it as a specific field of investigation was also tied to new perceptions of the radical *discontinuity* that punctuated human experience in the contemporary epoch. The phenomena of industrialization and of technological acceleration of the conditions of human life and the demise of traditional sociopolitical forms of organization in the aftermath of World War I are evident sources of this discontinuity. The emergence of vast collectivities and the transformations in the public sphere as well as in the mass media, which provide the principal source of communication in mass societies, engendered an ever-greater predominance of social, political, and economic contexts that are no longer structured on a local or communal level, ushering in our contemporary situation that has followed in the wake of the industrial, technical, and information revolutions, of the ever more rapid mobility of people and goods accompanied by mass migration toward urban centers and the integration of finance and markets on a global scale. Where smaller groups, families, and close-knit communities share similar kinds of experience that draw on a web of personal recollections interwoven with those of living generations who remain in close proximity, mass societies integrate groups whose modes of experience may well be unfamiliar to each other and whose relations are often characterized by an anonymity that distinguishes them from group interaction in smaller and more intimate social circles. The fragmented social contexts of mass societies are encompassed in the shared present, or what I term their common "horizon of contemporaneity." In this context of mass society the perspectives of different groups are rooted in symbol systems that may overlap, such as when they share a common language, but may also draw on diverse symbolic networks in relation to religious traditions, dialects, social practices, and other similar factors—that is, on a web of remembrance through which experience is oriented in relation to specific group assumptions and expectations. However great the similarity exhibited by the individual members of families, local associations, and small communities,[53] the public sphere, even in the most apparently homogeneous of mass societies, is marked by a mobility, a mutability of personal and social forms of existence, and an exposure to external influences that has not only propelled them beyond the sphere of traditional communal life, but has essentially modified the ways of being together in a common world.

In light of these changes, the transformed conditions of human existence in a shared world became a topic of intense preoccupation, above all in the years following World War I. A new, influential expression of doubt about the role of the public sphere and about the meaning traditionally accorded to a quest for collective continuity resounded in the work of Martin Heidegger—above all in his influential book *Being and Time* (*Sein und Zeit*, 1927). Heidegger's analyses in this work reflect a sensitivity to the recent transformations of public life. The development of new forms of public communication epitomized by the radio would bring about, according to Heidegger's prediction, an extension of the everyday environment (*alltägliche Umwelt*) that would impose what he termed an as yet "unforeseeable distance" from the world.[54] Moreover, the utilization of public information services, such as the newspaper, and public transportation, reinforced modes of public communication and interaction that tend to "level down all that is explicit and distinguishable among mortal beings (*Dasein*)" into ambiguous relations of everyday anonymity.[55]

According to Heidegger's interpretation, the reign of anonymous existence in the public realm tacitly serves a fundamental purpose: in fostering disregard for the irreducible singularity of mortal beings, group anonymity is ultimately engendered by silent collective dissimulation of singularity's ultimate consequence, which lies in existential finitude as being-toward-death. The public mode of existence tacitly arises from an inauthentic flight from mortal singularity and thus, in Heidegger's words: "The public realm (*Öffentlichkeit*) obscures everything and presents what it thus hides as well known and accessible to all."[56]

However pertinent Heidegger's descriptions of the essential anonymity of the public sphere might have been to the concerns of his period, the radical doubt he cast in *Being and Time* on any traditional significance that might have been accorded to the public realm did not intend to underscore the novelty of the age in which he lived and the radical transformations it had undergone. His purpose, indeed, concerned less the identification of an unprecedented mutation than what he took to be the latest form of an age-old quest. He thus focused not on the changing anthropological dimension of the public realm but on what he took to be the universal ontological scope of his investigations throughout human history. Viewed in this perspective, Heidegger's analysis of the forgetfulness of the finitude of human being was pursued not in relation to any particular epoch of the remembered historical past, but in relation to tacit expressions of this forgetfulness embodied in the predominant theoretical conceptions of truth throughout the Western tradition. According to this assumption, the Western tradition, which had taken truth to be a fixed attribute, or the result of a cumulative process of historical development, had forgotten the singularity of existence that is thrown into a world, absorbed in its present, everyday preoccupations, and obliged to choose a mode of being in the face of future death. For Heidegger, not only traditional metaphysics since Plato and Aristotle, which assumed that truth resides in what is eternal and self-same, but also the quest for spontaneous, trans-historical forms of continuity rising beyond historical flux were so many stratagems for avoiding and dissimulating mortal finitude. It is at this level that Heidegger brought into question the role traditionally accorded to the self-sustaining continuity of collective existence incarnated in the public sphere as well as in the articulations of world history. Neither absorption in publicly meaningful forms of development nor in the broader domain of history as a continuously unfolding process in the sense of Hegel or Dilthey, but only resolute choices in view of the finite future could reveal what is authentically meaningful in the past and worthy of repetition.

Where Heidegger's thought in *Being and Time* questioned the significance traditionally attributed to historical continuity and to the ongoing cohesion of public life without according any particular role to radical discontinuity in the conditions of human social existence, this latter topic inspired important reflection among numerous literary and artistic currents that bear directly on our theme of analysis. Here the essentially anthropological dimension of the modified conditions of human experience and remembrance and the radical discontinuity that sundered present forms of social existence from those of the past gravitated to the center of literary, artistic, and philosophical attention.

In his 1928 essay "The Conquest of Ubiquity" ("La conquête de l'ubiquité"), Paul Valéry identified what he took to be the grounds of this discontinuity and its implications for artistic creation, which were due to the sweeping changes that had occurred during the first quarter of the twentieth century: "Neither matter, nor space, nor time," he wrote, "are since twenty years what they were during all previous periods. We may expect that such great novelties will transform the entire technique of the arts, affecting in this way invention itself, and perhaps reaching to the point of marvelously modifying the notion of art itself."[57]

Valéry's remarks found eloquent confirmation in the writings of contemporary artists themselves. Here we may cite Fernand Léger's ruminations in 1914 concerning the relation between the "evolution of the means of locomotion and their speed" that modified perceptual habits and ushered in a wholly "new way of seeing" that painting depicts, or Piet Mondrian's reference to an alteration of contemporary awareness as a whole, leading to a metamorphosis in "all of the expressions of life," which had become "more positively abstract": these are representative testimonies of radical discontinuity between the present and past conditions of human life that affect the deepest levels of human sensibility and perception.[58]

Walter Benjamin's writings of the 1920s and 1930s focused on the theme of discontinuity, which placed the question of the significance and the scope of collective memory in a unique, contemporary perspective. For Benjamin, the decline in rural forms of life and, in a context of resolute secularization, of traditional beliefs in the sacred and the miraculous, signaled a radical metamorphosis in the conditions of human existence. Benjamin's essay "The Storyteller" focused directly on this transformation. The talent of the storyteller lies in the capacity to impart experience "from mouth to mouth," and it is exercised above all in contexts where experience can be readily exchanged, exemplified by predominantly rural or village life. By contrast, in large urban centers of the contemporary period, the isolation and anonymity of mass populations has given way to the predominance of "information." In this context, the traditional role of tales and stories is replaced by the factual sobriety of newspaper journalism, characterized by the disjointedness of the information presented, which is immersed in the ephemeral moment of its appearance before giving way to ever more recent material. Here there is an absence of the continuity that had been forged by collectively remembered and communicated experience that retained its significance over the course of generations. The cataclysm of World War I gave dramatic testimony to this contemporary situation: those who survived the horror were often reduced to a mute incapacity to communicate their experience in a way that might be recollected and exchanged with others as a meaningful source of group understanding.

Benjamin's broad approach to what he took to be the essential historicity of human existence, involving resolute transformation and secularization of all spheres of life, might at times give the impression that modernity marks a movement of decline from the rich context of experience that is exchanged and remembered among the members of traditional societies. And yet, Benjamin did not draw this conclusion. "Nothing would be more fatuous," he wrote, "than to see in it merely a 'symptom of decline,' let alone a 'modern' symptom. It is, rather, only a concomitant symptom of the secular productive forces of history, a concomitant that has quite gradually removed narrative from the realm of living speech and at the same time is making it possible to see a new beauty in what is vanishing."[59]

From the quasi-Marxist standpoint that Walter Benjamin defended, history curiously took on the structure of a process, propelled by changes in material conditions of existence and interpreted in light of a messianic outlook on the future. This orientation led him to regard the present as a period of transition announcing the emergence of radically different forms of social life. As in the past, collective ways of remembering were undergoing transformation corresponding to changes in the conditions of social existence themselves.[60] Paradoxically, however, the radical discontinuity between past and present, between past collective patterns of experiencing and remembering in relation to the present, brought into question all former philosophical models of historical development. The assumption of an ongoing cohesion between present and past, of a *Zusammenhang* spanning the epochs of history and available to historical memory, encountered a profound limit that the evidence of historical discontinuity itself brought acutely to the fore.

I have briefly evoked Benjamin's seminal reflection to suggest a tie between changing modes of experience in the twentieth century and the conception of memory in the collective sphere that began to emerge as a focus of investigation in the theoretical arena. The acute shift in the framework of experience between past and present generations, as Benjamin stipulated, set in relief the confines of the contextual horizon to which each generation's awareness is bound. Abrupt shifts in this horizon bring these limits into focus, revealing the distance of the present from modes of experience of the past and the problematic character of attempts to retrieve its significance in the context of the present.

In the decades following World War I and in a wholly different setting than that of Walter Benjamin, Maurice Halbwachs's concept of collective memory drew on methods of interpretation of collective representation elaborated by Émile Durkheim. His *Les cadres sociaux de la mémoire* (1925) and the posthumously published *La mémoire collective* (1950), written in the years before his death in 1945, set the terms for the discussion of collective memory as it is widely understood in contemporary usage. In presupposing the essentially anthropological scope of collective memory, Halbwachs posited a radical discontinuity between the historical epochs in which collective memory operates and to which it is bound. The conception of discontinuity that comes to the fore in his reflections on collective memory provides a *leit motiv* that is also found in his writings on group representations and social psychology. As he wrote, for example, in *The Psychology of Social Class*, published in 1938,

> We are in fact living in a period characterized by constant, rapid and fundamental change in all the circumstances of life; change that is powerfully affecting our modes of thinking and our ideas and beliefs. Social groups break up, lose their traditions and with them the possibility of surviving amid surroundings no longer favorable to them; they know they are on the wane; sometimes we actually watch them disappear. At the same time others start and develop, bit by bit taking over many elements of those that are on their way out, creating a new environment for men and imposing

new ideas and sensibilities on them. [. . .] Casting our minds back two or three generations, towards the middle of the nineteenth century, it looks as though the changes that have come about since then are probably bigger and more decisive than those we should see if we went back a further five or six centuries, or even more."[61]

Like the predominant theoretical approaches to memory of the late nineteenth century, both idealist and naturalist in orientation, Halbwachs's approach identified memory as the organ of continuity linking together the disparate moments of group experience. Yet, in positing a radical discontinuity between the historical epochs in which collective memory operates and to which it is bound, he limited the scope of collective memory to what living generations were able to recall. He thus distinguished between the two spheres of collective memory and history, corresponding to a breach between remembered continuities shared by contemporary generations and an historical past lying beyond the pale of living memory, which only historical research may reconstruct.

Halbwachs provided an original concept of memory in the collective sphere, due to the primacy he accorded to the capacity to recall *lived* experience in relation to all other forms of recollection. As he conceived of it, lived experience concerned not only personal experience, but that shared by social groups. Lived experience could be remembered and exchanged among such smaller groups but, as he was well aware, the events that were significant for vast associations, such as national groups, were usually too far removed from all but a few individuals who could experience them directly. In such a framework, what is termed "shared" experience is for the most part indirect and communicated by secondary sources; it is recalled in the form of what he termed "borrowed" memory.[62] In view of the primary role he accorded to remembrance among living groups, his principal focus was on collective memory shared by the members of smaller collectivities, and he considered this to be the source of group experience, constituting an intermediary zone between personal experience and that of vast collectivities. Each individual is in this perspective "immersed" (*plongé*), either simultaneously or successively, in several groups.[63] By means of this participation in the lives of different groups and of entanglements in different spheres of reminiscence, personal experience establishes lines of continuity between past and present that, through the unity of temporal context shared by different groups, lies at the source of its identity over time. In harmony with his sociological orientation, Halbwachs emphasized the central role of each social group as the source through which individual consciousness, as it is retained in memory, defines itself even at its most intimate levels. For the most part implicit and unperceived, the influences of the different milieus to which we belong are brought to awareness in situations of conflict. "A 'current of social thought,'" as Halbwachs wrote, "is ordinarily as invisible as the atmosphere we breathe. One only recognizes its existence, in normal life, when one resists it."[64] On the basis of the influence of diverse milieus, Halbwachs attempted to account for the different levels of self-consciousness, and even of the unity of self-awareness, among individuals who belong to them. If memory is always performed by remembering individuals, its sources and the frames of reference (*cadres*) through which it is stabilized and retained are essentially social phenomena.[65]

As recent critics have pointed out, Halbwachs's sociological theory comes close at certain points in his analysis to a form of collective determinism, which leaves little place for even a limited form of individual spontaneity and autonomy.[66] Nonetheless, it is by no means necessary to adopt such aspects of his sociological perspective in order to appreciate the importance of his insight concerning the temporal dimensions of collective memory in its relation to historical time, which plays a central role in the theory of collective memory that I elaborate in later chapters of this work.

For Halbwachs, the temporal context of collective memory is not limited to the immediate present, for it encompasses a past that existed prior to the birth of remembering individuals: it includes, most notably, the lived experience of previous generations with which they are in contact. He referred above all in this regard to the role of grandparents, who occupied a prominent place in his analyses of collective memory. Through grandparents we are able to establish intimate contact with the ways of being, the gestures and attitudes, that overlap a horizon of the past that eludes direct personal experience. Since they are communicated by older generations, younger relatives retain them in collective recollection. In their distinction from directly remembered experience, such memories are direct signs of shifts in temporal context. The demise of these older groups signifies not only their disappearance as individuals, but also that of the signs of a temporal context, which quickly fade from living memory. Through laborious efforts, the historian may reconstruct different aspects of this context. However, following the passing of generations, the "lived history" of their period that remembrance may still recall (he chooses here the example of popular magazines that belonged to the world of our grandparents) gives way to written history that relates what is beyond the pale of all living remembrance.[67] It is in this manner, for Halbwachs, that the disappearance of a living generation involves that of its temporal context, opening an abyss that collective memory is not able to bridge. This accounts for the radicalism of Halbwachs' distinction between collective memory and historical narrative. He writes, "If the necessary condition for the existence of memory lies in the feeling of the remembering subject, individual or group, that memories are retrievable in a continuous movement, how might history be memory, since there is a dissolution of continuity (*solution de continuité*) between the society that reads this history and the groups of witnesses or actors who, at a previous time, participated in narrated events?"[68] Halbwachs' conception of collective memory inaugurates a paradigmatic shift in relation to interpretations of the significance and scope of memory that predominated in the nineteenth century. This shift, which is of decisive importance for my present investigation, may be brought to light by means of an example that illustrates the originality of Halbwachs' notion of discontinuity between temporal contexts and accounts for the distinction he draws between memory and history.

In 1829 the *Mémoires* of Louis de Rouvroy, duc de Saint-Simon, in which he described life in the court of Louis XIV at the end of the seventeenth and beginning of the eighteenth centuries, was published for the first time in complete form. This publication was widely heralded in France and in the rest of Europe at a time when the historical novel was at the high point of its popularity. In the eyes of many contemporaries, Saint-Simon's *Mémoires* accomplished through a narrative of reminiscences what the historical novel aimed to achieve through fictive storytelling: a living connection, a line of continuity of present experience with an historical past that had long since disappeared. Commenting on this publication in his work, *Essais de critique et d'histoire*, written in the middle of the nineteenth century, Hippolyte Taine emphasized the almost contemporary quality of the work: "Here is one of the reasons that accounts for the popularity of Saint-Simon today: he describes the exterior, like Walter Scott, Balzac, and all of the contemporary novelists who willingly serve as antiquarians, auctioneers, and toiletry merchants. His talent and our taste encounter each other; the revolutions of the spirit have brought us to him."[69] Taine, in his historical works, such as the multivolume *Les Origines de la France contemporaine*, was among the authors in the second half of the nineteenth century who were most sensitive to changes in mentality that had occurred over the past centuries and that had become ever more pronounced since the period of the French Revolution. As he wrote in his *Histoire de la littérature anglaise*, "Every hundred years, the sources of passion, the degree of reflection, the kinds of motivation change. Who understands and appreciates today, unless he has received a long preparatory education, Dante, Rabelais and Rubens?"[70]

And yet, in spite of these changes that had intervened for Taine over the past two centuries, the gap was not too great to render Saint-Simon's *Mémoires* accessible to a nineteenth-century reader, who obtained through them the impression that he was reliving the times of Louis XIV and his court. As in the reading of historical novels, an act of imagination, even where it gleaned only an exterior veneer of appearances, could give the impression that the narrator of the story was bringing before remembrance living experience still accessible within the temporal horizon of the reader.

A century later, in a context animated by a generalized experience of discontinuity, Halbwachs highlighted less the possibility of a contemporary encounter with the spirit of the past than the foreignness of the mentality of the late seventeenth century to the contemporary French reading public: "The only effect of such publications," as he wrote, in referring to his own century and his own temporal context, "is to make us understand the extent of the distance that separates us from the writer and those he describes."[71] This comment concerning the distance of the present from a past beyond living remembrance reaches to the heart of the principal conviction that inspired Halbwachs' theoretical orientation. In view of the break with the past that had become immeasurably deeper during the first decades of the twentieth century, this conviction corresponded to a far more radical perception of discontinuity in temporal context than that typical of the predominant nineteenth-century paradigms of historical reflection. It is this perception that came forcefully to expression in his original theory of collective memory in its distinction from the historical past. In these terms Halbwachs justified the central methodological presupposition that I reexamine and reinterpret in the investigation that follows: in its contemporary significance and scope, collective memory essentially concerns the living remembrance of overlapping generations, and this remembrance must be distinguished from all secondary forms of recollection that are bequeathed by the historical past. Only a focus on collective memory as it is articulated within a given horizon of contemporaneity can adequately account at once for the anthropological foundations of collective memory and for the discontinuity that separates it from the historical past, which lies beyond its pale.

* Part 1 *

Symbolic Embodiment, Imagination, and the "Place" of Collective Memory

Is Collective Memory a Figment of the Imagination? The Scope of Memory in the Public Sphere

The historical introduction in the previous chapter advanced the hypothesis that the prominence of collective memory as a theme of theoretical reflection since the early decades of the twentieth century corresponds to a decisive shift in conceptions of collective experience that could no longer be accounted for through the principal paradigms bequeathed by the past. Over the modern period, as we have seen, the demise of traditional metaphysical presuppositions concerning the intelligibility of unchanging truths governing human society and the world in which it is situated brought to the fore a resolutely anthropological scope of reflection. The twentieth century witnessed a widespread questioning of all-encompassing spiritual or natural principles in their capacity to account for human historical development as an overall process. Parallel to the unprecedented transformation of the conditions of human life, beginning in Europe and North America, and a wide experience of discontinuity with the past, the preoccupation with collective memory reflected a shift in the modes of interpreting the phenomenon of social cohesion and human historical development. Here the historicist presuppositions that "historical memory" might discern a principle of cohesion uniting the epochs of history as a process or that the notion of an "organic memory" might explain historical development in terms of an inherited natural legacy gave way to a more limited perspective from which the topic of collective memory as an autonomous field of investigation provided a corresponding method of reflection.

After tracing the emergence of this new paradigm in the introduction, I devote my efforts in the following chapters to the development of a theoretical approach to the phenomenon of collective memory in the human social and political world. In this theoretical perspective, my primary concern centers on the precise sense that we might attribute to the concept of "collective memory."

I

Upon initial examination, the concept of "collective memory" presents an immediate difficulty as soon as we attempt to clarify it. According to its primary signification, remembrance is carried out in the original sphere of the self. In a strict sense, collectivities never "remember" any more than they have an autonomous, substantial being. And yet, members of a community, as vast as it may be, may share remembrances of what can be publicly communicated through word, image, and gesture. In the public sphere, however, it is not generally possible to convey what memory recalls in immediate personal experience: people and things, events and situations as they actually present themselves in a direct encounter or, so to speak, "in the flesh." My understanding of this phrase draws on phenomenological theory—above all on the work of Edmund Husserl, who equated original experience with what he termed experience "in the flesh" in a given, living present (*"leibhafte Erfahrung in einer jeweiligen lebendigen Gegenwart"*).[1] Other persons, as Husserl explained, present themselves to us "in the flesh." In a precise sense, this signifies that their bodies, movements, and gestures are displayed to us, and it is by this means that we gather in a secondary manner their inner thoughts and feelings. Moreover, Husserl also applied the phrase "in the flesh," *leibhaft*, to other things in the world, as to the givenness of the surrounding world itself. If photographs, paintings, or descriptions may revivify these encounters or publicly relate them through signs, images, or gestures, they can never replace this primordial capacity, which is unique to remembrance in the original sense. A brief example serves to illustrate this concept.

Autobiographical literature provides particularly vivid accounts of encounters in the flesh as, for example, in François-René de Chateaubriand's *Mémoires d'outre-tombe*. In this autobiographical memoir composed in different periods of the author's life and modeled along the lines of a confession, Chateaubriand proposed "to account for myself to myself [. . .]; to explain my inexplicable heart, in seeing finally what I will say once my pen abandons itself without constraint to all of my recollections."[2] With this aim in mind Chateaubriand, in an early chapter of the work, recalls his experiences as a young man when, in the early 1790s, he embarked on a voyage to the New World. After he arrived in Philadelphia, he was invited to the home of George

Washington, first president of the United States, who was in Philadelphia at that moment. Chateaubriand recounts their first meeting, before seeing him the next day at a dinner to which he was invited in the president's unassuming residence: "Large in size, appearing calm and cold rather than noble, he resembles his portraits." Regarding the dinner with Washington and a small number of his friends, Chateaubriand relates that while the president was "at his brilliant apogee," he himself was completely unknown; "I was happy, however," he writes, "that his gaze turned toward me! I felt enheartened by this encounter for the rest of my life!"[3]

Another example, this time a visual representation, will serve to complement Chateaubriand's reminiscence. In roughly the same period as Chateaubriand's visit to Washington, the United States Congress commissioned the French sculptor Jean-Antoine Houdon to fashion a marble representation of the first president of the United States. He made the trip from Paris to the New World to create this and other sculptures of Washington. The works were done in Washington's presence at his residence in Mount Vernon, Virginia, where the one commissioned by Congress stands today. The candidness of expression and the imposing demeanor of Houdon's representation of Washington corroborate Chateaubriand's description of the statesman. But here we come to our principle point: in spite of the vivid evocations of Washington conveyed to posterity by the talents of the writer and the sculptor, nothing permits us to recall an *original* encounter with Washington in the flesh, which Chateaubriand and Houdon each experienced at different moments and which it is the primordial capacity of memory to recall.

In our contemporary world, such a limitation of original experience to direct personal encounters might, of course, seem hopelessly narrow. Nowadays, we have immediate ways of conveying encounters through radio and television, and we can watch video interviews with public figures long after they have ceased to exist. Nonetheless, these media, even if they are able to record events for an untold number of spectators and preserve them for a seemingly indefinite period in film archives, cannot replace direct encounters in the flesh. What is missing in such reproductions or virtual representations is precisely the aura of a singular presence encountered in the plenitude of a surrounding "lifeworld" (or *Lebenswelt*). In its full sense, an encounter in the flesh signifies not only the perception of persons or things as single objects, but above all an experience of them in the lifeworld's immediately given horizon. Within this horizon, the foreground upon which the observer focuses presupposes a background, the plenitude of an accompanying context that is simultaneously given, even where the observer pays no attention to it. Where

FIGURE 1. Jean-Antoine Houdon, *Bust of George Washington*, 1789–1808, Louvre Museum, Paris. © RMN-Grand Palais (Musée du Louvre)/René-Gabriel Ojéda.

it is not explicitly noticed and stands in the background of the direct theme of attention, its passive presence may in many cases be made a topic of recall where an effort is made to retrieve it. Moreover, in the case of film or video presentations, it is rarely a matter of spontaneous encounters: even when they are, so to speak, "live," and not merely recorded, they are regularly organized or "staged," and they address a wholly *anonymous* mass audience with which there is only very rarely a possibility of interaction.[4] Even the social media that have become a popular means of communication in the Internet, where they make possible a measure of direct interaction, do so only through the mediation of a video interface that simulates personal encounters without being able to recreate them. As such, no "live," "prerecorded," or interactive media are able to reproduce the direct personal quality and the unique aura characteristic of situations and events as they are experienced in the flesh.

The cardinal importance we attribute to such direct encounters is clearly illustrated by the role that we generally accord to eyewitness testimony in everyday experience. Of course, witnesses may in certain cases be mistaken or may even attempt to mislead us in their accounts. Indeed, to return to our previous example, George Washington's records of his meetings during the month when Chateaubriand was in Philadelphia, which do not seem to corroborate Chateaubriand's account, have led some commentators to question the reality of this encounter, or at least the sequence of events as Chateaubriand recorded it in his work *Mémoires d'outre-tombe*.[5] In this regard, we cannot exclude the possibility that further evidence might eventually be uncovered proving that what Chateaubriand claimed to be an encounter in the flesh was actually a product of his literary imagination.

Beyond the possibility, however, of mistaken testimonies or those that invent or intend to mislead, reports of direct encounters are themselves manifestly of different kinds: eyewitness experience by passive bystanders presents a very different perspective than that of active participants in events, especially in violent or traumatic situations, such as war or similar occurrences. Involvement in traumatic situations has been associated with well-documented forms of memory loss and, in extreme cases, with aphasia.[6]

In all of these situations taken together, the fact that we can represent fictive constructions as real events, or that all sorts of imaginative constructions may lead us to distort the recollection of in-the-flesh encounters, and that traumatic experiences may cause us to repress them, encourages us to exercise great caution in interpreting such accounts. Here we must allow not only for the possibility that purely fictive creations may be represented as experienced "events," but also for the fact that experienced events themselves are always perceived in a particular perspective and are necessarily reconstructed through interpretative acts, raising the possibility that beyond the margins of the occurrences themselves, they may be subject to voluntary or unwitting re-elaboration, distortion, or suppression. Given the diversity of perspectives and the role of interpretative acts in the reconstruction of past experience, it would therefore be naive to claim that encounters in the flesh directly register the "reality" of events themselves, beyond the interpretative reconstruction of the viewer. And yet, in spite of this obvious limitation, eyewitness representations correspond to fundamental and irreplaceable kinds of experience. Far from recapitulating *reality* in some absolute sense of the term, they must constantly be complemented and corrected by other testimonies, which is why the comparison of numerous testimonies by different witnesses and their fit within the pattern of events remains the most reliable way to reconstruct the factuality of past occurrences. And here, not only in our everyday behavior, but also in the work of the judge or the historian, eyewitness reports are accorded a role of particular importance.[7]

In certain exceptional situations, publicly significant events may be experienced as encounters in the flesh, but only rarely and by a very small minority of remembering individuals who witness them directly. Even in such cases, direct experience of a given event does not necessarily entail comprehension of its *publicly* significant scope. In such instances, the unbridgeable gap between the recollections of individuals or of members of small groups and what might be termed "public memory" in the sphere of vast collectivities might well lead us to question the legitimacy of any application of the concept of "memory" to the public sphere as such. Large-scale public commemorations, indeed, almost always recall what is beyond any possibility of remembrance by those who participate in them since, for example, the foundation of a state or the occurrence of other politically significant events most frequently lie beyond the possibilities of what any living individual might have experienced and remembered. In all such commemorative ceremonies, as in any form of representation of publicly constituted collectivities, such as national groups, it might seem more just to refer not to "collective memory" but to images that are products or "figments" of the imagination. This consideration has led numerous theorists of the social world to follow the lead of Benedict Anderson in his book *Imagined Communities*, for whom such vast collectivities are "*imagined* because the members of even the smallest nation will never know most of their fellow members, meet them, or even hear of them, yet in the minds [*sic*] of each lives the image of their communion."[8] As a means of accounting for collective identity and group cohesion on a vast scale, insofar as it is rooted in reminiscence of a shared collective past, this recourse to the term *imagination* permits us to avoid the dilemma that the concept of "collective memory" would seem to introduce, since imagination as a capacity to maintain and revivify an "image of communion" on a large scale in no way requires that we invoke the most original feature intrinsic to remembrance of past experience, which is to have encountered what is remembered in the flesh.

Admittedly, however, the term *imagination*, as it engenders such "images of communion," raises another kind of difficulty: it might seem to blur any distinction between an interpretation of social cohesion that traces its source to blanket fantasy or fiction and one that admits that, if social cohesion draws on the imagination, it may also lay some claim to a basis in a "remembered" past, even where recollection is indirect and borrowed from past experience reported by others. We may, of course, deny the importance of such a distinction and claim, with Nietzsche, that all viable social existence and political cohesion depend upon roots in the mythical *Heimat* and mythical maternal bosom.[9] Indeed, as Nietzsche well appreciated, it may in many instances prove more in keeping with the requisites of a healthy vitality—and certainly of group contentment—to forget what is bothersome in the past or to recreate it along the lines of fiction. In referring to remembrance of the historical past, Nietzsche therefore frankly suggested that it is only when historical narrative is reframed as a "pure work of art" that it may sustain or even awaken vital instincts.[10] However, our experience with political myths of the most sinister kinds in the twentieth century necessarily leads us to moderate Nietzsche's radicalism and at least to distinguish between different varieties of myth on which collectivities may be founded; and here the delicate question of the relation of imagination to what is held to be a remembered past—even a past that has been remembered and related by others—must once again be asked.

To a large extent this question is of a semantic order. Ordinary language refers to *memory* or to *imagination* as if they were clear-cut and separate functions, whereas, even in immediate personal experience, they play multiple roles and are always interconnected. Far from designating simple operations, the words *memory* and *imagination* cover a wide range of capacities. A few cursory examples will suffice to illustrate this point.

In the original sphere of intimate life, the verb *to remember* is indifferently applied to very different kinds of experience, for I can remember a fantasy I have had, as I can recall all sorts of persons, events, or situations I am convinced I have experienced. On another level, I can remember an algebraic formula or how to ride a bicycle, just as I can remember how to use all kinds of skills I have acquired by learning, both purely intellectual and more corporeal and physical. The single term *memory* clearly covers a whole range of possible experiences, actual or fictive, sensuous or intellectual, passive or active.

In a similar manner, the word *imagination* carries multiple connotations that ordinary discourse rarely distinguishes in an explicit manner. We gener-

ally recognize the work of imagination in the production of fictive events—
the so-called "experiences as if" ("als-ob Erlebnisse")—as also in the more
incoherent flights of fantasy. From a theoretical point of view, the phenomenological research of Edmund Husserl has emphasized the fundamental
role of imagination at the heart of perceptual acts. Where perceived objects
always present themselves partially in a given field of view and from a given
standpoint, it is imagination, he explains, in an act of "fulfillment," that permits their identification as meaningful phenomena. Still another fundamental
capacity of the imagination is identifiable in what might be termed its *deliberative* capacity.[11] It is this activity of imagination that permits us to localize
past events in memory and place them in temporal sequence. If I have lost a
key or implement, I may apply this deliberative capacity of the imagination
to envisaging all of the places where I might have inadvertently dropped it in
order to find it once again. It would reach beyond the scope of the present
discussion to examine this topic in detail, which has been interpreted from
different theoretical standpoints since Aristotle, Hume, Kant, or Husserl, to
name only the best known interpreters. I limit my comments to the collective
sphere and remark that here too, if we are to interpret collective remembrance
by vast groups in public life, it is necessary to precisely identify its relation to
"imagination."

How might we understand the role of imagination in the realm of collectively remembered, publicly communicable experience? Certainly fantasy
and myth play a central role at all levels of social existence, but, as I interpret it, the social bond is not simply based on imaginary creations, for it must
be traced to a more fundamental function of imagination in the communal
sphere, which interweaves the very fabric of communal cohesion. Imagination in this sense is a precondition for social existence per se and, as such,
configures the basis for all that is communally significant. This primordial
role of imagination, as I interpret it, while distinguishing it from all other connotations of the term, renders what is collectively significant communicable
by embodying it in *symbols*. If I identify this work of symbolic embodiment,
however, with an act of the imagination, it is not imagination conceived as an
abstract function, but as part of a fundamental anthropological unity in which
memory is primordially intertwined. In the collective sphere, on the basis of
this original unity, imagination patterns a fund of remembered significations
in the form of communicable symbols. And here matters suddenly become
more complex, for imagination, through this work of embodying communicable symbols, lies at the source both of group fantasy and fiction and of what
is accepted to be communally significant reality.

To clarify this primordial role of imagination, we must describe precisely the conception of the symbol that we are employing. Symbols have most often been interpreted in two different ways in accord with two long-standing traditions: first, in a narrow sense where the symbol represents by virtue of sensuous images what lies outside of possible sense perception—the lamb, for example, as it symbolically represents the person of Christ or the flag as it stands for a given nation; second, in a broader sense that includes in the symbolizing function representational images, language, and gesture more generally. For our purposes in interpreting collective memory, this distinction is of secondary importance, since both of these conceptions of the symbol deploy an identical act of imaginative association: indeed, the first and narrower interpretation of the symbol, as representing what is absent in experience, presupposes and extends beyond the scope of experience the essential function that the broader interpretation of the symbol engages: its work as a collectively mediated organizing principle through which experience is endowed with a communicable sense. All symbols perform this minimal task, since they are all engaged in the transmission of publicly communicable experience through the activity I term "symbolic embodiment." According to this interpretation, it is *symbols* that confer spontaneous sense on experience by lending it communicable order at the primary level of its organization and articulation. This work of symbolic embodiment is for the most part spontaneous and commands our ability to confer sense on experience even before we reflect on it. It is not an aspect of experience that would be tacked onto it as a secondary addition, for symbols lend a communicable order to experience by patterning it in terms of spatial, temporal, numerical, and other conceptual relations.[12] Even before reflecting on them, we are immediately familiar with the spatiotemporal and conceptual relations that govern our everyday world: for example, the implicit distinction between the sacred space of a church and the banal space of a parking garage, the spontaneous distinction between the private space of a backyard and that of publicly accessible parks, the anticipation in given cities that markets will be closed on Monday mornings and not on Wednesdays.[13] Even the distinctions in the music I hear as it is piped into supermarkets and airports or played live at concerts involve the symbolic patterning of space and time, which, for the most part, are tacitly remembered as modes of orientation for immediate everyday activity. Symbolic embodiment renders communicable direct experience as it is remembered in the flesh, and, where it is set down in testimonies or other forms of narrative, it may retain this meaning long after the person or group who initially remembered it no longer exists to recount it in person; symbolic embodiment also sets fictional or mythical creations in communicable form.

And here we come to the crux of the matter. If the work of symbolic embodiment renders communicable both what we take to be fiction and what we identify as reality, both fantasy and remembered experience, what permits us to distinguish between these two realms? The most common answer given to this question is drawn from our everyday ways of making such a distinction, based on our capacity to reinsert what is purported to have been experienced into the broad context or web of reported events—including events in which we ourselves have participated and which we may have forgotten—in order to test the coherence of its fit within this larger web. Here Edmund Husserl's principal criterion for the distinction between remembered and fictive events proves particularly helpful. In theoretical discussion concerning time and temporal consciousness, Husserl elaborated on the distinction between remembered experience and fiction, and he remarked that remembered experience is characterized by its fit within the larger web of *temporal* relations to which all experience is necessarily bound. Fiction in a general sense, as he stipulated, is unrelated to this real temporal order, and where it displays temporal structure, it does so in a separate or—to use Husserl's term—a "quasi-time" (*Quasi-Zeit*).[14] Whereas what we take to be the reality of temporal events depends on our ability to fit them into the larger series of temporal relations in an overarching dimension of experience, such temporal relations have little significance for fictive events, which take on significance in relation to the make-believe temporal worlds that they construct. Following this line of reasoning, if I am able to determine that something is fictive, it is because, in an immediate sense, I find a discrepancy between a fictive event and the spatiotemporal and conceptual order in which it purports to fit. It is evident that in eyewitness testimony, a claim to have perceived something that goes against the logic of the spatiotemporal order is discounted, for if a certain person was seen by a large number of people at a given time in a given place, it is impossible for her to have been in another place at the same time.

Here, however, we must go a step further and specify that this "fit" within the web of events depends precisely on the prior organization of this web in relation to a symbolic order—or better, symbolic "orders"—which the public sphere presupposes. It is here, indeed, that the possibility of reinserting events into the web of the past presupposes the symbolic character of the temporal, spatial, or conceptual relations in terms of which it is organized. It is symbolically mediated in the sense that there is no experience in the abstract and that, as Ernst Cassirer has pointed out, even what are taken to be the most basic kinds of spatial or temporal perception and their concrete conceptual elaboration presuppose the work of symbolic embodiment insofar as concrete unities are isolated within the flow of experience and treated as equal or unequal quanta, of greater or lesser intensity, belonging either to uniform processes or to different or incommensurable orders, such as the utilitarian and the aesthetic, the sacred or the profane, the good or the reprehensible. We invest all such situations with a symbolic sense through which they may be meaningfully communicated to others and in terms of which the possibilities of their coherent fit into the web of reality may be explored. It is in this specific sense, therefore, that imagination shows itself to be intrinsic to the public construction of reality, but it is not for this reason that such constructions are "imaginary."

This idea may be illustrated more clearly if we briefly examine the most ubiquitous of all prerequisites of experience—that of time perception. In dealing with time, we must be wary of the categories of ordinary language, which, in referring to *time* in the singular, immediately lead us to interpret it as an autonomous, uniform medium of experience. We must employ the philosopher's skepticism concerning the persuasive power of ordinary language and inspect more closely what we mean by *time* and the *temporal web* of events. Unless we presuppose that time exists primordially as an undifferentiated *durée*, in the sense of Henri Bergson, which, as such, can be the basis of no articulation and of no communication, temporal relations, as soon as they are brought to awareness and divided into numerical units, are necessarily mediated by *symbols*, for they are always ordered according to some communally intelligible numbering system. Such temporal relations are further charged with symbolic meaning when they are fit into the web of time in calendar form, be it in the Christian, Jewish, or Moslem frame of temporal reference. To be remembered and publicly communicated, all events that are placed in a temporal web of relations depend on imagination in its fundamental way of situating them in the symbolic order to which they are bound. Let us frame this idea in more technical philosophical terms. What Kant took to be the uniform schematizing work of pure imagination in the early part of the transcendental analytic of the *Critique of Pure Reason* is more comprehensively characterized—without any necessary recourse to Kantian or neo-Kantian epistemology and its reference to the uniform transcendental subject as the source of all meaning-constituting acts—as the work of symbolization in its broadest sense, through which embodied symbols schematize experience by organizing it, at its most fundamental level, in terms of concrete, collectively mediated modes of interpretation. In the final analysis, it is therefore on the delineation of the concrete symbolic structure of the public world of interpretable events, persons, and things that the possibility of distinguishing between fiction and reality depends. It is in terms of this delineation also that we may approach a past that lies beyond all contemporary memory—the remote memory borrowed from the testimony of others and attested by their traces. Insofar as it speaks to us at all, it does so from out of a network of embodied symbols in relation to which we may interpret its real or fictive character. This fund or network of embodied symbols, prior to any codified tradition or historiographical elaboration, underlies what I term "collective memory," with which the self-interpretation of groups in each successive present must grapple.

Symbols, of course, as I have pointed out, may be understood in two principle ways: either in the broader sense, as fundamental organizing principles of experience or, in a more narrow sense, as representatives or signs of something that cannot present itself before immediate perception. If this distinction, as I conceive of it, presupposes that the basic task common to all forms of symbolic embodiment lies in the collectively mediated organization of experience, through which experience is given a communicable sense, the different articulations of the symbol, both broad and narrow, correspond to a plurality of interrelated orders in which they are embodied.

III

We may illustrate this complex stratification of embodied symbols if we pursue a bit further our interpretation of the symbolic embodiment of time. In an earlier reference to the elementary ways of dividing and enumerating time, I referred to the broadest sense of the symbol as it lends schematic structure to experience to render it communicable. In this sense, to return briefly to Chateaubriand's account of his dinner with George Washington, to which I referred at the outset, it is possible to fit this encounter into the simple temporal sequence in which, within the larger web of events, their lives were interwoven. This, however, designates only the most rudimentary and general level of succession and simultaneity in the web of events corresponding to a broad symbolic interpretation of experience. As a personal record, it might be narrated in a diary or journal. Its particular significance to a broader public, however, conveyed by Chateaubriand's evocative style, lies not only in his personal impressions of Washington in the context of his voyage to the New World but, at another level of symbolic elaboration, in his interpretation of

Washington's unique role as a statesman. Here we enter a symbolic order of another and more specific kind, in which temporal relations are not only organizing principles in the immediate web of experience, but are interwoven with a topic of reflection in which the symbolic interpretation of Washington's simplicity and imposing stature were taken to be attributes of the new political regime he represented. Chateaubriand's reminiscence of Washington stimulates musing, as he himself recounts, on the world-historical symbol that Washington incarnated in his eyes, which the author developed in a comparison of Washington with his contemporary, Napoleon Bonaparte. As Chateaubriand wrote, "Washington cannot be characterized, like Bonaparte, as a being rising beyond all human stature. There is nothing astonishing about his personality. Far from being engaged in a vast theatre of action, [. . .] he defends himself with a handful of citizens on land without fame, in the narrow circle of domestic hearths. He does not wage wars to renew the triumphs of Arbelles and Pharsale; he does not overturn kingdoms to reward others with their remains."[15] Here we recognize a powerful source of the imagery— indeed a variety of "political myth"—that Chateaubriand developed in detail in the course of his narrative: he juxtaposed what he took to be the corrupt old world with the untarnished simplicity of the new, and proposed a vision of regimes and of times which, in his eyes, Bonaparte and Washington symbolically exemplified.

My purpose in relating the concept of collective memory to the symbol through the work of imagination in this chapter has been twofold: first, I have argued that memory on a collective scale corresponds to what can be symbolically embodied and communicated; second, I have stipulated that collective remembrance in the public sphere depends upon imagination for translation into symbolic expression, yet it is not for this reason simply imaginary. Only the skeptic can deny the nuances between different articulations of the imagination and, in view of ever-present possibilities of distortion and manipulation, invariably treat remembered experiences that are communicated among vast groups as so many *fables convenues*.

CHAPTER 2

Analyzing Collective Memory

In our investigation of the concept of collective memory thus far I have equated it with transmission of shared experience which has been retained by a group. Beyond this rudimentary sense, as I stipulated, the concept of collective remembrance exhibits a seemingly infinite complexity in relation to the level at which it is analyzed. At the primordial level, memory necessarily refers to the original sphere of experience in the intimacy of personal life; in any strict sense of the word, therefore, collectivities never "remember." On another level, when we focus on group experience in which personal life is interwoven, memory appears in a very different perspective in relation to a small group, such as a family or professional association, or to a more extended collectivity, such as the public sphere of national identity and of public commemoration. When seen in terms of such heterogeneity at the different levels of its expression, we may wonder according to what principle it may be identified, or in what "place" it might be located.

The previous chapter situated this locus of memory in relation to what I termed the *web of experience* among individuals and groups, in which, at its different levels, memory is entangled. It is in terms of this web, as we have seen, and of the possibility of fitting it into a coherent spatiotemporal and conceptual order, that we are able to establish the reality of the remembered past and to distinguish it from fictional creations that do not belong to this web. Far from a static configuration, we have emphasized the mobile character of this web, which is constantly being re-elaborated by those whose experience is entangled in its symbolic ramifications.

My task in this chapter is to examine more closely the articulations of this web of remembered experience as the locus in which collective memory finds its bearings and its unity as a coherent and therefore "real" system of relations. An example that is particularly appropriate to elucidate this "place" of collective memory is suggested by the famous speech of Martin Luther King Jr., "I Have a Dream."

I

Martin Luther King Jr. delivered this speech on August 28, 1963, during the March on Washington, which drew more than two hundred thousand participants. The demonstration was called in the name of the civil rights movement, which was protesting the conditions of political and social inequality to which black Americans were subjected. This event also marked a commemoration: assembled before the Lincoln memorial, it recalled the centenary of the famous Emancipation Proclamation by which President Abraham Lincoln, in the midst of the American Civil War, proclaimed the liberation of the black slaves. Martin Luther King Jr. called attention to this commemoration in his speech, and he also reminded his hearers that the promise of equality made by Lincoln had never been kept.

Dr. King presented this speech on a very hot and humid Wednesday under clear and sunny late-summer skies, during which the tension was palpable because of the unusually large number of police on duty that day. To an observer who witnessed this speech "in the flesh," even from afar, the circumstances making up the context of the speech were everywhere in evidence. Prior to the speech itself, a number of civil rights leaders representing different organizations, along with Dr. King himself, accompanied a large assembly of demonstrators, both black and white, of different ages and from different walks of life, to the site where the speech was delivered. Dr. King and other leaders wore dark suits and ties, but some of them wore Ghandi-style white hats. Observers of the event "in the flesh" might have simultaneously seen not only this focus of interest, but myriad other details, including the attentive silence of the forces of order, the casual apparel of many of the demonstrators, their enthusiasm and generally upbeat mood, all of which belonged to the surrounding lifeworld, within the horizon of which the speech was presented. Even if many participants in the event paid little or no attention to these circumstances, and perhaps later forgot them, in certain cases they provided themes for explicit recall and reflection.

The March on Washington was a momentous event not only for those who participated in it or observed it directly, but also for a large number of television viewers who followed it from afar. Indeed, the March on Washington and Martin Luther King Jr.'s speech were one of the earliest events in American history that had a broad television impact that complemented radio transmission and subsequent newspaper reports. Direct observers beheld the event from near or from afar, in relation to the orientation of their bodies, and they were able to simultaneously view both the central focus of the scene and its broader context; television viewers' perception of the event was mediated by the camera's field of vision as it zoomed in on and out of selected images and scenes. The vicarious presence made possible by a technical medium excluded the sensuous givenness of the surrounding lifeworld because its narrow field of vision cropped out the full scope of its environing horizon, while enabling a virtual proximity to the center of interest, which in most cases greatly increased its visibility for the spectators.

For all who viewed the event, whether present "in the flesh" or in the mediated format of a video broadcast, the significance of the remembered experience was conveyed through symbols at different levels of expression. Situated in the large mall before the Lincoln Memorial, the space in which the speech was delivered was symbolically embodied in the broad sense I identified in the previous chapter, for it was spontaneously recognizable as the public space of an urban park, as opposed to the semipublic area of a shopping mall or the private space of a residential yard. In the course of his speech, King invested the public space with a sacrosanct quality, referring to it as "this hallowed spot."[1] In the more narrow sense of the symbol, where it designates in sensuous form what is absent from all possible immediate perception, the space of commemoration drew its significance from the large statue of Lincoln sitting in the immediate background, to whom King referred in the opening words of his speech as the "great American in whose symbolic shadow we stand today."[2] This provided the ideal topographic setting for the presentation of his message.

If we turn for a moment to the symbolic configuration of the temporal setting of the speech, we similarly recognize implicit signs that are so much a part of the habitual lifeworld of those who belong to it that they ordinarily go unnoticed. Nonetheless, all collective experience and subsequent recollection presuppose, at the most general level, myriad signs that designate a given *present* and permit observers to identify it as a unified temporal context. In everyday life, we spontaneously wear clothing, make gestures, use implements, or employ specific words for a variety of reasons, in conformity with pragmatic, aesthetic, religious, or other factors. All of these are identifiable in terms of the concrete temporal context in which they are rooted, or what I have termed their *horizon of contemporaneity*.[3] If it is possible to use outmoded implements, to wear unfashionable clothes, and to use outdated gestures and language, it is always in reference to a particular context or "horizon of con-temporaneity" that the unseasonable, the anachronistic, or the outmoded be-come perceptible as temporally rooted signs. Moreover, this context concerns not only direct experience in the everyday lifeworld, but is also the essential reference through which the current immediacy of television broadcasts fits into the broader *present* context. Our belief in the reality of news programs that claim to bring us up to date on the latest events depends in important measure on the spontaneous correspondence of what they report with (or at least its noncontradiction of) the overall horizon of contemporaneity origi-nally rooted in the everyday lifeworld of "in the flesh" encounters.

Fifty years after Martin Luther King Jr.'s "I Have a Dream" speech, a host of signs in the video recordings permit us to recognize that this event no longer belongs to our present context, but to one of the recent past: the hair styles, the women's long skirts, bobby socks, flat tennis shoes, and the cars in the street are all part of this contemporaneous context of the recent past, as is the language of Dr. King himself, whose references to the "negro" and to the con-dition of "negro Americans," in the aftermath of changes in attitude toward blacks that Dr. King himself helped to bring about, are no longer considered to be appropriate terms of reference. As habitual aspects of the world of early 1960s America, such phenomena were rarely noticed by contemporaries, for they fit into a specific context of contemporaneity that they took as much for granted as the air they breathed. By contrast, those who stand in a different context immediately apprehend the signs that differentiate it from their own. This symbolically configured context forms the basis for the "web of events" making up the locus of collective memory.

I myself recall Martin Luther King Jr.'s speech, which I watched on televi-sion as a young boy. Through the recollections of those who lived through this period, generations born after the 1960s are able to be aware of the event and also of the context in which it occurred. In this sense, as Maurice Halb-wachs clearly appreciated, there is an overlap in the contemporaneity of liv-ing generations, even if, in the case of younger groups, we must refer to an indirect memory borrowed from the living recollections of older generations. Overlapping living generations, as Halbwachs understood, are able to share through their contemporaneity a basis for experiential *continuity* that quickly fades when no living memory remains to recount past events and to elucidate the nuances of the temporal context in which they were situated.[4]

This circumstance may be elucidated if we look for a moment outside the sphere of the recent past to evoke an example drawn from the historical past beyond the possibilities of recollection of currently living generations. Chateaubriand provides a poignant illustration of this at an early point in his *Mémoires d'outre-tombe*, where he evokes his youthful experience of the first years of the French Revolution in Paris. He recalls in vivid terms the effervescence and enthusiasm of the years 1790 and 1791 during which, for a short period, an unprecedented liberty in clothing styles, in demeanor, and in expression prevailed in the French capital. In a period of rapid and radical upheaval, even the most ordinary aspects of life entered into a state of flux. We can assess the utter distance from us of this past context if we reflect on the complexity of habitual temporal references of that momentous time where, in everyday fashion and demeanor, the new stood alongside the old. Among the many facets of this situation, Chateaubriand records what he presented as a typical occurrence: "Beside a man in French dress, with powdered head, sword at his side, hat under his arm, pumps and silk stockings, walked a man with short, unpowdered hair, in English tail-coat with American tie."[5]

Who today, centuries after this event, might be able to evoke in memory, even in the borrowed recollection of a former time, not simply isolated events or their general interrelations, but the profounder nuances encompassed in the myriad situations intertwined as a concrete "web of experience" within the horizon of contemporaneity in which such events transpired? Even flights of the imagination within the temporal bounds of our contemporary world, insofar as they are limited in scope to the lifeworld of living generations, could hardly recapitulate the concrete plenitude of such everyday past situations.[6] We are able to discover these past possibilities and, above all, the experiential horizon in which they are rooted, only through narratives that speak to us from the historical past, complemented by the historical research that subjects them to scrutiny in the framework of their contextual horizon.

II

In dealing with Martin Luther King Jr.'s speech thus far, I have evoked the broad symbolic details making up its spatial and temporal context, but not the impact of the specific symbols that account for its epoch-making significance. Their singular meaning derives from Dr. King's ability to draw on what stood outside the immediately given web of events and to evoke, on different symbolic levels, the repercussions of the unfulfilled promise made to black Americans. In this vein, King recalled the principal topic of Lincoln's speech a hundred years earlier: the idea of equality upon which, beginning with the Declaration of Independence of 1776, the American nation was founded. "We hold these truths to be self-evident, that all men are created equal," are words from this document that were cited by Lincoln and evoked once again by Martin Luther King. On another level, the founding fathers of the United States did not limit themselves to a purely *political* legitimation of this principle of equality; they also grounded it in what they considered to be a divine sanction. Lincoln did not hesitate to refer to this religious basis of the principle of equality, and Dr. King recalled with singular eloquence its profound eschatological source. Thus, after envisioning an end to racial strife in the American south and the possibility that black and white children might walk peacefully hand in hand, the Protestant pastor evoked the prophetic vision— drawing on the New Testament gospel of Luke, which explicitly recalled the Old Testament words of the prophet Isaiah: "The glory of the Lord shall be revealed, and all flesh shall see it together."[7] The unusual force of Dr. King's speech arose from his ability to draw on political and theological symbols from different levels of stratification that, in their familiarity to his audience, touched on deep sources of group identification and provided a decisive point of orientation for future collective remembrance.

In situating the "place" of collective memory as illustrated through this example, we can elicit at once the recollections retained by those who experienced the speech on August 28, 1963, both among contemporaries who were present at the event and who saw Martin Luther King Jr. "in the flesh," even if at a distance, and those who followed it as it was conveyed through the media. As a young schoolboy, I recall how vividly this discourse moved me as I watched it on television. I remember the tense context in which it was presented in the year 1963, which, less than three months later, would witness the assassination of John F. Kennedy. The demonstrators, the schoolboy who viewed it on television, and the contemporaries who learned of the event through the media would all remember a contemporaneous experience that was either directly or indirectly apprehended at various points of distance from the event itself. Through the imaginative act of symbolic embodiment, the significance of the event was open to subsequent interpretation from a variety of possible perspectives: contemporaries who appreciated the profound significance of Martin Luther King Jr.'s speech initially grasped the importance of the event and his contribution, which is today the object of official commemoration on a national scale.

The example provided by Dr. King's speech permits us to situate the "place" of collective memory more closely through a clarification of the concepts of sedimentation, stratification, and fragmentation of symbols that collective memory embodies. In employing the concept of the stratification of sedimented symbols, I refer to the complex layers of symbolic signification, rooted deeply in the past and referring less to the configuration of direct experience than to what lies beyond its immediacy. In view of the complexity of symbolic layers in Martin Luther King Jr.'s speech, the mere fact of having witnessed this event, whether "in the flesh" or through the media, in no way guaranteed that its collective significance had been grasped. Here immediate personal experience of an event must be distinguished from an apprehension of its symbolic implications. It would have been possible, indeed, to listen to the speech without comprehending its public significance. One might have failed to pay attention to its words, as many often do while listening to political utterances, which are for them a source of infinite boredom. One might in such a case recall ancillary or even trivial phenomena—the beautiful sun that illuminated the August sky, the unusually large number of police called in for the occasion, or the tension that could everywhere be felt on this momentous occasion. To my mind, it is essential not to confuse the recalled personal impressions of an event that has been directly experienced, or the recall of impressions that have been indirectly conveyed, with the grasp of diverse levels of embodied symbols that underlie its collective significance. Here I must draw a distinction that is essential to our discussion. I distinguish between the multitude of perspectives retained by personal memories of a collectively experienced event and the symbolic embodiment of memory, constituting a collectively significant locus for past experience. And the point that I seek to make is that "collective memory" can be reduced neither to one nor the other of these moments, but gravitates between them as modes of recall of the remembered past. At one extremity is found the singularity of perspective that roots all collectively significant experience in the web of personal remembrance; at the other extremity, symbolic incorporation raises remembrance beyond personal experience to confer upon it significance and communicability in the collective sphere. At one extremity, it is possible to limit remembrance so completely to the realm of personal experience that its collective significance is blurred ("the beautiful sun that illuminated the August sky, the unusually large number of police forces called in to maintain order, the tension that could everywhere be felt on this momentous occasion"); at the other extremity, even after all personal, living recollection of the event has vanished, its symbolic embodiment as a specific occurrence can be recalled and reenacted to lend significance to later collective experience (Martin Luther King declaring, "I have a dream").

At the level of symbolic embodiment of remembered experience, the concept of "fragmented" collective memory accounts for the different and even contradictory ways in which the same symbolically embodied memories may be interpreted. Southerners hostile to the message of the black pastor or the head of the FBI, J. Edgar Hoover, who was implacably hostile toward Martin Luther King and his cause, accorded a very different symbolic significance to the event than did his supporters. This hostility toward the legacy of Martin Luther King Jr. also came clearly to the fore in the decades after his death, above all on the occasion of the vote in Congress concerning the establishment of a national holiday on Martin Luther King's birthday. A number of southern congressmen vehemently opposed this bill, and Senator Jesse Helms threatened a filibuster of the bill while accusing Dr. King of having harbored communist sympathies. In spite of President Ronald Reagan's ambivalence toward Martin Luther King Jr., he signed the bill into law in 1983.[8] In this sense collective memory is, from the very point of its genesis, fragmented memory.[9]

Amid this diversity of interpretations, it is in the thickness of its many stratifications that symbolic embodiment confers on collective memory a perdurability extending well beyond the lives of those who directly experience a moment in its ongoing and changing articulation. And this perdurability indicates a dimension of symbolic incorporation of language and bodily gesture that constitutes a meta-personal fount of personal and interpersonal interaction.

CHAPTER 3

Thresholds of Personal Identity and Public Experience

The theoretical analysis undertaken thus far has proposed to interpret the significance and scope of collective memory in relation to the imagination and then to situate its place at different levels of articulation, extending from small groups to the vast domain of the public sphere. The conception of collective memory I have developed has focused primarily on it as a public phenomenon, since memories retained among smaller groups presuppose the existence of publicly communicable symbols comprising a web of interwoven significations that successive generations take up and modify in overlapping contexts of contemporaneity that gradually fade into the historical past. The conditions of continuity between these contexts, as I have illustrated, are forged at different levels of the temporal articulation through which collective memory assumes its ongoing patterns.

This concluding chapter of the first section shifts its focus in order to explore the *limits* of collective memory and to more directly situate what lies beyond its scope. It takes as its theme the "place" of remembered experience that has fallen into oblivion and no longer circulates in the reservoir of recollections upon which, in a given present, group experience spontaneously draws. It is here too that, in highlighting the modes of latency and of forgetting at the different personal, small group, and public levels, we may further elucidate the unique status of collective remembrance in the public sphere, most notably in the identification of the specific modes of inadvertence, opacity, and oblivion lying beyond the scope of what is acknowledged to be publicly significant communal recollection.

In order to sound the depths of collective memory and underscore its limits, I first focus on the bounds of recall in the original sphere of personal experience and place in relief its specific difference in regard to the various levels of group experience with which it is entangled. This latter topic involves a closer scrutiny of the bounds of what might be legitimately termed collectively remembered experience—above all in its public scope.

I

As I briefly indicated in the introduction, the question concerning the status of incidents or objects in past experience that are forgotten and fall into oblivion played a role of singular importance in the genesis of modern reflection on personal identity. In this light I introduce the theme of inadvertence and of forgetting of past experience by placing it in relation to its genesis as a topic of modern philosophical reflection.

Among the sources of the theoretical investigation of memory, this theme of inadvertence and of forgetting of past experience became a primary issue of debate following Locke's interpretation of the relation between memory and personal identity in his *Essay Concerning Human Understanding*. This theme assumed a wholly new form in the wake of his epoch-making critique of traditional metaphysical assumptions concerning the intelligibility of the human soul as a substantial being. As noted in the introduction, Locke's assumption that self-understanding is achieved only through experience, and that experience provides no occasion to confirm the existence of a substantial soul, led him to conclude that the only source of self-knowledge and of personal identity lies in the memory it retains of itself and its experiences over time—the capacity of the self to "consider itself as itself, the same thinking thing in different times and places."[1]

This conclusion, however, carried with it bewildering implications. For Locke, indeed, the corollary that corresponded to this conclusion was that *only* what the self retains in remembrance belongs to its ongoing identity; what is no longer remembered, by contrast, no longer belongs to the realm of self-experience. "If there be any part of [my] existence," as Locke wrote, "which I cannot upon recollection join with that present consciousness, whereby I am now my*self*, it is in that part of its existence no more myself, than any other immaterial being."[2]

Subsequent reflection on the theme of personal identity revealed the problematic consequences of this conclusion. All remembrance depends upon a selection from a vast and, indeed, infinitely varied multiplicity of events that might serve as topics of recall. This consideration led critics of Locke, such as the eighteenth-century philosopher David Hume, to point out that only a minute selection from the multiplicity of experienced events is later available to recall. If I try to reconstruct in memory all that I did in the recent past, for example on a given day or a given week of the previous year, most of my recollections are at best confused and vague. Aside from momentous events that may permanently mark my life, most of the myriad episodes of personal experience are no longer subject to recall and, in many cases, have faded into oblivion. On the basis of the conscious retrieval of past experience, memory would thus seem to be far too weak to constitute the identity of the person. From the standpoint of present awareness therefore, according to Hume's telling statement in *A Treatise of Human Nature*, "Memory does not so much produce as discover personal identity."[3] And, given the fact that our experience of ourselves and of our doings in the past has so often been forgotten, the logical conclusion for Hume was that the self we discover, rather than a tangible entity, turns out to be a fictive creation of the imagination.

We need not accept the radicalism of Hume's skeptical conclusion concerning personal identity to appreciate the deep dilemma his philosophy placed in evidence. And if we attempt to draw consequences from this debate on memory and personal identity for contemporary reflection, it is perhaps not to Hume but to Locke's contemporary, Leibniz, that we must turn. Leibniz criticized Locke's theory from a different perspective which, as I interpret it, anticipated and set the ground for theoretical reflection that bears not only on the theme of personal identity, but on that of remembered experience in the collective sphere.

In his interpretation of memory in relation to personal identity in the *Nouveaux essais sur l'entendement humain*, which presented a direct response to Locke, Leibniz advanced the hypothesis that past experience, even when it is forgotten, continues to exercise a role in the delineation of the present identity of the forgetter. To support this conclusion, Leibniz pointed out that *obliviousness* does not only concern *past* experience, but also encompasses experience in the original plenitude of the living present. What I retain of personal experience in the past depends in large measure on the *attention* I paid to it while it was still being experienced. Indeed, all present experience involves a focus on given aspects of the present and, therefore, a measure of inadvertence or unmindfulness in regard to myriad other aspects standing in the foreground or background of a given context in which experience transpires. All conscious apprehension, indeed, is accomplished against the subliminal background of an infinite multitude of minute perceptions (*petites perceptions, perceptions inaperçues*) that are ordinarily not noticed. If, therefore, the infinite plenitude of experience generally escapes notice, Leibniz at the same time readily acknowledged that even that part of experience to which attention has been lent quickly loses its sharpness and clarity. But where this is admitted, it does not allow us to conclude, as Hume would later do, that minute and even unperceived aspects of the present and forgotten aspects of the past do not continue to mark our identity.

In my elaboration of a theory of memory in its anthropological scope, I do not delve into the metaphysical basis upon which Leibniz sought to establish his theory: from the assumption concerning the continuing presence in memory of an infinite manifold of perceptions that constitute personal identity, he postulated the ongoing subsistence, beyond all conscious apprehension or memory, of an underlying substantial soul. What remains fruitful from the anthropological standpoint of our present investigation are two orders of reasoning that Leibniz's considerations anticipated, at once psychological and ethical, to which I limit my reflection.

The ethical argument brought forth by Leibniz's objection to Locke's theory may be stated simply: Locke's assumption that personal identity is entirely constituted by the recollection of past acts allows no distinction between what one has done in the past and what one later *believes* one has done. This not only excludes what has been forgotten, but also those aspects of the past that have subsequently been misrepresented or distorted. "Memory after an interval may deceive," wrote Leibniz; "we have experienced it often."[4] Moral identity, however, requires that we account for acts that we have *really* committed, even if we have forgotten them or distorted them in our recollection. In extreme situations, we may even entertain the possibility that consciousness of our past life as a whole has been obliterated; yet even in such cases our past continues to constitute our *moral* identity. Leibniz subtly formulates this idea in his *Nouveaux essais sur l'entendement humain*: "Yes, even if I had forgotten all of the past," he wrote, "so that I had forgotten everything, even my name, and even had to relearn to read and to write, even then might I learn of my past life in my earlier state from others, as I would retain, in the same way, my rights, without requiring that I divide myself into two persons to inherit what I bequeath to myself. All of this suffices to maintain moral identity, in which personal identity consists."[5] The decisive consideration that Leibniz introduced here lay in his conviction that even if I have completely forgotten my past acts, a reliable witness or group of witnesses are capable of giving testimony in regard to what truly happened in the past. For this reason, even if I have forgotten my past acts, *others* may be able to give reliable testimony to restore the factual occurrences of the past in which I participated. As Leibniz wrote, "The testimony of others may fill the void of my reminiscence," and this account may, indeed, be invoked in legal proceedings.[6]

The second response to the question concerning the role of the forgotten past places particular emphasis on the dormant or unconscious status of recollections, which, although no longer present, continue to influence personal identity. Where Leibniz underlined the profound theoretical significance of latent experience for the constitution of personal identity, he anticipated a theme that reemerged as a central preoccupation in the late nineteenth century, at least in part due to the ongoing influence of his reflection. It would extend beyond the purview of our present investigation to deal with the genesis of more recent schools of reflection over the past century and a half concerning the theme of dormant or unconscious aspects of experience. I briefly pursue two ramifications of this theory for the interest they present for our immediate topic: the extension of dormant or unconscious memory beyond the personal sphere to that of collective memory.

Within the framework of personal experience, I may refer to this notion of dormant recollection in the general sense of latent memory. A person I meet for the first time, for example, may make an agreeable impression on me, but she might at one point in our conversation let fall a disparaging or incongruent word in regard to me or my acquaintances, or might make an unexpected and almost involuntary grimace betraying deep-seated feelings that are not brought to more explicit expression. On such occasions, I might take no heed of this sign, yet at a later point, as I become more thoroughly acquainted with this person, words or gestures to which I paid little attention may be recalled from the latent recesses of my awareness, and they may thus take on a new significance. To this form of recall, however, which may suddenly dawn upon us without the exertion of a conscious effort, we may also add those long-forgotten recollections that, at unexpected moments and in wholly unforeseeable ways, make their *involuntary* return.

Marcel Proust was particularly attentive to this *mémoire involontaire*, which he eloquently described in his novel, *A la recherche du temps perdu*. Proust emphasized this virtual existence of the long-forgotten past, entangled in the totality of awareness, which present associations draw out of the obscure reaches of our being. "Memory," as he wrote in a suggestive passage, "rather than being a second copy, that is always present before us, of the diverse facts of our life, is rather the nothingness out of which a present resemblance permits us at times to draw dead remembrances, as resurrected; but there are still a thousand small facts that did not enter into this virtuality of memory, and which will always remain uncontrollable for us."[7] Proust's notion of the *mémoire involontaire* brings to the fore a dimension of personal identity in which, for the definition of selfhood, the obscure, the latent, and the forgotten episodes of our experience play an essential role: "We are only what we possess; we only possess what is really present, and so many of our remembrances, of our moods, of our ideas embark on voyages far away from us, and we lose sight of them! We are unable to account for them in that totality making up our being. But they find their secret paths to return within us."[8]

Proust's ruminations on the role of the *mémoire involontaire* did not limit it to the sphere of personal experience. Indeed, in his subsequent commentary on *A la recherche du temps perdu*, Proust contrasted his conception of memory with that elaborated by his great predecessor, Henri Bergson. Against Bergson's identification of genuine memory with the singular image drawn from personal experience, Proust emphasized the fundamental status of involuntary memory: as elaborated and situated in a later context of the remember, these memories, precisely because they are involuntary, "are the only ones that bear the mark of authenticity."[9] And, since they arise from the hidden depths of the personal self, the unwilled resurgence of these memories at the same time resuscitates a network of interrelations with others. In the famous scene of the madeleine that provides an occasion for the introduction of the topic of the *mémoire involontaire* at the beginning of the novel, the senses of taste and smell restore to the protagonist, Marcel, a past that, unlike these sensations, is not limited to a realm of personal impressions, but reaches out to encompass a world of shared experience: "The good people of the village and their little dwellings and the church and all of Combray and its surroundings: all of this that takes on form and consistency arose, town and gardens, from my cup of tea."[10] Walter Benjamin emphasized precisely this interconnection between different levels of personal and collective memory in his analysis of Proust's notion of *mémoire involontaire*. As he wrote, this memory marks the return not only of the personal past but a retrieval of the cohesion of "certain contents of the individual past with material of the collective past."[11]

Psychological and, particularly, psychoanalytic theorists, as I remarked in the introduction, have placed a similar emphasis on the tacit dimension of remembrance underlying conscious experience, above all in regard to the pathological hold that memory may exert on conscious life. The well-known therapeutic aim of Freud and his followers emphasized the role of working through repressed unconscious memories with the intention of liberating individuals from their obsessive grip. Freud, moreover, as I noted, was convinced that such repressed unconscious impulses did not only concern individual patients, since for him group trauma and frustration were decisive factors that also characterize vast collectivities. In his theory of mass psychology, as we have seen, Freud proposed that the dynamics of vast groups and mass movements are essentially extensions of individual and family relations that do not fundamentally differ from them, but result from a phylogenetic tendency to repress or sublimate memory traces inherited from the archaic experiences of the primitive horde in prehistoric times.

Both ethical and psychoanalytic considerations place in evidence the role of memory as a source of identity, at both personal and collective levels of experience, above all where it is *virtual* and no longer explicitly brought to mind. The ethical light in which Leibniz initially placed the theme of a forgotten past, involuntary memory in the sense of Proust, and unconscious memory in its psychological dimension each indicate the limits of personal awareness, nourished by conscious memory, as a source of selfhood. In the case of the moral philosopher and the psychologist, we may at the same time evoke the essential role of the *other* in permitting us to resuscitate the past. For the intervention of the other, as a witness or a therapist, aims at the retrieval of what has been lost. Virtual experience may in such cases be restored through the capacity of the other to bring it back from oblivion, uncovering an implicit "place" of experience, an extra-individual and supra-personal dimension of our being from which, to use Proust's metaphor, recollections "find their secret paths to return within us," permitting us to delineate the hidden contours of personal identity. And this brings us to the decisive point: when it is a question not only of personal identity or that of small groups, but of remembered experience among large collectivities amid the diffuse reaches of the public sphere, who may be called upon to serve as this other?

II

In previous chapters, I designated the diffuseness of public experience and public recollection as the principle trait that distinguishes personal and small-group recollection from remembrance in the public sphere: whereas the former draws in important measure on direct encounters "in the flesh," such a possibility only rarely concerns group experience of publicly significant events. I lived in the United States during the difficult period of the Vietnam War, but my "experience" of that trying event was essentially limited to viewing war films diffused by the media and to occasional conversations with war veterans. Nonetheless, even where we are dealing with a soldier who participated directly in the combat, to what extent might we claim that his remembrances, gravitating between the particularity of personal impressions and the viewpoint of his immediate peer group, corresponded to politically significant "experience"? To a certain extent, as in the case of direct testimony relating a publicly significant event, diffuse public memory may depend on the recall of personal experience and, when in such cases it is forgotten, it may be, as in Leibniz's example, retrieved by the testimony of other witnesses. Yet, in spite of this possibility, there remains an irreducible difference between public memory and all other kinds of memory: actions and events in the public sphere are of such a complexity that their significance can hardly be accounted for on the basis of simple personal recollections of individuals, or even of given groups.

Here we arrive at the decisive point, for we apprehend that, in the public sphere, the symbolic sense of events depends less on the direct experience of contemporaries than on the elaboration of events—their configuration as "information"—by the mass media. We thus discover a deeper source of the distinction between remembrance in the public sphere and that of smaller groups, such as families or other associations: while memories of a smaller group most often arise from direct perception, or may be related to such perception, publicly significant collective memory essentially depends on diffuse, indirect experience, in which imaginative reconstruction and transfer play a preponderant role. And here the function of imagination in the crystallization of a symbolically embodied meaning may be appreciated in a still more comprehensive scope. This symbolizing function may, indeed, incorporate in certain circumstances both direct experience and individual and group fantasies; without this function, however, no experience or fantasy could attain to a perdurable *public* significance. On this basis, collective memory provides content both for political commemoration and for historical representation.

For the members of a political community, the absence of direct perception highlights what I have described as the unique role of imagination in the constitution of public memory, whereby significance is collectively conferred upon reported events. In the sphere of personal memory and of the recollection of small groups, as I noted, the other, whether as witness or therapist, plays a decisive role in the reconstitution of obliviated experience, and in the identification of those aspects of memory that are products of illusion or mere fantasy. In the public sphere, however, where group recollection can rarely rely on direct perception, the regulatory role of the other is far more problematic. Here ideological claims of a national group may easily contest the recollections of the limited number of eye witnesses to an event, especially where the media pass over them in silence. This is why correctives to fantasies and illusions in the public sphere are particularly hard to identify and to apply.

Does this, however, signify that there are no correctives to the rule of collective fantasy and illusion, above all in situations where they are reinforced by the representations of the media? Is there no other in the public sphere who might permit us to distinguish between imaginative reconstruction and the distortions of fantasy? Are not direct experience and eyewitness reports of decisive importance in the framework of vast mass societies? Of course, even in the public sphere the role of the other can be fulfilled by the juxtaposition of conflicting testimonies and original traces in the hope of attaining a comprehensive representation of events. But the analogy between the public sphere and more limited levels of personal and collective memory should not be exaggerated. The very complexity and diffuseness of the public realm and the fragmentary character of its symbolic configuration render the status of testimony and reporting highly problematic. If the public significance of acts and events draws less on an assemblage of personal or small-group recollections of immediate experience than on the symbolic configuration of recounted events, then here again, at the level of public reality, the principal corrective to distortion lies in the *coherence* of the larger web of recounted events from which remembered experience draws its specifically public scope.[12] In this sense, the role of the other in retrieving the forgotten or misrepresented past depends on an essentially political intention in which the symbolic function of distortions in the web of recalled events is decoded. This is by no means to contest the claim that massacres that are passed over in silence and leave behind only a motley group of mute survivors are the result on a collective scale of psychopathological aberrations or legally punishable criminal acts; it is to interpret their significance predominantly in terms of the political symbolism of particular ideologies or of given politico-theological aims that serve as the fundamental source of their public intelligibility. And here the role of the other as witness or therapist must be supplemented by the judgment of a political theorist whose methods are adapted to the public sphere.

It has often been emphasized, and justly so, that the originality of the contemporary mass media lies in their capacity to disseminate information in a context of virtual absence of personal contact between communicators and spectators. As Niklas Luhmann has suggested, the novel quality of the mass media lies in the situation of anonymity that they create by technical means.[13] This notion of general anonymity, however, should not obscure the unique symbolic power that, already at the level of language itself, mass information wields. This unique capacity of the contemporary mass media accounts for the profound difficulty that all attempts at political deciphering of information face—above all in cases where it is not simply a question of interpreting information disseminated by our own media but by those belonging to political collectivities very different from our own. And this underlines an essential feature that characterizes the contemporary globalized situation: the emergence of a world thoroughly permeated by the media, in which, for the first time in human history, the possibility exists of simultaneously referring to radically different and even contradictory information systems. This mode of simultaneity of different information systems, and of the immediate presence of the most variegated kinds of information originating in radically different contexts highlights the unique temporal structure of the virtual forms of remembered experience in the public sphere that I explore more fully in chapter 5, which concerns the mass media and the configuration of collective memory in the public sphere.

The identification of the qualitatively unique place of public memory leads us, in conclusion, to insist on the paradoxical role that collective memory has assumed in the public sphere in our present era. In our contemporary world, despite the immediacy of media coverage, the chasm between personal experience and the public realm has tended to widen. With the multiplication of political agents in our mass societies, as Alexis de Tocqueville already anticipated in *Democracy in America*,[14] the centers of political action become increasingly diffuse, creating an ever wider chasm between political events and those who seek to recall and explain them. On one hand, public remembrance serves as a primary vehicle for political identification; on the other hand, the events on which remembrance focuses become ever more elusive as concrete contents of representation. It is perhaps this paradox that accounts for the increasing proliferation of monuments and archives seeking to collect and to preserve traces of public memory. They provide tangible symbolic images to reinforce the precarious ties between personal experience and the public sphere of political action, which has become opaque.

This quest has its own inherent dangers. Where memory is assigned a task it cannot hope to fulfill, that of bridging the abyss between personal identity and a mass public, this may lead in extreme forms to a denial of the reality of events that recollection cannot hope to fathom. Where the many-layered complexity of the public sphere is forgotten, fragmented recollections may all too readily be manipulated to promote the illusion that they are direct "experiences," capable of symbolically configuring the coherence of events as a whole. The deliberative task of imagination as it deciphers the evanescent context of symbols, permitting us to situate and reconstitute the past, is contaminated by collective fantasies that radically distort its factual texture. The abyss between memory and political reality is all too readily filled by fictional representations of public identity, which, in the guise of political myths, have become an all-too-familiar facet of our contemporary political world.

Critical Reflections:
The Contemporary Theories of
Edelman, Ricœur, and Nora

We have reached a point in our analysis at which we may clarify the conception of collective memory that has been elaborated thus far by engaging in critical scrutiny of contemporary theories that, from very different perspectives, have played a significant role in orienting it in recent years. Three such theories, above all, have served as matrices for the study of collective memory in the contemporary human, natural, and cultural sciences, encompassing hermeneutics, the neurocognitive, and sociohistorical disciplines. I first deal with the hermeneutic philosophy of Paul Ricœur and with the way in which, after elaborating a critique of the Freudian theory of the symbol in his early work, he shifted his angle of approach and adapted this theory to his later conception of group identity and collective memory. This examination is followed by a critical appraisal of Gerald Edelman's application of neurobiological and evolutionary theory to the domain of collective experience and collective memory and by an analysis of the concept of collective memory in the historical writings of Pierre Nora. Each of these methodologies presents an approach to collective memory that is difficult to reconcile with the others. Let us briefly examine their respective claims and subject the presuppositions of each to critical analysis.

I

Paul Ricœur's interpretation of Freudian psychoanalysis in his early book, *Freud and Philosophy: An Essay on Interpretation* (1970), and in the different perspectives of his later writings has a direct bearing on the topic of the symbol and of its relation to collective memory. At the beginning of *Freud and Philosophy*, Ricœur elaborated a conception of the symbol in terms of which he then subjected the Freudian theory to critical scrutiny. As Ricœur defined it in the opening pages of *Freud and Philosophy*, the work of the symbol lies in its capacity to represent what is absent and, above all, what cannot be presented in the sphere of direct sensuous experience. At earlier points in the present work, I have highlighted this concept of the symbol, corresponding to what I characterized as its narrower function, deriving notably from its Christian sources and its subsequent re-elaboration in the philosophy of Kant. The goldfinch as a symbol of resurrection or the flag as a symbol of the nation represent in this manner what stands beyond the possibilities of direct sensuous apprehension. Ricœur's hermeneutic reference to the symbol in this narrower sense led him to exclude the broader idea of the symbol developed by Ernst Cassirer in his *Philosophy of Symbolic Forms*.[1] For Cassirer, as I have noted at earlier points in my analysis, the function of the symbol was not limited to representing extra-sensuous spheres of meaning, but was extended to encompass the spatiotemporal and conceptual preconditions of experience as a whole.

As Ricœur pointed out, Freud's psychological conception of the symbol also defined it in terms of this narrower function, since symbols stand for what is not manifest in experience, but remains hidden, operating in the form of signs that must be deciphered by the competent therapist. In considering Freud's psychological interpretation of the symbol's representative function, Ricœur, however, entertained doubts concerning what he took to be Freud's one-sided conception of this function in terms of psychic processes, whereby it was reduced to the expression of repressed unconscious drives in the form of symptoms. Here Ricœur sought to determine the limits of this psychoanalytic theory of the symbol. He pointed out that while symbols may indeed represent symptoms of neurotic illnesses, an essential component of their meaning may be lost when they are examined too exclusively in this light. While symbols may be signs of regression and symptoms of illness, they may also, according to Ricœur's terminology, convey a "progressive" significance serving to communicate inspiration, as in the work of art, a religious doctrine, or an original political foundation.[2] Ricœur sought to place in evidence a multiplicity of significations intrinsic to the symbol and to indicate a plenitude of symbolic nuances that the psychoanalytic method overlooked.

A decade and a half following the publication of *Freud and Philosophy*, Ricœur modified his theory of the symbol. Indeed, in the first volume of his *Time and Narrative*, he claimed that human action is "always symbolically mediated." To support this premise, he explicitly drew on the theory of the symbol developed in Ernst Cassirer's *Philosophy of Symbolic Forms*, as on the work of anthropologist Clifford Geertz.[3] In this context, he more or less embraced the broader concept of the symbol that he had previously rejected, for he now conceived of it not only as a means of representing what is absent, but as a mode of structuring experience as a whole.

In light of my interpretation of collective memory, these different approaches to the symbol, the narrower and the broader, are compatible with one another and, as I have emphasized, stand at different levels of the social construction of reality. At different levels, each contributes to the minimal task of rendering experience communicable. Be this as it may, Paul Ricœur, after a cursory reference to the theme of the symbol at the beginning of *Time and Narrative*, did not further clarify this theme in the two volumes of this work that followed, nor did he return to it in his principal later writings, such as *Oneself as Another* (*Soi-même comme un autre*, 1990) or *Memory, History, Forgetting* (*La mémoire, l'histoire, l'oubli*, 2000). In view of the central role accorded to the topic of collective experience and collective memory in *Memory, History, Forgetting*, this absence of analysis of the symbol is puzzling; for, as I interpret it, only an adequate theory of the symbol can account for the complex levels of mediation that lie between personal experience and memory in the collective sphere.

In the brief section of *Memory, History, Forgetting* that deals with the phenomenon of collective memory, in which Ricœur examined the problem posed by the cohesion of the collective sphere, his analysis did not immediately touch on Freudian theory. Nonetheless, following his critical appraisal in this section of a number of classical models of social cohesion, he integrated a Freudian perspective into later parts of the work. In his examination of collective memory, he criticized on one hand the Lockean model of society composed of a collection of atomized individuals united only on the basis of a social contract. On the other hand, Maurice Halbwachs's conception of social cohesion, in emphasizing social factors as the source of personal consciousness, seemed in his eyes to underestimate the role of the individual in the social framework.[4] In attempting to steer between these extremes, Ricœur returned to one of the earliest sources of his philosophical work, the phenomenology of Edmund Husserl, above all to the fifth of Husserl's *Cartesian Meditations*, which examines the possibility of comprehending other persons in a communal context. For Husserl, the condition of possibility of grasping the other lies in an *a priori* appresentation, or in what he termed an "analogical apperception" of the other in terms of the self; and Husserl conceived of this constitution of the other, "in me, yet as other," not in terms of the simple perception of a multiplicity of atomized individuals, but as the possibility of immediately apprehending others as communal others.[5] This constitutive act serves as the starting point for a theory of intersubjectivity at the different levels of articulation of the social world, from interpersonal interaction to the "higher intersubjective communities" that designate larger collectivities.

Ricœur was well aware that Husserl did not resort in his analysis to any form of collective *memory* to ground his theory of the constitution of communities.[6] Indeed, as Ricœur well appreciated, collective memory could never have played a fundamental role for Husserl as a principle of cohesion of collective identity, for it could hardly furnish an *absolute* basis for meaningful interaction in the common lifeworld, independent of historical flux and contingency, which Husserl sought in the self-certitude of the transcendental ego. The central role that Ricœur accorded to collective memory in his final period is entirely consonant with a more modest conception of the self, inspired since his earliest works by the metaphor of the "wounded" cogito, who can make no claim to absolute certitude of the "exalted" subject.[7] As a more humble alternative to the transcendental ego, collective memory could adopt the vocabulary of Husserlian idealism, while definitively renouncing its absolute transcendental claim as the basis for understanding the other and for the configuration of an intersubjective cohesion. Nonetheless, this ambiguous relation to Husserl was not without its paradoxical consequences. Indeed, even where Ricœur renounced the absolute basis Husserl claimed for personal consciousness, he maintained the fundamental idea that Husserl sought to elaborate on this basis: the idea that in terms of an analogical relation to personal consciousness, communities may be made intelligible. It is this analogy that Ricœur employed to elaborate his conception of social cohesion and collective memory. Hence he wrote in *Memory, History, Forgetting*, "It is only by analogy, and in relation to individual consciousness and its memory, that collective memory is held to be a collection of traces left by the events that have affected the course of the history of the groups concerned, and that it is accorded the power to place on stage these common memories, on the occasion of holidays, rites and public celebrations."[8]

This analogical relation between individuals and groups came to expression in the two principle categories of analysis of memory that Ricœur adopted: on one hand, the moral category of the "debt" and of the "obligation to remember"; on the other hand, the psychological concept of the "work" of memory, modeled on psychoanalytic therapy. In each case, the theory of collective identity and collective memory depended on a strict analogy between individual and community that, while making reference to Husserl, simultaneously drew on the methodology of Freud. Ricœur's doubts concerning the transcendental basis of Husserl's justification of this analogy coincided in his later work with a renewed appreciation for the Freudian psychological method as a support for this analogy in his understanding of collective memory as a source of social cohesion.

My purpose here, as I have previously emphasized, is in no way to deny that analogies drawn between individual and collectivity may in certain cases be legitimate; for communities, in a manner that is analogous to individuals, may undergo collective trauma, just as responsibility may be imputed to them for acts that they collectively commit. Nonetheless, without the transcendental grounding Husserl proposed to justify such analogies, categories primarily applicable to individual moral understanding or to the relation between patient and therapist would hardly seem adequate to the task of placing in relief the complex levels of intersubjective cohesion required by a theory of collective memory. To perform this task, Ricœur nowhere follows Freud's own appeal to the phylogenetic sources of what he took to be inherited social dispositions deriving from archaic trauma and the subsequent repression or sublimation of the unconscious drives that engendered it. Here, however, it seems striking that Ricœur, in his preoccupation with relations that can be analogically applied to individual and community, neglects the fundamental role of the symbol that such relations presuppose. Symbols, indeed, precede individual awareness. At a fundamental level, they lend awareness communicable form as a source of intersubjective cohesion refracted in the fragmented perspectives of the groups that are engaged in collective relations.

To illustrate what I take to be the problematic implications of Ricœur's dependence on Freudian categories in the interpretation of the analogical relation between individual and society that he mobilizes in his theory of collective memory, I return for a moment to the earlier example provided by Martin Luther King Jr.'s epoch-making "I Have a Dream" speech. It would be possible to characterize Dr. King's civil rights movement in psychological terms by underscoring the traumatic collective experience of centuries of slavery, followed by a century of injustice during which blacks were deprived of elementary civil rights. Subsequent to the changes in legislation that were largely due to the moral persuasiveness of this movement's nonviolent tactics, one might continue to underscore the ongoing inequalities that have persisted following the institution of political equality. Or, on the contrary, one might signal what certain authors have described as an "abuse" of memory and, in extrapolating from Freud's theory (albeit not always in accord with Freud's intentions), advance this assumption on the basis of psychological arguments analogically applicable both to individual relations in the nuclear family and to vast groups. From this perspective, the initial success of the civil rights movement might appear to be the source of a new strategy among the black minority insofar as it seeks to convert a situation of past injustice into a new privileged status. Did Dr. King himself, in his "I Have a Dream" speech, not proclaim that the American people had a debt to pay to black citizens and that he had come to Washington, D.C., to "cash a check"? And once civil rights had been granted, was it not all the more convenient to be able to "place oneself in the position of the victim," in order to legitimate further claims to reparation? As Tzvetan Todorov wrote, applying the psychology of family therapy to the political domain, "To have once been a victim gives you the right to complain, to protest and to make demands."[9] And in adopting a similar psychological perspective in *Memory, History, Forgetting*, Paul Ricœur, while stressing that he did not want to overstate this point, echoed Todorov's claim that the posture of the victim "engenders an exorbitant privilege, which places everyone else in the position of owing a debt." This is why Ricœur abandoned the idea of a moral "duty to remember," preferring instead, in accord with his interpretation of the Freudian terminology he adopted, a "working through" of the collective memory of past trauma.[10] But, whether we are referring to black Americans or to any other minority group (Todorov and Ricœur had most immediately in view the posterity of Jewish victims of the Shoah), does this preoccupation with the psychological dimension of collective memory provide us with the best way to interpret this phenomenon? As I understand it, such strict application of the analogy of individual psychic processes to collective remembrance runs the risk of reducing unique aspects of communal existence to uniform models of psychic explanation. It is in danger not only of overlooking the intrinsic legitimacy of claims that are made but, in applying uniform models to unique situations, of oversimplifying the singular complexity of fragmented symbolic nuances in the collective remembrance of groups that coexist in our contemporary mass societies. At a metapersonal level, it is the virtual force of embodied symbols underlying the particular expressions of communal life that, amid the transformations and meanders of finite collective existence, accounts for the persistence of collective memory at its profoundest levels.

If we evoke in the final analysis the example chosen by Ricœur and Todorov of the Nazi extermination of European Jewish communities during the Second World War, the inadequacy of categories such as the "debt" and the "duty" to remember, as well as the "work" of memory, becomes singularly apparent. Here we are faced not only with the deaths of vast numbers of individual persons but also, at another level, with a radical break in continuity in the European world itself. What is essential here eludes the comparison with "debtors" and "creditors" or "patients" and "therapists." The true problem concerns less a carrying out of the "work" of memory in order to remedy an excess of memory or of forgetting, than the general awakening of comprehension that this radical break touches the vibrant fiber of Europe stemming from antiquity, which the genocides of the twentieth century have irrevocably denatured.

I I

In the introductory chapter, I noted the lively interest that Freud maintained in the somatic sources of psychological processes, even if he focused his clinical work on the psychological explanation of mental phenomena. The cognitive scientist, who analyzes the neurological functions underlying experience, centers investigation on these somatic sources. In recent decades, Gerald M. Edelman has proposed provocative hypotheses in this field of investigation and has provided noteworthy philosophical arguments to support his method of analysis of human consciousness and of the phenomena of personal and collective memory. His neurophysiological theory has had wide influence on this discipline, not only in the United States but in Europe, notably among the members of the school of Jean-Pierre Changeux.

Edelman's philosophical presuppositions can be summarized by a quotation from the book *Quiddities*, by W. V. Quine, which he used as an epigraph at the beginning of his work, *The Remembered Present: A Biological Theory of Consciousness*: "Whatever it precisely may be, consciousness is a state of the body, a state of nerves."[11] By this statement, Quine, and with him Edelman, aimed to challenge all forms of dualism whereby mind and body were taken to be separate entities or substances. This proposition identified mind and body as a unity, and intended in this manner, in Quine's words, to "repudiate mind as a second substance, over and above body." Taking this principle as his starting point, Edelman sought to rigorously explain consciousness in terms of natural functions. In line with this assumption, Edelman asserted that individual consciousness and memory, as well as language and symbols—consequently all that might be placed under the heading of collective memory—are means by which human organisms naturally adapt to their environment in an ongoing evolutionary process. The capacity to remember past events and to communicate them through language is naturally useful, and favors adaptation in permitting humans to liberate themselves from the constraints of the immediate temporal moment in order to recall past experience as a basis for deliberation on a future course of action. The temporal consciousness with which the development of memory is intrinsically connected constitutes a uniquely human capacity that Edelman termed "higher-order consciousness." And he sought to account for the emergence of this capacity through biological and neurological laws of natural selection that govern the general process of human evolution. In his words, "With higher-order consciousness, the ability to plan a series of actions, more or less free of immediate time constraints, must have enhanced fitness. In hominids, at least, primary consciousness must have had evolutionary efficacy, insofar as it is required for the development of a self concept and of language."[12]

In its general line of argumentation, Edelman's attempt to explain the workings of consciousness, and more precisely the phenomenon of collective memory, highlights the essential role of neurophysiological functions that underlie all forms of human awareness. But this method hardly can be said to remain within the bounds of scientific inquiry and of philosophical plausibility, where Edelman adapts the language of empirical investigation to what are clearly speculative hypotheses. The claim to reveal neurophysiological preconditions *necessary* for explaining the physical capacity to represent and to retain images or sounds, as well as for their communication, may well be an empirically grounded conclusion. But the claim that the laws of natural selection or, for that matter, any general laws of nature, might provide *sufficient* grounds to account for personal consciousness, as well as for group experience and collective memory, remains entirely hypothetical. Even where such propositions are dressed up in scientific language, they do not operate at the level of empirical science, but of metaphysical hypotheses that are not empirically verifiable.

Edelman himself has admitted this point in acknowledging that, in the final analysis, his speculative theories depend on materialist presuppositions. Here, insofar as he moved beyond the basic proposition that mind and body form a unity to indulge in speculation concerning the substantial nature of this unity, he parted company with the original source of his philosophical inspiration, the theories of W. V. Quine. Quine, indeed, steadily refused to account for consciousness and the phenomena of memory, imagination, or perception in terms of neurophysiological hypotheses. He explicitly adopted Donald Davidson's principle of "anomalous monism," signifying that the idea of mind as an expression of body did not warrant the further possibility of accounting for a complex of mental events in physiological or neurological terms.[13] In a seminal essay entitled "Mental Events," Davidson further clarified this point when he included among mental events moral properties that, in his opinion, defy reduction to physical or neurological processes. He acknowledged that "dependence or supervenience [of the mental in regard to the physical] does not entail reducibility through laws or definition: if it did we could reduce moral properties to descriptive, and this there is good reason to *believe* cannot be done."[14]

In dealing with this distinction between the mental and the physical, Davidson's remark underscores, above all, the principle of *validity* of normative standards in the mental sphere, which no logically coherent theory can reduce to biological functions or to natural laws. From this perspective, the neurophysiological claim to account for consciousness and, more specifically, for the phenomenon of memory, discounts what is most fundamental: the premise according to which symbolic structures, the locus of embodiment of collective memory, possess a significance whose validity cannot be derived from neurophysiological laws or vital functions. Where neurophysical processes are contingent and depend on the organization of the human species at a given stage of development, logical and moral truths depend on a necessary validity that is not a function of contingent processes, but which the possibility of understanding these processes presupposes. Indeed, logical principles or the norms of social justice and the symbols through which they are expressed are ultimately convincing in virtue of what we take to be their *intrinsic* truth, which, in the final analysis, is of an order that cannot be reduced to the psychophysical laws or the natural processes that may claim to account for them.[15]

III

The specific character of what I term the "sociohistorical" approach to collective memory lies in the historical methodology through which this phenomenon is set in relief. Sociohistorical methods set aside any claim to account for historical variability in terms of natural laws or all-encompassing systems, which they trace instead to the irreducible historical singularity in the ways of being human and in the corresponding modes of collective remembrance of the past. From this perspective, the role of memory varies in relation to its social function, and to understand its contemporary significance, it is first necessary to identify its social function following the rationalization and urbanization of the predominant sectors of modern society. Over the past centuries, this development has brought in its wake the decline of rural communities and the disappearance of oral traditions that, in a premodern context, were a primary source of collective remembrance. Over the course of the twentieth century, this conviction has inspired a broad variety of interpretations of the phenomenon of collective memory in philosophy and the human sciences. As I noted in the introduction, Walter Benjamin, in his essay "The Storyteller," provided salient insight into the decline of the oral traditions of rural society and into the subsequent mutation in collective memory. What is of particular interest in Benjamin's insight lies in the novel perspective he explored concerning the essential historicity of collective human forms of remembrance corresponding to concrete social situations in which they emerge.

In his multivolume work *Les lieux de mémoire*, Pierre Nora and his collaborators have adopted a similar assumption concerning the radical divergence in the function of memory between premodern and modern, between traditional rural and modern rationalized forms of society. In my brief examination of sociohistorical conceptions of collective memory, I limit my comments to a critical appraisal of Pierre Nora's influential theories, elaborated in his different contributions to this multivolume work, which includes the essays of a large number of contemporary historians, and in his later articles on this theme.

In harmony with the premise concerning the radical break with the past inaugurated by modernity, Pierre Nora, in his general introduction to *Les lieux de mémoire*, "Entre mémoire et histoire: La problématique des lieux," underscored the fragility of collective memory in the contemporary context. With the decline of the social function of collective memory, the lines of continuity linking the present to an ongoing, living memory of the past have been severed: "One speaks so much of memory," according to Nora's hyperbolic phrase, "only because it no longer exists."[16] The disappearance of collective memory, according to Nora, corresponds not only to the decline of its social function due to the urbanization of modern society, but to the phenomenon of secularization that has accompanied urbanization and rationalization. Collective memory in traditional societies was sustained by the continuity provided by ongoing religious practices, by the rituals and liturgies that were an integral part of traditional life. The rationalization of human existence in the modern world has engendered a radically different approach to the past: in the chasm left by the demise of previous forms of collective memory and of the religious practices that kept it alive, modernity seeks to resurrect the past through historical-critical methods of analysis that hold such practices at a distance. "Memory," as Nora writes, "situates recollection in the sphere of the sacred. History, as an intellectual and secular operation, elicits analysis and critical discourse."[17]

The relation that Nora established in this manner between collective memory and the "sphere of the sacred," equating the decline of collective memory with the secularization and urbanization of modern political society, raises the question concerning the precise conception of collective memory he employed. Oral traditions were admittedly an essential spur to collective remembrance in previous rural societies, and they have declined with the advent of mass urban culture. Nonetheless, if the contemporary predominance of mass urban culture has marked a clear break with earlier forms of traditional life, can this indeed be correlated with a "decline" in collective memory? The point might just as well be made that, on the contrary, collective memory and the symbolic meanings it embodies exhibit a vitality that is in no way restricted to traditional rural environments. As the ongoing influence of political pronouncements such as the speech of Martin Luther King amply attests, collective memory shows an ongoing capacity to revitalize past religious and political experience in the contemporary world.

In light of this ongoing role of collective memory, Nora's assertions seem puzzling, and raise the question whether his inspiration does not lie elsewhere—in the ideal of *tradition* with which, in his vocabulary, collective memory is manifestly conflated. His general claim concerning the loss of "memory" more precisely underscores the disappearance of *tradition* and of certain forms of collective memory that traditional practices nurtured and sustained.[18] Nora's own pronouncements, indeed, seem to confirm this interpretation where, in his introductory essay "Entre mémoire et histoire," he equated the death of the remembered past with a "tearing away from what was lived in the warmth of tradition."[19]

Although Nora tends to associate collective memory and tradition, the task of clarifying the concept of collective memory requires that we investigate the possible point of demarcation between these two orders. If, indeed, "memory establishes the chain of tradition" (*Erinnerung stiftet die Kette der Tradition*), as Walter Benjamin admonished, in recalling the adage of Herder and of Hegel, collective memory nonetheless remains fluid and multivalent, whereas tradition has been codified and set in a unified conceptual framework. Nora himself comes close to acknowledging this point in his introduction to the third volume of *Les lieux de mémoire*, where he wrote that "a tradition is a memory which has become historically conscious of itself."[20] Nevertheless, where the two orders are conflated, as in Nora's "Entre mémoire et histoire," the danger arises of reifying collective memory as a monolithic structure. In such instances Nora's perspective has tended to underplay the essentially *fragmentary* character of collective memory as a source of divergent public interpretations and of group conflict. Indeed, this danger is nowhere more in evidence than in the overall conception of the multivolume work *Les lieux de mémoire*, where specific presuppositions concerning the French national tradition risk hardening into a rigid and nostalgic perspective. The choice of topics for the different articles contained in this work clearly favors a picture of a secular and Republican France that has emerged since the French Revolution, while downplaying the more negative aspects surrounding such national mythologies as the Napoleonic heritage or such painful topics as French colonialism and the genealogy of political right-wing extremism.

Harsh reproof of the selective nature of *Les lieux de mémoire* has been voiced by numerous critics, including the French deputy of Guyana, Christiane Taubira, who was named French Minister of Justice (*Garde des Sceaux*) during the presidency of François Hollande. Madame Taubira rebuked this work for what she considered to be its near silence in regard to centuries of slavery and French colonial history.[21] As a deputy, Christiane Taubira introduced legislation, which was subsequently passed into law, favoring the official proclamation that the centuries-long practice of enslavement of black Africans constituted a crime against humanity. The law has further encouraged the teaching of black and colonial history in the French public schools.

This political initiative was met with sharp criticism by Pierre Nora and other historians, and the historical scholarship published by his associates has sought to nuance the political pronouncements of Madame Taubira and of more radical political activists. In 2004, French historian Olivier Pétré-Grenouilleau published a work entitled *Les traites négrières*, in which he argued that slavery, whatever moral considerations might be advanced against it today, was undertaken for essentially commercial reasons. As a commercial enterprise, its proliferation over the course of several centuries can in no way be equated with an intention to commit genocide in the contemporary sense, which indicated for him the problematic character of comparisons between the centuries-long practice of slavery and the "crimes against humanity" constituted by the deliberate extermination of vast populations during the Shoah. Following the publication of *Les traites négrières*, a group of activists from the French overseas domains (principally from Guadeloupe, Guyana, and Martinique) pressed charges against its author in the French courts. A large number of historians, led by Nora, responded by signing a petition rebuking these charges that was published in a newspaper article entitled "Liberté pour l'histoire."[22] They argued that legislation regarding the kind of history that should be taught in the schools, decisions to press criminal charges against historians in the courts, and the general climate created by the criminalization of historical writings were in danger of curbing intellectual freedom. In the aftermath of this petition, the activists withdrew their legal charges.

Pierre Nora analyzed the general situation symptomized by this conflict in a short essay entitled "Malaise dans l'identité historique." He sharply criticized what he termed the "omnipotence of memorial hegemony," and he thus placed the phenomenon of collective memory in a different light in comparison with the interpretation of it he had developed in the essay "Entre mémoire et histoire."[23] Memory now appeared as a danger which, in fueling the claims advanced by political pressure groups, risked distorting the past it claimed to represent. In opposition to the fluid and changing field of history, memory assumed an ahistorical quality that "denies by definition differences and temporal transitions, [and] suppresses the factors of transformation and the conditions of change."[24] In this way, the memory of collectivities is in danger of undermining the historian's critical quest for an impartial perspective in regard to the past, beyond the claims of particular groups anchored in the perspective of the present.

In this brief essay Nora cogently argued for the separation of historiography from the claims of collective memory. Nonetheless, in spite of the clear merits of Nora's plea for the autonomy of historical judgment in the face of political pressure, his argument, as I interpret it, calls for further clarification of the concept of collective memory, above all in relation to national traditions. Indeed, his manner of limiting his criticism of "memorial hegemony" to the position of his opponents raises questions concerning the conceptual structure he has chosen to adopt. From Nora's standpoint, the "rememberers" were those who insisted on the negative aspects of the French past, and against them he dreaded the prospect that "this past as a whole" might be cast into the "shadows of history to which one turned one's back."[25] Was it, however, legitimate to draw such a rigid line between the "memorial hegemony" of his adversaries and his own form of historical judgment? Did his claim, like that of Christiane Taubira, not obey a logic that was at least to a certain extent nourished by the "collective memory" of his own group? In taxing his opponents with "memorial hegemony," Nora side-stepped the issue of the memorial sources of his own position and of its relation to the preconceptions of a predominant French national tradition he sought to uphold.

The questions arising from this debate illustrate to my mind the complexities of political judgment, while underscoring the importance of a clear theoretical distinction between collective memory and tradition. Where tradition is codified and tends toward unity, the fragmentary and fluid character of collective memory lends expression to a variety of conflicting experiences and claims. The conflation of the two spheres, which seeks to impose a codified position on the remembered past, necessarily overlooks the essential dynamics that the exercise of collective memory brings to the fore.

* Part 2 *

*Time, Collective Memory,
and the Historical Past*

CHAPTER 4

Temporal Articulations

My investigation of the place of collective memory in the preceding chapters has placed it in evidence as a web of remembered experience embodied in collectively communicable symbols. In evoking this web, I have referred to what I term moments of "sedimentation," "stratification," and "fragmentation," all of which convey spatial metaphors. As spatial metaphors, however, they do not intend to suggest that collective memory is primarily elicited through association with physically extended objects, which resuscitate collective remembrance as so many haphazardly encountered sites. These metaphors situate the web of experience retained by collective memory as a symbolic interspace through which physical things assimilate their publicly communicable significance. Sedimentation, stratification and fragmentation of symbolically embodied memory draw on a reservoir of remembered experience that is brought within the horizon of a common present and is beheld from its perspective.

The simultaneity of sedimented, stratified, and fragmented experience that collective memory retains arises through group apprehension of the ongoing presence of past experience within a shared horizon of contemporaneity. It is the apprehension of a tie between past and present, and thus of a line of continuity in time. If it is also in time that mutation and discontinuity with the past occur and are later brought to mind, group perception of discontinuity nonetheless presupposes an underlying continuity or sameness in the remembering collectivity in relation to which discontinuity may be placed in relief. Collective memory is in this sense the matrix of cohesion of the remembering group, however vast it may be, through which its continuity in time is at once attested, consolidated, and reaffirmed. Within an essentially anthropological range of apprehension, collective memory identifies amid dislocation, discontinuity, and flux the margins of collective continuity over time. In close association with the imaginative work of symbolic embodiment of experience, the specific, meta-personal province of collective memory lies in the articulation of the modes of temporal synthesis through which the web of remembered experience shared by groups is interwoven in a given present and recalled as *common* experience. My purpose in this chapter is to examine the temporal articulations of collective memory as the source of continuity and collective cohesion in a shared horizon of contemporaneity. This analysis of the temporality of collective memory permits us at the same time to demarcate more precisely the limits of collective memory and, in delineating its specific province facing the abyss of discontinuity, to interpret what lies beyond its temporal scope.

I

To situate the place of collective memory involves first and foremost an investigation of its role in the temporal synthesis of group experience. It requires an adequate theory of social time in which the synthetic work of memory in the collective sphere may be brought into focus. As I conceive of it, the temporal dimension in which collective memory is deployed is not *primarily* identifiable with cosmological time derived from the movement of the heavenly bodies, nor with the clock time that is regulated in accord with this movement and in terms of which collective interaction is organized. Moreover, it cannot be equated with the biological rhythms of organic growth, maturity, senescence, and death. Certainly human temporal experience at all of its levels is interwoven with each of these forms of temporal organization, without which temporal sequences could not be patterned or measured as distinct phases or unities. And yet, in their generality, cosmological, clock, and biological time are hardly sufficient to account for the specifically *social* sphere of temporal articulation in terms of which the time of collective memory exhibits its concrete contours.

To illustrate what I mean by this specifically social sphere of time, I draw on an example, which I present in the guise of a thought experiment. For this purpose, the preoccupation with time by a man stranded on a desolate island and artificially severed from social existence admirably places in relief the temporal preconditions of experience that collective memory continually marshals and that historical interpretation, at a secondary level, presupposes.

The example is taken from a fictional account presented in the celebrated eighteenth-century tale of Robinson Crusoe and relates to Robinson's earnest attempt to keep track of time.

> And now being about to enter into a melancholy Relation of a Scene of silent Life, such perhaps as was never heard of in the World before, I shall take it from its Beginning, and continue it in its Order. It was, by my Account, the 30th of Sept. when, in the Manner as above said, I first set Foot upon this horrid Island, when the Sun being, to us, in its Autumnal Equinox, was almost just over my Head, for I reckon'd my self, by Observation, to be in the Latitude of 9 Degrees 22 Minutes North of the Line.
>
> After I had been there about Ten or Twelve Days, it came into my Thoughts, that I should lose my Reckoning of Time for want of Books and Pen and Ink, and should even forget the Sabbath Days from the working Days; but to prevent this I cut it with my Knife upon a large Post, in Capital Letters, and making it into a great Cross I set it up on the Shore where I first landed, viz. I came on Shore here on the 30th of Sept. 1659. Upon the Sides of this square Poste I cut every Day a Notch with my Knife, and every seventh Notch was as long again as that long one, and thus I kept my Kalander, or weekly, monthly, and yearly reckoning of Time.[1]

The stranded Robinson Crusoe, after being severed from all social relations, seeks to maintain contact with his previous world by observing the temporal schema governing his normal social existence. This temporal order is regulated in terms of the revolutions of the heavenly bodies and the passage of days and nights, accompanied over time by changes in the seasons. In due course Robinson would have noted biological transformations in his ageing body. Yet the immediate temporal rhythm that preoccupies him sets in relief a more specific sphere of activity that is distinguishable from more general temporal rhythms: his concern for the temporal sequences established by the calendar through which he might obey the injunction not to forget to distinguish the "Sabbath days from the working days." The time that is here remembered, even as depicted in the bare outlines of Defoe's narrative, is not an abstract sequence but a concretely experienced and socially instituted whole, articulated through the symbolic separation of sacred from profane as it is inscribed in the Christian calendar. It is this contact that permits Robinson, even in his state of isolation, to maintain his ties with the collective past.

One aspect of this thought experiment is of particular importance for our analysis of the time of collective memory: Robinson's concern makes explicit what in normal social circumstances remains implicit. His example illustrates that our everyday modes of temporal reckoning belong to what is most commonly given as a *passive* basis of experience, where the interpretation of time and its sequence need not be a theme of reflection but belongs to the implicit horizon of group experience that is most often taken for granted. All of the rhythms of collective life presuppose this socially instituted temporal horizon as the passive basis of experience around which contemporaneous social existence coheres and which collective memory deploys. Passivity is what lends group activity spontaneous temporal pattern. The passive ubiquity of the temporal horizon in an environing world, forming the concrete context in which activity is situated, is at the same time never completely sundered from potentially active recall, even where it is not explicitly acknowledged.[2]

At the basis of social existence, which is for the most part passively articulated, the temporal spheres of collective life bring to light a fundamental characteristic of collective memory as it lends pattern to time: Robinson's aim in recalling the sequence of days and the need to separate the Sabbath from the working days is to maintain *continuity* with the social world from which he has been severed. This continuity is not experienced as a bare succession of nameless days punctuated by changes in the position of the sun, nor through lunar phases and star-filled nights; it is most immediately given as socially instituted time in terms of which the ongoing connection with the past comes to the fore. In its full sense, collective memory is deployed not only where it directly anticipates or engages the temporal framework of events, but where it also draws on the sedimented and stratified passive reservoir from which group dispositions and habitual activities are spontaneously reenacted, forging tacit links between communal past and communal present in view of the future. This concept of the role of collective memory in the synthesis of a common temporal horizon is at the same time consonant with what I have earlier described as its fragmented character, leading different social groups to remember in different and at times opposing ways and, as I illustrate in greater detail below, involving different references to the temporal ordering of the past in its relation to the present. If we admit such differences in the ways of asserting continuity with the past that the collectively channeled reminiscences of each group mobilize, such divergences nevertheless presuppose a contemporaneous horizon that is common to them all.

Far from having a uniform structure, the temporal articulations of memory correspond to different interwoven orders of group experience that lend pattern to the active recall of socially meaningful and symbolically embodied events. These different orders may be distinguished by the manner in which they are passively structured and by the depth of their inscription as sources of short- or long-term cohesion of social existence. In terms of group experience and of collective memory, the passive patterning of collective activity transpires in a variety of ways. In each of them, collective remembrance engages acts of *presentification* through which the past is drawn into the horizon of the present. The acts of presentification involve at different levels what I term the "temporal intentionality" through which a synthesis between group past and present is brought about. Intentionality identifies the pattern of group temporal synthesis whereby the collective present that emerges from the past is delineated, not by a simple succession of moments, each of which constitutes a point in group experience, nor in terms of a constant process of updating in which elements enter into and fall out of currency, for it comprises complex layers of interpenetrating temporal spheres in which acts of group presentification are undertaken. In this work of temporal synthesis, memory does not operate as an isolated faculty, but interrelates with a primordial unity of human capacities. It is here in the synthesis of group past and group present that group fantasy may open the way to a legendary vision of past experience, serving to fill in those perspectives of the group past that have become obscure, or to set aside those which, in their disturbing quality, are painful to acknowledge. Such fanciful or fictionalized visions of past group experience are familiar aspects of collective identities, which I evoke in the course of the analysis that follows.

My interpretation of the temporal articulations of collective memory centers on three interwoven spheres: the rhythms of habitual practices of everyday life, the periodic, socially organized commemorative recall of symbolically charged events, and the ongoing subsistence of group dispositions that customary practices mold into long-term propensities that span generations. Since each of these spheres comprises a mode of temporal synthesis through which remembered group experience is brought into the horizon of a given present and transpires as a *shared* present, they are each sources of group identities over time. It is a meta-personal sameness that, unless interrupted by new social patterns and institutions, extends beyond the scope of memory retained by all contemporaneously living generations. This sameness in the modes of temporal articulation of group experience provides a semblance of long-term continuity and of ready translatability of the past into the horizon of the present, "as if" the group were able to remember the distant collective past in a manner that is analogous to reminiscence of what is given in the context of living generations. In interpreting these spheres of temporal articulation of collective memory, my purpose is to depict their temporal form and, following this, the temporal intentionality that, on the basis of these articulations, lays bare a deliberate quest for group continuity with the past that collective memory projects.

II

As expressed in the habitual patterns of everyday life, I call "reiterative" those practices that collective remembrance patterns in terms of the continually recurring cycles of social activity: the rhythms of everyday life that conform to specific habits, even though they may vary among different sectors of the population in accord with particular kinds of activity. The division between hours of work, of recreation and sleep, between working days and rest days, the regular intervals at which, in given social contexts, market days and other similar social institutions are enacted, exemplify the reiterative rhythms that punctuate social life. All such reiterative rhythms, if they are regulated through cosmological time and through the natural cycles upon which it depends, are *socially* instituted and, as myriad instances in recent memory attest, are subject to modification according to the decisions adopted by members of the societies in which they predominate. Where, however, reiterative rhythms prevail, they serve as quasi-automatic regulators of everyday social activity. At moments when they are not directly anticipated or enacted, they fade into the passive temporal recesses of collective life.

Like reiterative temporal rhythms, commemorative practices, if they recur in accord with the calendar regulated by cosmological time, are likewise socially instituted phenomena. They also recur at regular intervals, but their periodicity corresponds not to habitual everyday activities, but to *unique* past events that are generally recalled on a yearly basis (or of groups of years marked off in decades and centuries) to designate symbolically meaningful occurrences and to reaffirm collectively held ideals through which groups renew their cohesion. Such commemorations may depend on publicly proclaimed decisions of the sovereign political authority, or they may bring to expression the commemorative will of unofficial groups, which are charged with publicly interpretable meaning. In all forms of commemoration, the symbolically charged dates of enactment are invested with a temporal intentionality through which a given line of continuity between past and present is reaffirmed. At times when they are not enacted, they are generally not themes of explicit reflection and fade into the horizon of latency until, at regular intervals, their symbolic charge is summoned anew in view of solidifying group cohesion and orienting group identities in a current context.

Where reiterative and commemorative rhythms that punctuate collective life are, in their multifarious expressions, straightforward and readily recognizable, long-term group dispositions are more difficult to situate, since they span all reaches of the public sphere and, for the most part, spread over the implicit layers of group life. Here we encounter the deeper strata of collective existence, which, by virtue of the symbols in which they are couched, trace the links between past and present elaborated in successive moments of contemporaneity, lending continuity to group experience and to collective self-conceptions as they are mobilized in view of what is to come. In virtue of these passive recesses of group experience, the present in which the public life of a collectivity is sustained bears within it a past that informs the present in its currency.

Rooted in an underlying network of passive dispositions that encompass the different sectors of social life, these long-term customary patterns constitute the deeper and usually implicit horizons of temporal continuity residing in collective memory. Beneath the surface strata of group existence, these diffuse levels of group existence, from the latent reaches in which they perdure, account for the anonymous threads of social cohesion that are woven amid changes, shifts, and upheavals. The acts of collective remembrance that come to expression in commemorative ceremonies, on monuments, and in museum displays presuppose the symbolic recesses situated at the deeper levels of collective existence. These continuities, drawing on the reservoirs of sedimented group experience that have been symbolically elaborated over the long term, are not to be confused with secondary elaborations, such as codified traditions or an organized "cultural memory," which presuppose this fundamental experiential dimension. In view of their mostly latent character and their diffuseness, these long-term collective continuities are not so much the direct objects of historical representation as patterns of regularity accounting for the social cohesion of experience that historical representation presupposes. As a vast fund of symbols upon which we collectively draw and to which each individual gives a unique and personalized expression, such continuities of group life, inscribed in the recesses of collective memory, are not so many monolithic structures but, like living languages themselves, arise in a dynamic movement of re-elaboration and re-adaptation over time. Language, indeed, in the plenitude of its metaphorical expressions, gives most immediate testimony to the ongoing and mostly implicit presence of the collective past, and to the temporal articulations of long-term continuities between group past and present, in view of an anticipated future.[3]

From the latent recesses of symbolic structures underlying and providing coherence to public life, I bring together heterogeneous phenomena that are activated in a variety of ways. My purpose here cannot be to propose an exhaustive interpretation of these deeper strata of social existence, but to focus on them as indicators of the temporal concatenations of collective memory, and also of its limits. To serve this aim, I emphasize above all the role of the "*êthos*," or "habitus," lending cohesion to contemporaneous public contexts over time. In its long-term temporal scope, the *êthos* concerns not only manifest continuities but also embraces ongoing group visions of what is taken to be a lost collective past, potentially serving as a spur to orient collective activity in the present in view of the future. It is here that they marshal a temporal intentionality that aims to forge continuity between past and present, to summon the past in the horizon of the present. The long-term temporal continuities of the *êthos* depend on the uncanny resiliency of embodied symbols which, amid transformations and breaks, may serve as rallying points for collective remembrance that reach over centuries.

The classic theoretical interpretation of an ongoing temporal ground of continuity of group experience draws on the concept of *êthos* (often translated as "custom") that Aristotle elaborated in the *Politics*. In identifying it with long-term group temporal continuity, Aristotle equated it with specific patterns of group cohesion arising from common experience in a same context which, over *time*, is the source of specific shared habits, attitudes, and dispositions. In interpreting variations in the customary practices among peoples, Aristotle underlined the role of patterns of collective interaction in the public world as it is configured through institutions and laws. The public existence of a people draws upon such dispositions, on an *êthos* in the full political sense of the term, and it is for this reason, according to his judgment, that it is advisable to change the laws governing public life only with the greatest caution: "for the law has no power to compel obedience," as he stipulated, "beside the force of custom (*êthos*), and custom only grows up in a long lapse of time, so that lightly to change from the existing laws to other new laws is to weaken the power of the law."[4] Aristotle's statement is of particular interest for our interpretation, not due to the conservative conclusions that might be drawn from it, but to the importance he attributed to customary practices, laws, and institutions over time for the molding of the specific way of being together and of interacting in the political context of public life. Aristotle's theory emphasizes the essentially *political* sources of group dispositions as they come to expression over the long term, which set the framework for ways of living together in a common world. He traced the divergence in the modes of collective life among peoples to the specific ways in which, over the long term, social forms and institutions mold shared dispositions. As Aristotle pointed out in the *Politics*, coexistence in a political society in which the public sphere has become the instrument of private factional interests, where individuals and groups hesitate to openly question the ruling interest, and where, in extreme instances, they must fear for their lives if they do so, cannot fail over the course of time to have an impact on group dispositions and the collective *êthos*. By contrast, the possibility of engaging in public debate without fear for the consequences of freely sharing opinions cannot but leave its mark on the way in which, over the long term, individuals and groups coexist in a common political society.

If we focus on the ways in which long-term dispositions of the *êthos* are articulated in time, we note that such perdurable continuities may persist over extensive periods in the passive reaches of collective symbolic networks. Once, indeed, group dispositions and expectations are set down as foundations for public life and are firmly embedded in the language and systems of symbolic interaction of a given collectivity, they may continue to influence attitudes that prevail in it well after the sociopolitical or cultural context of the group itself has changed. This theme, indeed, has long provided a spur to reflection on long-term social and political dispositions. Machiavelli, to cite a noteworthy example, underlined in his political analysis the resilience of long-term collective dispositions, which in many situations remain latent and implicit. Machiavelli focused on the power that the memory of a collective past may exercise, above all in situations where a long-standing order of political independence has been violently disrupted and political liberty undermined. In chapter 5 of his work *The Prince*, Machiavelli cautioned that a ruler who seeks to conquer a people accustomed to life in a free republic runs a great risk, and that he might succeed only if he chooses to live in their territory or to destroy or completely uproot them:

> In fact, destroying cities is the only certain way of holding them. Anyone who becomes master of a city accustomed to a free way of life, and does not destroy it, may expect to be destroyed by it himself, because when it rebels, it will always be able to appeal to the spirit of freedom and its ancient institutions, which are never forgotten, despite the passage of time and any benefits bestowed by the new ruler. Whatever he does, whatever provisions he makes, if he does not foment internal divisions or scatter the inhabitants, they will never forget their lost liberties and their ancient insti-

tutions, and they will immediately attempt to recover them whenever they have an opportunity, as Pisa did after enduring a century of subjection to the Florentines.[5]

The present in which the life of a collectivity perdures bears within it a past that infuses it and lends it contemporary form. This long-term customary pattern of group experience, rooted in an underlying network of passive dispositions, constitutes the deeper recesses of temporal articulation, which are often implicit, and are the anonymous, extrapersonal sources from which "collective memory" draws its sustenance.

In the modern period, reflection on the sources and nature of long-term collective continuities that had traditionally been conceptualized in terms of the *êthos*, or habitus, have been a continuous spur to theoretical reflection in the framework of divergent conceptual systems. Following the emergence of novel Enlightenment conceptions of these continuities as a community of "spirit," as in the spirit of the laws or of the nation, and then of the Hegelian "phenomenology of the Spirit," I noted in the introduction the emergence of broad speculation that attributed shared dispositions or characters among national groups to biological and organic causes. Here the conception of "organic memory," above all in the theories of Richard Semon and Ewald Hering, attempted to account for social dispositions in terms of biological inheritance, which is slowly modified over the course of generations. The period following World War I, as we have seen, witnessed the emergence of more sociologically oriented theories of collective memory in the ideas of Walter Benjamin and, above all, of Maurice Halbwachs; at that time, theorists also renewed interest in classical interpretations of social dispositions and social cohesion, above all as formulated in the Aristotelian conception of the *êthos*. In cultural and aesthetic theory, to take a noteworthy example, Erwin Panofsky stressed the role of acquired social dispositions and mental habits to account for the deep and often unconscious interrelation of different forms of cultural production.[6] In France, the sociology of Émile Durkheim also focused on the sociological functions of such acquired collective dispositions and habits, and his eminent student, Marcel Mauss, explicitly traced this theoretical insight to Aristotelian sources.[7] In an insightful sociological application of this theory, Mauss interpreted this long-term basis of social cohesion as an *êthos*, or habitus. In his essay entitled "Techniques of the Body," for example, written in 1934, Mauss identified this deep level of social cohesion, not with a "mysterious 'memory'" taken in a metaphysical sense, but as an essentially sociological articulation that generally corresponds to dispositions of the body and "varies not simply among individuals and their imitations [but] especially among societies, forms of education, styles and fashions, notions of prestige."[8]

In the framework of a pluralistic ideal of contemporary mass society, the more recent sociological conception of the habitus proposed by Pierre Bourdieu is particularly instructive. Drawing on the original Aristotelian concept of the *êthos*, on Durkheim's notion of automatic and unconsciously performed social patterns of activity adopted from past generations,[9] as on the insights of Erwin Panofsky and Marcel Mauss, Bourdieu has defined the habitus as a system of "lasting, transposable dispositions which, integrating past experiences, functions at every moment as a matrix of perceptions, appreciations and actions" in terms of regular social patterns.[10] Bourdieu's work has emphasized the role of posture, gesture, and corporal disposition as the locus of socially mediated symbolic expressions, and, in more recent years, the theme of the body as a vehicle of long-term articulations of collective memory has provided a seminal topic for anthropological theory.[11]

I draw loosely on these more recent interpretations of the *êthos*, or habitus, to corroborate my quest for an anthropological conception of the temporal articulations of collective cohesion and continuity, which I situate in the context of vast and often multi-ethnic populations, organized in the midst of fragmented group perspectives in an increasingly globalized world. The introduction of this topic is at the same time animated by a different approach to the phenomenon of social cohesion than that employed in sociology or in political theory, for the topic of the temporal continuity of a passive symbolic network underlying group contemporaneity seeks to place in relief, not so much a social or political dynamic, as its role as a specific modality of temporal articulation that collective memory brings into play. In concrete practice, moreover, the reiterative and commemorative modalities like that of the *êthos* are not isolated domains, but are interwoven as a unity. Reiterative rhythms most often comport a commemorative dimension, especially where they are affiliated with holidays and customs drawn from long-instituted ceremonies like Christmas, Mardi Gras, Lent, or Easter; as instituted in social contexts based on the Christian calendar, they assume a recurring temporal form. In a pluralistic social context, this temporal reference may be broadened to encompass Pesach, Ramadan or other celebrations, but the principal is in any case the same. Reiterative and commemorative rhythms at the same time depend on the long-standing *êthos* of corresponding groups.

As passively shared by members of vast groups, the temporal articulations of collective memory, at its different levels of deployment, underlie explicit awareness through which past group experience is brought within the horizon of the present. Groups do not only act in concert in virtue of automatic reflexes and implicit shared preconceptions; they also bring shared beliefs and behavior to awareness in the aim of extending in a given contemporaneous context ways of being and of acting that are identified with the legacy of past generations. This temporal intentionality operates in lending unity to the three modalities of temporal patterning of group experience, which, if they are generally taken for granted as spontaneous patterns of activity, are nonetheless essentially conventional in character. As natural as they might seem, the temporal articulations of collective memory obey artificially instituted ways of mobilizing the quest for temporal continuity between collective past and present.

At this point in my analysis, I further elucidate this conventional basis of the three modalities through which collective experience and collective memory are lent temporal pattern and group continuity is forged. I do so by means of a second thought experiment intended to compliment and extend the earlier example of Robinson Crusoe. This second thought experiment, however, is drawn not from fiction but from historical record. It concerns not one stranded individual severed from his social context and from the socially instituted temporal articulations that constitute it, but the attempt during the French Revolution to radically alter the predominant temporal rhythms through which social reality had previously been constructed. The unparalleled significance of this example lies in a wide-scale attempt to reorder the temporal framework of everyday experience, as well as the modalities of collective recollection, as a means of sundering lines of continuity with the old regime and of reestablishing temporal continuity on a fully new basis.

III

The deliberations of the revolutionary French National Assembly in 1792 associated the political and theological authority of the old regime with the prevailing ways by which, over the centuries, it had organized *time*. The daily commemoration of saints and martyrs, arranged according to specific dates on the calendar, holidays of every sort, and even the rhythm of market days—promoting abstinence from meat, for example, on Fridays and during Lent—rigorously conformed to the ordinances of the Catholic Church and constantly evoked them in everyday activities. To break with the Church and with the traditional political order, it was necessary to radically modify the temporal order that reinforced their domination. This was the intention of the National Convention when it introduced the *Calendrier Républicain*, which aimed to subvert the Christian temporal order and to replace its religious content with the Republican gospel (*Évangile Républicain*) as a means of assuring the newly won principle of popular sovereignty.[12] The poet Fabre d'Eglantine, one of the two framers of the new calendar, elucidated this policy in his presentation of the new system for ordering time: "We can no longer count the years when the kings oppressed us, as a time when we had lived. The prejudices of the throne and the Church, the lies of the one and the other, soiled each page of the calendar that we employed."[13]

Fabre d'Eglantine and Gilbert Romme, the coauthors of the new calendar, modified the names of the days and months to recall the order of natural events, related to sowing and to the harvest, to plants and animals, which they arranged in terms of a new decimal system. As a means of dechristianizing everyday life and of ending centuries-long subservience to the theological and political authority of the ancien régime, the habitual rhythms of the market days were deliberately modified in view of creating among French citizens new dispositions favorable to the Republican form of government. Later analysts of the French Revolution, such as the nineteenth-century historian F.-A. Aulard, appreciated the weighty impact of such intentions to contravene habits that had been instilled over the centuries. As Aulard astutely commented, "The establishment of the Republican Calendar was the most antichristian measure that the Convention initiated."[14]

Well after the end of The Terror in 1794, which had claimed the lives of both of the framers of the new calendar, Fabre d'Eglantine and Romme, it continued to organize the temporal order in France and in territories under French domination. A decree of the *Directoire* of 14 Germinal, year 6, reiterated the public authority of the Republican Calendar, stating that municipal administrations were responsible for determining the market days in their districts, which were to respect the new organization of days of work and rest. According to the decree, "They will be especially careful to break any relation of the fish markets with the days of abstinence designated by the old calendar."[15] The *Directoire*'s decree further admonished that, as far as possible, the new Republican holidays should not fall on the same days as those fixed by the old Gregorian calendar. The new calendar was to be the public reference for coach transport schedules, for the opening of navigation locks, for setting rest days in workshops where tasks were undertaken for the state, for the dates of leases and contracts, of theater representations, and of the publication of newspapers.[16] In succeeding years, as the rigidity in its application was gradually relaxed,[17] the Republican Calendar continued to symbolize the new order in contrast to the ancien régime. Not only in the aftermath of The Terror, but even following Napoleon Bonaparte's rise to power after the 18th of Brumaire, the new calendar continued to provide the official measure of public time in France and in territories it occupied.

In 1806, during the third year of the empire, Napoleon, as a concession to the Catholic Church, finally proclaimed that France would revert to the traditional temporal order. Official use of the Republican Calendar was abolished. As a symbol of the new order, however, its charm survived long after this date, as is attested by successive attempts to restore to it, during the Revolution of 1848 and, once again, at the time of the Paris Commune of 1871. Nineteenth-century enthusiasts of the revolutionary heritage, such the historian Jules Michelet, continued to express a lingering disdain for the "absurdity" of traditional measures of time. In Michelet's opinion, the *Calendrier Républicain* marked a true caesura between past and present, and in his classic history of the French Revolution, published between 1847 and 1853, he wrote, "The struggle between the two calendars, the Republican and the Catholic, was a struggle of the past, of tradition, against the eternal present of mathematics and of nature."[18]

Among the original framers of the Republican Calendar, the intention of this remarkable project was not limited to modifying the ways in which time is publicly perceived, nor to transforming the objects of periodic commemoration and the habitual rhythms of everyday life. In his original elucidation the new calendar's purpose, Fabre d'Eglantine insisted on a still more essential aim that the new system was to promote: new forms of temporal imagery, indeed, were introduced to reorient public memory. "We conceive only by means of images," as he wrote. "In the most abstract analysis, in the most metaphysical combinations, our understanding proceeds only by images, our memory is based on and is supported only by images. You must therefore employ them in your new calendar if you want the method and the whole of this calendar to penetrate easily into the understanding of the people and quickly impress itself on its memory."[19]

This reorientation of remembered images was intended above all to deflect popular remembrance from past illusions, which Fabre d'Eglantine characterized as prejudices that had long been inculcated by a superstitious priesthood. The redirection of public memory through images aimed to fix it on natural and rural objects, the most dignified topics to which a free and sovereign citizenry could devote its attention:

> It is easy to see that by means of this method there will not be a citizen in
> France who, from his earliest youth, has not imperceptibly and inadver-

tently made a study of rural economy; there does not exist a single urban dweller who, at a mature age, cannot learn from this calendar in a few days that which to the shame of our customs he was previously ignorant. He will learn, I say, at what time the earth gives us one product, at what time another. I dare say here that this is what many people who are educated in more than one luxurious, urban, and frivolous science have never known.[20]

This project employed a theory of association and of memory as a pedagogical tool on a national scale to enforce radical discontinuity with the old regime and with what were taken to be the fundamental illusions of the past. The reorientation of public modes of accounting for time in all of the spheres of its articulation aimed to establish a radically new and rationally formulated basis for social experience and social remembrance as a source of collective continuity in the new age.

I V

The example provided by the radical change in temporal schema in all spheres of public life during the French Revolution underlines the essentially *conventional* basis of continuity that bridges the distance between different temporal contexts of collective existence. The longevity of such schema over centuries reinforces their habitual practice at the level of deeper strata of passivity orienting social interaction. As familiar patterns of everyday collective life, they may then appear to be endowed with a stability much like the natural variations in cosmological time with which they are interwoven. At all levels of the temporal articulation of experience and of remembrance, they enable the ready translation of past experience into the horizon of a given present. They orient the temporal intentionality through which groups consciously summon remembrance of the past in an attempt to forge continuity between past and present. In this section I focus on this theme of temporal intentionality— involving a variety of aims that presentification of the past seeks to fulfill—in relation to the three temporal modalities of collective memory. It is here that our investigation will broaden its scope to analyze the ways in which fragments of past experience, or of given configurations of past social existence retained in group memory over the centuries, may be invested with a symbolic charge of a particular intensity as they seize the imagination of large groups. The temporal intentionality of collective memory thus concerns the ideological uses to which it is subject in our contemporary globalized period.

Christian temporal ordering principles, taking the birth of Christ as their reference, provide a possibility for spontaneously interpreting temporal continuity which, beyond the existence of living generations, encompasses the succession of generations reaching back to antiquity. In the domain of socially constituted reiterative rhythms, as in recurring festivals and holidays that may be located on a calendar, the distant past may be spontaneously transposed, through the symbolic embodiment of time, into the horizon of the present. If, for example, we read documents originating in past centuries, such as the late seventeenth-century letters of Madame de Sévigné to her daughter, we are able to spontaneously translate the temporal rhythms that regulate her social context into those which are familiar to our own. When on February 5, 1674, Madame de Sévigné wrote to her daughter to tell her that, due to the war with England, the carnival in Paris was not particularly joyous, we need not understand anything about the historical events surrounding the third Dutch war, which pitted Louis XIV against England, in order to immediately grasp the *temporal* reference to the carnival, which is immediately familiar to us as a holiday preceding Lent, forty days prior to Easter Sunday. This temporal reference that Madame de Sévigné included makes it immediately transposable into the present nearly three and a half centuries later: "We had one or two balls in Paris during the whole carnival; there were some masks, but only a few. There is great sadness."[21] Such an immediate possibility of transposing the temporal schema of the past into our contemporaneous context becomes considerably more difficult if we must deal with dates based on wholly unfamiliar schema—for example, dates on the revolutionary calendar such as "Duadi Verdermaire of the year 4" or "Octidi Messidor of the year 6"!

If we briefly turn our attention less to the continually recurring schema of socially instituted time and more to the unique objects or events that are commemorated, here too the symbolic embodiment of time in terms of memorable dates that retain a collective significance enables us to spontaneously transpose them from the collective past into the horizon of present experience. In previous chapters I have referred to this temporal intentionality of commemoration through the example of Martin Luther King Jr. and his followers, who aimed to bring to fulfillment in the present what had remained unfulfilled in the past. In such instances, as I emphasized, the symbolic charge that emanates from such events and sets in relief what are taken to be long-term lines of continuity serves to bring past experience into the immediate present context. Symbols, however, as a basis of commemoration, need not have a firm basis in fact; the present intentionality that draws on what is taken to be remembered experience of the past may correspond to orally transmitted recollections and recorded events and also to the reconstituted experience that has been fanci-

fully rearranged on the basis of legends. In the framework of long-term continuities that reach over centuries, it may indeed be, as Ivo Andrić has written
in his historical novel *The Bridge on the Drina*, that remembrance of events
over long periods among broad segments of the population, above all in times
when literacy was not common, depended on the possibility of converting
them into legend: "The people only retain in memory and recount what they
are able to grasp and transform into legend. Anything else passes them by
without deeper trace, with the mute indifference of nameless natural phenomena, which do not touch the imagination or remain in memory."[22]

Transformed into legend over the course of centuries, such sagas are not to
be conflated with "collective memory" in the sense of recollected experience
that is transmitted among contemporaneously living generations, since here it
is less a question of remembered experience than of recollection of an oral tradition based on distant events that have been reembroidered as their record
was handed down. Nevertheless, the intentionality that refers to such recollection as "memory" is of singular importance in accounting for the intensity
of its symbolic force. This figure of speech, indeed, concerns less the retrieval
of identifiable past "experience" than the quest for *temporal* presentification
through which embodied symbols rooted in the distant past are transposed
into the present and commemorated *as if* they were objects of direct group
recall. By means of acts of commemoration of a past that is treated as *remembered* group experience, the sense of continuity with the past is reinforced,
and its symbolic charge endowed with a singular intensity. If such acts of
commemoration are, in general, an integral part of national life that come to
expression in all manner of sagas and legends, we have also become familiar
with the violent force that symbols may unleash in situations of group conflict,
often eliciting archaic images that fuel political mythologies.

The symbolic charge that, over a period of centuries, may accompany the
commemorative temporal intentionality may be illustrated through a particularly evocative example presented by Ivo Andrić in *The Bridge on the
Drina*, composed in Belgrade during World War II. Writing in what was then
German-occupied Yugoslavia, Andrić referred to a notable commemoration
in Serbia that he himself had experienced as a young man, the festival of the
"Vidovdan," or Saint Vitus, which is the principal Serbian national holiday.
The festival recalls not only the day of the saint but, above all, the famous
battle of Kosovo that took place on June 28, 1389 (Gregorian calendar), marking the loss of Serbian independence and the beginning of their domination
by the Ottoman Turks, which lasted until the nineteenth century. According
to the historical record, both the Serbian general, Prince Lazar, who has since

become a sacred hero for the Serbian Orthodox Church, and the Ottoman general, Murad, were killed in this battle. In subsequent centuries, Vidovdan was commonly considered by the Serbs as a sacrifice that they made in the hope of maintaining their national integrity and the borders of the Christian West facing the Moslem East. During the Middle Ages, the battle inspired a rich oral tradition recorded in the Kosovo Cycle of Serbian epic poetry, which, in later centuries, fascinated authors like Herder, Goethe, and Walter Scott.

In an event depicted in *The Bridge on the Drina*, which he drew from his own experience, Andrić recalled the annual commemoration of the Vidovdan on June 28, 1914. During the festivities in Serbia, their Austro-Hungarian rulers suddenly ordered that the celebration immediately cease, for on this symbolic day, recalling the loss of national independence that many Serbians longed to regain, Gavrilo Princip assassinated the Austro-Hungarian Archduke Franz Ferdinand during his official visit to Sarajevo. In the framework of his historical novel, Andrić related the catastrophic events that followed: the wave of persecution of the Serbs launched by the Austro-Hungarian authorities, followed by the outbreak of World War I.[23]

Beyond the context described by Andrić, the symbolic force of the Vidovdan has continued to arouse nationalist sentiment in recent years. After having been downplayed in the decades following World War I and, after World War II, during the Tito regime, it regained its force as a symbol of Serbian national identity when Yugoslavian unity weakened in the 1980s. In 1989, on the occasion of the six hundredth anniversary commemorating the battle of Kosovo, the remains of Prince Lazar circulated throughout Serbia in national festivities, and on Vidovdan 1989, at the site of the battle at Amselfeld, S. Milošević rallied more than a million followers and delivered the speech that provided a first premonition of the armed conflict that would ensue.

My purpose in citing this example is not to single out the Serbian people or to suggest that the archaic force of their national symbols was the only source of violence in the recent Balkan wars. Indeed, as is well known, analogous legends and symbols also animated the claims of Serbia's opponents. It would reach beyond the framework of the present study to examine the political myths of the Croatians and the devastating effects they had at the hands of the fascist Ustashe who, under the encouragement of the Nazi occupiers, persecuted the Serbs during World War II. Nor do I mean to suggest that the evocative force of legends and symbols in Europe is limited to the Balkans or to other zones of recent conflict. Even a cursory glance at the current political platforms of the extremist political parties in other parts of Europe indicates that the singular potency of political mythologies is by no means peculiar to the Balkan region, even if in recent years their murderous force has been calmed in Western and Central Europe.

As an illustration of the symbolic potency of commemorative events, this example highlights the temporal intentionality that animates them, permitting large collectivities to recall events that lie far beyond the possibilities of remembrance of living generations. In its commemorative guise, the temporal intentionality that aims to construct lines of continuity between the distant past and the present and to treat the distant past as if it were an object of direct collective recollection, may arouse a long-standing symbolic force drawn from its deeper legendary origins.[24]

In identifying the *êthos*, or habitus, as an articulation of long-term continuities in the symbolic reservoir upon which collective memory draws, I have traced its source to the passive reaches of group experience, which, in their diffuseness and latency, are often difficult to set in relief. Since Aristotle, as I have indicated, such grounds of continuity have preoccupied theorists of the social world, and they have been revived in a twentieth-century context by thinkers like Marcel Mauss and Pierre Bourdieu.

What I term the "temporal intentionality" of the *êthos,* however, concerns less this passive dimension on which I have dwelt, than the way in which it is interpreted and made both a topic of reflection and a spur to action. Ernest Renan's conception of the nation as a "rich heritage of memories," to which I called attention in the introduction, bears a close affinity to this conception of the *êthos,* as a heritage lying at the source of national identity. Renan, as we have seen, also specified that one must be capable of forgetting past experiences when they stand in the way of national unity. National identity, moreover, must be confirmed by an ongoing *contractual* relation between citizens—a "plebiscite every day." In the later sociological reflection of twentieth-century thinkers like Mauss or Bourdieu, the *êthos,* or habitus, as a precondition of social unity was consonant with contractual principles that aimed to reconcile the long-term dispositions of collectivities with the pluralistic framework of modern social existence.[25]

All such theoretical reflections on the long-term "heritage of memory," or the transmission of social dispositions, concern the ways in which remembered group experience, emanating from the broad, passive reaches of the collective past, are activated in the horizon of a given present. And this temporal intentionality may also play a singular ideological role where it is brandished in reaction to changes in social context, to the influx of new and heterogeneous members of the national community, and the organization of political life in terms of contractual ideals to which considerations of the *êthos* are subordinated. To an ideology founded on the *continuity* of the *êthos*, however, such modern conditions are so many sources of discontinuity that contravene the traditional quest for stability in the sociopolitical order. The ideology of the *êthos* seeks to counteract such tendencies as a means of safeguarding what is taken to be an original continuity of group identity. It places a premium on rootedness in the *longue durée*, or what is taken to be the organic cohesion of social existence, in which remembrance of the past and conscious appropriation and reinforcement of an inherited *êthos* fuels a sociopolitical program.

This temporal intentionality of the *êthos* takes on a radical ideological form where the aim to transpose the past into the horizon of the present is inspired not only by the conservative quest to sustain and nurture in the present an essential continuity with the past, but by the aim to maintain what is taken to be the national heritage conceived in terms of social homogeneity. The ideal of social homogeneity that is taken to reside in the deeper recesses of collective existence bequeathed by a long succession of generations has animated for more than a century the ideology of the radical right, which, in successive waves, has reacted against the effects of the industrial revolution, wide-scale migration toward urban centers, social mobility, social heterogeneity, and the fundamental principles of parliamentary democracy. The ideal of social homogeneity and continuity with the heritage of the past, and the devalorization of the contractual ideal of equality of all members of society regardless of ethnic origin have been essential features of this ideology since the extreme right in its contemporary form began to emerge at the end of the nineteenth century. What interests me in this ideology, however, is not its historical genealogy but the way in which, from its beginnings, the idea of collective memory shared among vast national groups has become a central feature of its discourse. For this reason I focus my analysis on what has often been taken to be an original paradigmatic form of this ideology in the works of Maurice Barrès, which continue to orient its expressions in the contemporary world.[26] Indeed, since at the moment of inception of this ideology in the late nineteenth century, the language of memory and of the *êthos* came to the fore in his novels and essays, they illustrate with particular clarity the temporal intentionality of this ideological use of memory.

Barrès's novel *L'appel au soldat*, the second of his trilogy *Roman de l'énergie nationale*, is set in the Lorraine, his own native region in eastern France. At the time of its publication in 1900, parts of the Lorraine had been lost to Germany following the French defeat in the Franco-Prussian war of 1870–71. Barrès presented his meditations on national and regional identity in this novel in the form of a fictive dialogue between two young friends who travel through this region on bicycles. In the course of their conversation, as they evoke the theme of their origins, one of the friends presents his ideas on the importance of their regional roots; forgetfulness of roots, he admonishes, is tantamount to the loss of a collective identity that was increasingly threatened by the rootless ideal of cosmopolitan life. During their trip, they recall the medieval folk legend of Geneviève de Brabant, who was accused of infidelity by her husband and, after undergoing many difficulties, proved her innocence to him. This legend, as the narrator in Barrès' novel explains, reflects the social realities of regional life: a long record of common existence constituted by the virtues of fidelity and sacrifice bequeathed by an ancient feudal heritage. Such legends speak to these two friends immediately and move them deeply. Barrès adds,

> This tradition of the Mosel [. . .] dates perhaps from 724; certainly it was known in 1472. It belongs to a cycle of stories which, from the noblest of estates, were imparted to the grandchildren. In areas that had been shaped by feudalism, they have a deep effect on them, as long as Paris has not distorted them and it is possible to communicate to them the preferences of their fathers. But these young people will not maintain these legends for long over the chasm of forgetting; they will no longer feel them to be national, since they themselves will have been emptied of their ancient nationality.[27]

The cosmopolitan melting-pot of Paris and the forced Germanization of French territories are two dangers that threaten to obliterate the heritage that has been tempered by centuries of national existence. In an essay that Barrès wrote shortly after the publication of *Le Roman de l'énergie nationale*, entitled "The Earth and the Dead" (*La terre et les morts*), he placed the long chain of successive generations on a common terrain (*la terre*), forging a line of continuity between the living and the dead (*les morts*) and constituting the common national legacy that he sought to invest with a new vital force. "To enable the consciousness of a country like France to emerge," as Barrès wrote, "it is necessary to root individuals in the earth and in the dead."[28] This legacy transmits a cluster of sentiments, of attitudes, and of manners of reasoning that are not chosen by individuals but are typical expressions of their milieu; as he stated in a further elaboration of his argument, appropriately titled "That Nationalism Is the Acceptance of a Determinism," this cluster is ultimately a product of "very ancient physiological dispositions."[29] Here Barrès set in relief a clear statement of the ideology of the *êthos*, which he readily formulated in terms of physiology and of blood (*sang*).[30] And yet, if the legacy of deeds and of models rooted in ancient dispositions is inscribed on the "temple of Memory,"[31] this is because it is through conscious remembrance—the aim not to let the national heritage fall into oblivion—that the conditions are created for assuring continuity with the past in the present.

The will to found national identity in a long heritage of collective existence ultimately rooted in physiological dispositions was coupled in Barrès's writings with a curious appeal to a more mystical and mysterious source of national identity, which he resolutely opposed to theories of society founded on the notion of the social contract. During a speech delivered on the bicentennial commemoration of the birth of Jean-Jacques Rousseau, he stated this conviction in unequivocal terms: "Ah! Gentlemen, we all very well know that society is not the work of pure reason, that it did not originate in a contract, but in more mysterious influences which, outside of all individual reason, have founded and continue to maintain the family, society, all order in humanity."[32]

There are striking affinities between Barrès's original expression of the ideology of the *êthos* and similar attitudes that have emerged with a renewed vitality among adherents of the extreme right in Europe and elsewhere, and historians have not failed to notice them.[33] Beyond the question concerning Barrès's ongoing influence on the contemporary extreme right, however, it is noteworthy for our discussion of the ideology of the *êthos* that a similar language of communal "memory," and of the ongoing presence of the past it assures, is marshaled to support the ideal of social homogeneity allegedly constituted over the centuries.

In his writings, Jean-Marie Le Pen, founder and former president of the French extreme right party, National Front (*Front National*), does not hesitate to invoke the "sacred rights of the collectivity in regard to its continuity."[34] It is in this vein, too, that in an editorial in his bimonthly journal, *La Lettre de Jean-Marie Le Pen*, entitled "Memory and Hope" (*La mémoire et l'espérance*), he has alluded after the manner of Maurice Barrès to remembrance of the ancestral past and communion with the "earth and the dead" (*La terre et les morts*) as a prerequisite to integration into the ongoing national group.[35] Where Le Pen has not refrained from invoking racial sources of national homogeneity, political analysts have also pointed out that, according to the public to which the party message is directed, it may at times express a more open view of the nation that stresses, in the fashion of Renan, the role of common remembrance of the past and of the ongoing decision to affirm national unity.[36]

Whatever nuances might exist in the party program of the National Front, for the purposes of our analysis of the ideology of the *êthos*, Le Pen's populist

pronouncements are particularly instructive where, in his view, collective remembrance nourishes historical continuity of the nation over the ages. In one
of his best-known texts, "Hear the Song of the French People" (*Entendez le
chant du peuple français*), published in 1996, Le Pen wrote, "Memory is our
most precious possession. We don't need to barter our most ancient memory
for a 'new-look,' sterilized morality, in conformity with 'political correctness'
and the aims of a foreign imperialism which does not dare speak its name.
[. . .] When we say that we want to defend our roots, [. . .] when we warn
against the demographic peril, when we denounce the terrible danger of the
immigration-invasion, we speak on behalf of our ancient memory."[37]

Memory in this sense, as Le Pen made clear in other proclamations, corresponds to what he took to be the "historical homogeneity" of the French nation, forged "over a thousand years."[38] In 2002, Le Pen outscored the socialist prime minister, Lionel Jospin, in the French presidential elections and, in
the second round of the election, ran against the previous French president,
Jacques Chirac, who beat Le Pen in a landslide victory. In spite of this political setback, his anti-contractualist notion of the nation as the "guardian of the
popular soul" (*guardien de l'âme populaire*) that is "mandated with an historical mission" (*historiquement missionnée*),[39] has become a commonplace
assumption in the ideology of the *êthos* of the extreme right in France and in
Europe, where the homogeneity and unity of individual nations is seen to be
the source of a strong European federation.

In more recent years, Jean-Marie Le Pen's successor as leader of the party,
his daughter Marine, has sought to gain a new respectability for the National
Front by attenuating her father's radicalism.[40] Nonetheless, the ideology of
the *êthos* has lost none of its force among members of the French and European extreme right. Among the more radical recent expressions of such
convictions, the ruminations of established French writer and critic Richard
Millet, who has played a significant role in French cultural and publishing
administration, provides a particularly unsettling example. Millet, who has
gravitated toward ever more extreme right-wing positions, stirred up a highly
publicized debate in France, due to his manner of publicly lamenting what
he described as the loss of cultural and social homogeneity in Europe. He
did this in the form of a eulogy for the Norwegian mass-murderer Anders
Breivik who, on a summer day in 2011, in protest against multiculturalism
and European immigration policies, bombed Norwegian government build-
ings and killed seventy-seven of his fellow citizens. In his eulogy for Anders
Breivik, Millet wrote, "We who each day measure the lack of culture of the
native population, like the abyss that separates us from the extra-European

peoples who inhabit our territory; we know that it is language that suffers from this, and with it memory, blood and identity."[41] If Millet's statement was too extreme to find endorsement among groups such as the National Front, I do not concern myself with such nuances among the positions of the radical right and retain for analysis one general assumption that they share, which is pertinent for the theory of collective memory: their common conceptions of social homogeneity arising from long-term shared memory and underlying group dispositions that have developed over the ages. Here we must investigate more closely the specifically *ideological* character of this temporal intentionality of collective memory, which seeks to establish long-term continuity with the past in the horizon of the present. This will permit us in the concluding section of the present chapter to extend our query concerning the place of collective memory to a more comprehensive investigation of its limits.

V

In previous chapters I have interpreted collective memory as a contemporaneous horizon of experience and remembrance shared by overlapping, living generations. Collective memory flows from a reservoir of sedimented, stratified, and fragmented symbols that are preconditions for continuity between past and present in view of a common future. Far from being a uniform block, collective memory constantly undergoes re-elaboration in the plurality of perspectives of living groups who, in drawing on a vast reservoir of symbols, are continually brought to reappraise the past in its relation to the present. However homogeneous a group may believe itself to be, the transition between generations is never one of simple continuity, since the passage from one horizon of contemporaneity to another is punctuated by divergences in the concrete situations in which living groups find themselves and by transformations in the corresponding modes of group existence. Such modifications affect the finite perspective of group experience and of group recall at all of its levels, and introduce divergences in the communal sense of continuity itself. This transition of temporal horizons is not only accompanied by metamorphoses in *explicit* modes of group awareness, for radical contingency also alters the passive levels of symbolic articulation: independently of the express will of living generations, and often without their awareness, they undergo constant and for the most part unforeseeable modifications over time.

Amid the shifts in forms of group existence that intervene within the life span of contemporaneous generations and place in relief the conditions of their collective finitude, the cohesion of the remembering collectivity is nourished by the capacity to relate to the past as a common past. In what way, however, might this cohesion be interpreted? And what, indeed, is *common* in the past? Amid gaps, fissures, and discontinuities, the remembered experience of larger groups is necessarily dismembered along the lines of different perspectives in a given present of the smaller groups that compose them. And, if groups in their heterogeneity remember the past from different present perspectives, any possibility of referring to a *common* identity depends not on a reified shared substance, but presupposes first and foremost group awareness of the temporal link between past and present, a shared manner of drawing past group experience into the horizon of the present and of endowing it with a publicly recognized symbolic significance. Here common recollection concerns not only isolated persons, things, or events but also—even if in an implicit manner–the temporal horizon of a common past; a previous temporal position that is presentified and mobilized in view of shared future possibilities.

Given the impossibility of recalling a past that lies beyond all living memory, any reference to "historical" remembrance of the long concatenation of past generations can only be metaphorical. This usage signals the imaginative transfer of what is beyond all possible recall into the imagery of lived experience and vivid recollection, and it lends affective tone and rhetorical weight to the sense of continuity with the past. Yet, in any literal sense, it promotes the often implicit and wholly illusory assumption that the distant past may be brought into the horizon of the present as if it were an object of living remembrance. The historian's deliberative use of the imagination, supported by contextual analysis, may in some measure reconstitute the temporal horizon of the past on the basis of traces left by past generations, yet this possibility is always limited.

Where the metaphorical status of remembrance as it is applied to the historical past is overlooked and its finite scope discounted, it readily falls prey to extravagant claims, notably where beliefs in the substantial homogeneity of the group *êthos* over time draw on the language of ethnic traits, physiological dispositions, or blood and race. Here the ideal of the *êthos* presupposes a form of group remembrance enabling the presentification of the past in an unambiguously direct and concrete sense. This usage, however, intends to fulfill ideological aims that should not be confused with the prudent avowal that shared dispositions may indeed span centuries and draw on deep, if often unperceived sources in the reservoir of shared symbols. Such dispositions come to expression in the symbolic forms communicated in all aspects of daily life: in the idioms we employ, the stories we tell, the gestures we make, the melodies that move us, which have been handed down by past generations beyond living memory and recorded chronicles. The extravagance of any attempt to fix this *êthos* in the mold of a substantialized group identity and of its collective remembrance lies in its manner of projecting the assumptions of a reified social homogeneity onto the past, thus ignoring the moments of radical contingency through which, over time, discontinuity separates different horizons of contemporaneity, rending the very fabric of collective existence. Such extravagant illusions are particularly well suited to the promotion of ideological positions where they ignore the possibility that continuity in dispositions over the course of generations, far from emanating from an underlying substance, is modulated in terms of modifiable structures of interaction governing ways of being together in a common world.

In the third novel of Barrès's *Roman de l'énergie nationale*, entitled *Their Countenances* (*Leurs figures*), one of the two protagonists who, in the previous novel, *L'appel au soldat*, engaged in a dialogue on national identity during a bicycle trip through their native Lorraine, sends a letter to the other protagonist in which he further elaborates on this topic. In this letter, introduced in the chapter entitled "Letter of Saint-Phlin on the 'food' of Lorraine," the young man provides an eloquent illustration of what I refer to as the ideology of the *êthos*: "You smile, Sturel. Not at all, I realize, at the *regenerative virtue I attribute to the historical sense*: you hope, as I do, that our provinces will emerge from their oblivion and stop forgetting themselves, that *our children will recognize themselves to be in continuity with their parents.* [. . .] We so totally misunderstand the law that I embrace! In other words, *that the human plant only grows vigorously and fruitfully where it remains under the conditions which formed and maintained its species over the centuries.*"[42]

According to this passage, national character is nurtured by collective existence in a common locality, and group integrity maintains itself through a conscious effort not to forget the legacy bequeathed by the long chain of past generations. Remembrance of the past is here equated with the "historical sense." This conception of the historical sense is noteworthy, for it hardly concerns the historical past in its singular and unique quality, through which it is necessarily distinguished from the present. On the contrary, any historical concern for the singular texture of the past is subordinated to another, eminently *present-oriented* aim: the quest, by the supposedly homogeneous group that forms the most recent link in the long concatenation of past generations, to collapse the distance between past and present and, through self-understanding derived from the past, to bask in the past's regenerative powers. Here we encounter a quasi-mystical vision of communion with the ancestral world in which the ideology of the *êthos* reveals the full scope of its temporal intentionality: in aiming to bridge the chasm between the distant past and the horizon of the present that no finite anthropological vision is capable of penetrating, it places in a wholly illusory light the opacity of the historical past lying beyond the limits of all living collective memory.

CHAPTER 5

Virtual Experience, the Mass Media, and the Configuration of the Public Sphere

As I have delineated it in previous chapters, collective memory, beyond the scope of personal and small-group recollection, is primarily articulated at the level of what can be publicly interpreted and communicated. From this perspective, specific ways of publicly organizing collective experience and collective remembrance, as they are projected toward a shared future, correspond to what we commonly term the "public realm." In its different manifestations in our contemporary mass societies, the public realm has undergone a series of fundamental transformations over the course of the past century and a half. A comparison of the present-day organization of the public realm with that which predominated among earlier generations illustrates that these changes correspond to metamorphoses in the ways of communicating and of retaining in collective memory what is deemed to be significant in public life, a role which, in our contemporary mass societies, is predominantly assumed by the "mass media."

In chapter 3, I suggested that the mass media, in bringing events to public visibility, organize public experience and collective remembrance by portraying what ordinarily lies beyond the purview of immediate experience and direct recollection for the vast majority of individuals and groups who take cognizance of them. In this capacity, the mass media select what are deemed to be significant events out of the diffuse and highly complex manifold of available data, while shaping and disseminating accounts of them in the public sphere. In the present chapter I extend and deepen this analysis by exploring how the media, in bringing to visibility what ordinarily lies outside the range of vision of all but a small minority of direct witnesses, confer on public communication a spatiotemporal and logical order that is specific to them. This spatiotemporal pattern and logic bear no direct analogy to individual modes of experience and remembrance, nor are they simple replicas of the spatiotemporal pattern and logic of personal experience in the flesh, or of remembrance of that experience. In ways that are specific to mass existence, they precede and pattern the personal sphere by lending it a specific symbolic order. As such, the spatiotemporal pattern and logic of mass communications constitute an autonomous mode of symbolic embodiment through which public awareness is channeled that infuses the overarching horizon of con-temporaneity in which the public realm is situated. Far from a fixed property, this spatiotemporal pattern and logic are subject to modification in relation to the technical organization of the media through which information is com-municated. Over the past century and a half, the emergence and development of the mass media has brought a series of transformations in the modes of public presentation of information and in the ways in which, as it is invested with symbolic significance, it is made part of shared experience and collective remembrance. The symbolically configured spatiotemporal and logical order of the evolving technical structures of the mass media, to which experience and remembrance in a mass society continually adapt, reveals the scope and significance of the way in which the mass media bring them to visibility in the public sphere.

I

In selecting, organizing, and communicating information on a vast scale and in bringing it to public visibility, the media have appropriated and trans-formed what had been performed on a more limited scale by flyers, almanacs, and news pamphlets in an earlier sociocultural framework. If the invention and spread of the printing press initially brought print and image to public visibility on a mass scale, the advent of modern mass societies in the nine-teenth century, accompanied by momentous technological innovations, has not ceased to recast the very foundations of public life. From the first trans-atlantic telegraph cable in the 1850s to the transatlantic telephone and com-munications cables in the early twentieth century and contemporary satellite transmission, the reach of the information network has spanned the globe in ever more comprehensive fashion. The acceleration of the conditions of modern existence, associated with the greatly increased mobility of persons and goods, is complemented by immediate access to information, placing a premium on its rapid turnover, which has vastly increased in its variety and quantity over the course of recent generations. These changes, however, do not only concern the geographic reach of the media or the speed with which information is transmitted, but above all the *form* according to which it is organized: from the newspaper and the illustrated journal, to film and newsreel, televisual image, the World Wide Web, and accompanying kinds of digital communication, this form concerns the incessant evolution of the media in relation to novel technological capacities that lend pattern to the public ways of experiencing and remembering. This change, moreover, is not limited to selection, configuration, and acceleration of communication by the media of an ever-growing quantity and variety of events; still more essential is their role in making people, objects, and events publicly visible while interweaving their visible representation in the broader web of what may be collectively recalled. Beyond their use as a means of instructing, entertaining, or influencing commerce, the mass media both mirror and pattern ways of experiencing and remembering, as well as future expectations, through which the public sphere assumes its contemporary configuration. In bringing to visibility what ordinarily lies outside the range of direct vision, and in conferring on it public significance, the media constitute the essential vehicle through which current preoccupations and events are publicly accounted for and retained in memory. In this they exercise what might be termed a reflexive function.[1] If we consider the different kinds of public communication that have developed, roughly speaking, over the past century and a half, including newspaper, film, video, or, more recently, digitalized computer technology, it would be possible to distinguish nuances in the spatiotemporal pattern and logical form that characterize each of these media. I touch on these nuances in the course of my analysis. According to the central argument of this chapter, however, any such nuances presuppose an underlying *similarity* in the modes of spatiotemporal and logical configuration that, in the context of mass society, enable each of them to endow collective experience and remembrance with public significance. This similarity concerns first and foremost the news, current events, and information functions of the media that, as I argue, are paradigmatic in the exercise of their reflexive role and their mode of public diffusion.

How might we qualify these novel conditions of the public visibility of communicated and remembered events? Several elements are above all pertinent for our analysis, since each concerns the means of configuring public communication, whether newspaper, film, video, or digitalized information. The first element has often been emphasized, and justly so, for it concerns the *anonymity* of mass audiences to which communication is directed. Note that the theme of the anonymous reader or viewer is by no means specific to *mass* communications and has, indeed, long been associated with all that is represented before undifferentiated audiences. In an ancient context, for example, Plato called attention to the impersonal character of writing and of the image more generally: unlike the dialogue in a direct encounter, fixed word and image do not allow for interaction on the part of the reader or viewer, and, as he stipulated, they may be addressed to anyone at all, regardless of whether or not the receiver is capable of properly understanding the communicated message.[2] If the most recent interactive computer technologies, such as those employed in the social media, have striven to overcome this situation, anonymity also concerns another aspect of mass communication that cannot be avoided by the generalized format of technologically programmed responses: in the situation of mass society, this impersonality is dictated by the way in which communicated words and images are tailored to the concerns of a vast number on a mass scale. Here the horizon of contemporaneity of overlapping generations is distended to accommodate the symbolic structures of information that may be expanded to address the widest possible variety of receivers. In recent years, thanks to information sold by the social media, mass marketing can be targeted to correspond to specific interests of smaller regions and groups, and this refines the appeal, but does not essentially alter the form of mass production. In such form, goods are adapted to an order that characterizes mass consumer products more generally. In the early twentieth century, Georg Simmel described this process in his analysis of the newspaper as a consumer product: "The more functional and impersonal a product is, the better it is suited to more people. Such consumable material, in order to be attractive and enjoyable for a very large number of individuals, cannot be designed in view of the particularity of subjective desires, while on the other hand only the most extreme differentiation of production is able to produce objects cheaply and abundantly enough to satisfy the demands of mass consumption"[3]

Second, in accord with this anonymous mode of presentation, the mass media open the public horizon of contemporaneity to simultaneous contact with symbolic networks at different levels, from the local levels, in which symbolic expression of group experience is immediately familiar, to national levels with which local groups share overlapping, readily interpretable symbolic networks and, finally, to foreign contexts, encompassing often unfamiliar symbolic structures that are not readily comprehensible. Here a given public is largely dependent on media accounts that translate and interpret what would otherwise be incomprehensible. In this manner, the media simultaneously bring to visibility the concentric spheres of community, collectivity, and global totality that, whether communicated through print or visual image, endow with public status what has been directly witnessed by a small minority, while opening it to the global reach of the information network. Where personal and small-group experience is embedded in the web of symbolic cohesion of the life-experience of overlapping, living generations in the context of a given horizon of contemporaneity, what is brought to public visibility by the mass media is not necessarily commensurable with the symbolic web of this context. The anonymous mode of organization of information, which simultaneously orders the local and familiar as well as the foreign and unfamiliar according to a uniform scheme of presentation, favors a principle of selection that leaves the broader context of communicated information undefined. Although those who are immediately familiar with events and with the symbolic web from which they draw their significance may be able to recontextualize them, this is not possible for much of the information that the media convey that is abstracted from this weave and presented from the outside. It is primarily in this decontextualized order that information circulates and is received by those who retain it as remembered experience.

Third, in the framework of newspaper journalism, information is organized in sections, in which the types of information are most commonly juxtaposed in haphazard fashion: advertising may border reports of foreign affairs, a miscellaneous news item may abut stock market reports or the letters to the editor column.[4] Similarly, information and news in more recent digital interfaces are "hypermediated": moving images on the main body of television screens are bordered by mobile printed strips on the lower margin of the display in contemporary CNN-like television announcements, and these mosaics have more recently been multiplied in an ever more elaborate mix of words and images that appear on the constantly shifting display of the World Wide Web.[5]

Fourth, in news reporting, if events are for the most part haphazardly arranged, they are not randomly selected, for their interest to a general public lies in their immediate relevance as current events or "breaking news." This simultaneous and ubiquitous status brings first and foremost before the public eye preoccupations that are presently at hand, which are decontextualized not only in the spatial terms of mixing together local and familiar contexts with foreign and unfamiliar ones, but in the temporal sense of portraying events in their immediacy and without necessary continuity with what predates a short-term past. The principle of selection of events requires a continual process of updating in which a premium is accorded to what is most recent.[6]

All of these forms of visibility before a mass public impose a specific order on publicly remembered representations. It is a *symbolically* configured order not because it assumes the form of a sign or emblem, but because of the immediate spatiotemporal pattern and logic it deploys: anonymous, decontextualized, and haphazard modes of presentation that, in their currency, are continually subjected to a process of updating format information as current events that are, so to speak, capable of grabbing the public eye. As it is displaced from its original context, the condensed format and heightened immediacy of media news transposes information from the horizon of contemporaneity of given groups in which original experience transpires and is remembered and communicated to what might be termed its "field of currency." In the field of currency, the anonymous, decontextualized, haphazard, and continually updated mode of presentation lends information a spatiotemporal pattern and logic that formats it for mass dissemination.

The abridged, condensed, and reconfigured format of the field of currency introduces a gap between the mode of mass-media presentation and the horizon of contemporaneity in which everyday experience and remembrance transpires. This does not mean, however, that information communicated in mass-media format would somehow remain separate from the *Lebenswelt* of direct everyday experience. On one hand, assumptions arising from the web of collectively remembered, embodied symbols shared by a given group, notably a predominant social group, orient the selection and arrangement of events that are communicated in the field of currency. Here, if essentially current events, or events immediately pertinent to the field of currency, are portrayed for their public significance, this by no means excludes an orientation in terms of long-standing group assumptions or biases—for example, of a religious or national order. On the other hand, the field of currency, in the framework of its specific format, infuses and restructures the horizon of contemporaneity in which these assumptions are embedded, providing the broad context in which they confront the perspectives of other groups. In this context, events depicted in the mass-media format of the field of currency, as they are received within a given horizon of contemporaneity, may often assume greater importance than what is immediately experienced in the common, everyday *Lebenswelt*.

The reflexive function of the mass media becomes operative in the act of bringing to visibility, according to their specific spatiotemporal pattern and logic, what ordinarily, for the vast majority of individuals and groups, lies beyond the purview of face-to-face experience and direct remembrance. It is in this quest to "mirror" what is publicly significant and to fill in the gaps of what for the most part lies beyond the pale of ordinary experience that the media constitute a unique mode of public awareness and self-awareness; in organizing the field of currency, they virtually parallel and infuse the broader horizon of contemporaneity that, in its continuity and cohesion in public remembrance, interweaves the web of symbolic significations as it is configured over time. Where in the decontextualized framework of mass-media accounts reported information goes out of currency and no longer provides a focus for public interest, it falls into forgetfulness and neglect. Amid the diffuseness and vast complexity of the public sphere, decontextualized information that has no ready relation to an overarching horizon of contemporaneity is all the more capable of being marginalized or simply ignored, opening the door to possibilities of dissimulation, manipulation, and exclusion.

In referring to the reflexive function of mass communication in its field of currency, I have assigned, since the beginning of this chapter, a paradigmatic role to the *news* media and their manner of selecting, organizing, and communicating events that are deemed publicly significant. If the role of newspaper, magazine, radio, and above all television and World Wide Web is by no means *limited* to the communication of current events, the act of conferring public visibility and engendering public self-awareness nonetheless remains their indispensable purpose. The format of the mass media is most directly adapted to journalistic reporting, which at the same time structures other sectors of activity in which the mass media are engaged. The anonymous, haphazard, decontextualized format in which reported events are continually updated may admit of variations when it is a question of entertainment or advertising. Above all, the requirement for continuous updating in the shifting field of currency is not necessarily as stringent in these sectors. Entertainment, for example, may allow for a more sustained dramatic presentation (even where interrupted by commercials), and commercials often resort to the repetition of a recognizable message. Yet even in these sectors the viewers' attention is drawn to the "latest" sports results, to ever-renewed entertainment programming, and to "new and improved" commercial products. If, as I understand it, the field of currency predominantly accommodates the format of journalistic reporting, other sectors involved in mass communication are essentially oriented in terms of its general structure.

In regard to the concepts of a "field of currency" as the format of mass communication and of a "horizon of contemporaneity" with which it interacts, encompassing the experience and shared, symbolically embodied memories of overlapping generations, I must emphasize a further consideration in order to avoid misunderstanding. As I interpret them, these concepts delineate the public dimension of group experience and collective memory, and, at all levels of their deployment, they must be distinguished from specifically *historical* categories of analysis that apply to more extensive and qualitatively different temporal regimes. If at first sight, therefore, they might seem to bear a certain resemblance to historical categories of analysis, notably to the concept of the present as a "space of experience" (*Erfahrungsraum*), as understood by Reinhart Koselleck, a cursory look at Koselleck's concept will set in clear relief the essential difference in the respective interpretative regimes of collective memory and history.

In referring to the historical experience of a given present as a "space of experience," Koselleck sought to account for the emergence of a typically modern way of relating present time to the past and future. According to his argument, the modern experience of historical time emerged in the eighteenth and nineteenth centuries, as history was perceived to be a self-sustaining, autonomous process that actualizes itself in the "space of experience" of a given present and projects itself onto the horizon of expectation (*Erwartungshorizont*) of an anticipated future, toward which it was believed this process was leading.[7] The governing idea of history as an overarching, cohesive whole—a "collective singular," in Koselleck's terminology—thus commanded the novel modern mode of unification of the three temporal fields of historical experience, opening the way for an idea of history as an objective agent bringing forth change and development.

As I employ them in relation to collective memory, the concepts of the horizon of contemporaneity and the field of currency, respectively limited to the time-span of living generations and to the ephemeral lapse during which news retains its novelty, might both be encompassed in the "space of experience" as Koselleck understood it. Indeed, for the historian, all contemporary history is set within what is, from the perspective of the collective memory of contemporaneous generations, a relatively long time-frame. This historical time-frame provides for no specific categories of temporal articulation to delineate the interwoven networks of collective memory in relation to the public sphere. Therefore, my primary focus concerns not general categories of historical time, orienting the ways in which a given present anticipates a corresponding future, but a plurality of temporal perspectives that, in a mass social framework, distinguish group orientations among overlapping generations. As uniform as the format of mass communication may be in a given field of currency, its interaction with the weave of remembered experience spanning successive living generations, concerns not such protracted categories of historical experience and expectation but common and fragmented visions of different future possibilities that are mobilized in relation to a plurality of present group perspectives and divergent ways of remembering the collective past.

Koselleck's viewpoint has been relativized in more recent theoretical work, where the argument has been advanced that the experience of history in the current framework of collective life has been propelled beyond its modern form into a still more recent mode of relation to historical time, a new "regime of historicity" that François Hartog characterizes as "presentism."[8] According to this conviction, the modern experience of history, governed by a variety of modes of expectation of the historical future, has given way to an increasing contemporary submergence in preoccupations dictated by the present. According to this argument, historical "presentism" accounts for the contemporary decline of modern ideologies that, in terms of class or nation, sought to establish long-term lines of continuity between past and present, and provided specific orientations toward the future. Absorbed in present preoccupations, our contemporary societies subordinate both the remembered past and the anticipated future to the short-term vision encompassing current projects.[9] The concern with collective memory in recent years, in particular among historians, is taken to be a further symptom of contemporary presentism, insofar as the interest in long-term historical continuities, such as an ongoing national identity, is inspired less by an aim to realize future projects and goals than to resuscitate collective identities that are so thoroughly submerged in the preoccupations of the present that they have lost their traditional historical range and depth.[10]

In highlighting the increasing orientation of our contemporary societies toward the present, this theoretical approach has, I believe, identified a significant tendency of our times. This tendency, however, corresponds to a highly complex phenomenon, and its different ramifications, if they may confirm a broad temporal orientation of our epoch, must be more closely tied to the concrete situations from which they arise. It is debatable, indeed, whether the general temporal category of presentism can account for the diversity of sociopolitical perspectives in our contemporary mass societies, in which, in the same horizon of contemporaneity, different groups may marshal diverse kinds of temporal understanding.

If, as I interpret it, the suggestive category of presentism is to be made fruitful as a means of characterizing a predominant tendency of the contemporary world, it requires investigation at a more basic level: not only on the plane of ideas but also, and primarily, in relation to contemporary productive processes and to a variety of attitudes toward time that they promote in an increasingly globalized world. From this point of view, different forms of progress, whether economic, technical, or scientific, depend on a constant process of updating, whereby what does not conform to the most recent standards is set aside as obsolete. Outdated computer programs; medical procedures prior to Pasteur, Fleming, and Salk; physics before Newton—these may be of academic interest to small groups of historians, but they remain ancillary to the present quest for technical and scientific results. On a similar note, the mass media are an essential by-product of technological innovation, without which mass communication in word and image, as we know it today, would be unthinkable. Yet, as dependent as the media have been upon a long series of technological innovations, the temporal schema of the field of currency in which the mass media operate should not simply be assimilated to the predominant temporal orientation of contemporary productive processes and technology. If the mass media, indeed, place a premium upon current events and upon an approach to the past submerged in the perspective of current preoccupations, their reflexive grasp engages a temporal order that is oriented in terms of the specific symbolic framework of the public world they bring to visibility.[11] The spatiotemporal patterns and logic through which the mass media operate are therefore not one manifestation among others of an overarching category of presentism that infuses them, nor are they mere symptoms of present-oriented societies that have lost their historical sense. The autonomous symbolic order they create is not only one aspect of a more general postmodern condition, but corresponds to a fundamental status lying in their manner of patterning the public sphere from which shared experience and collective memory draw their sustenance. The concept of the field of currency seeks to nuance and differentiate the specific orientation toward the present fostered by the mass media and by the modes of public experience and collective memory that mass communications engage.

The autonomous symbolic order configured by the mass media is not a hermetically sealed order. The orientation of the mass media toward the present, while it continually patterns the larger context in which the mass media operate, is also nourished by the broader horizon of contemporaneity of given groups or peoples, which is by no means limited to the present but continually draws on a past beyond its purview. The reflexive selection of meaningful events in the present, as they are charged with symbolic significance, by no means excludes a nostalgic and traditionalistic outlook that, in a given field of currency, may engage non-contemporaneous assumptions that, even where latent and unacknowledged, essentially distinguish them from the kind of present orientation animating the quest for what is technologically up-to-date.[12] As I have stressed in the preceding pages, the format of the mass media, as it draws words and images into the field of currency, is by no means incompatible with a quest for religious identity or a nationalistic drive for ethnic homogeneity.[13] Even where the temporal intentionality of such a quest issues from essentially present-day sociopolitical preconceptions that, in their aim to establish continuity, are hardly concerned with the specific texture of the historical past, it is difficult to comprehend how such general categories as "presentism" in a postmodern age might account for the singularity of their ideological appeal.

I I

If we are to pinpoint the essential dynamic governing the mass structuring of public experience and public memory underlying anticipations of a common future, a decisive factor lies in the role that the *image* has come to play in our contemporary world. The emergence of a culture of the image over the course of the twentieth century has signaled a break with all earlier forms of public visibility that has at the same time reinforced and extended on a new basis the primary tendencies that characterized an earlier mass literary culture.

How are we to understand the singular potency of the image and, through the web of embodied and remembered symbols, its relation to the transformation in the conditions of public visibility in the era of mass communication? If the image has assumed an ever more prominent role in the mass media, this role at the same time involves an essential transformation in its traditional vocation in the visual arts in conformity with the spatiotemporal pattern and logic of mass communication. In the era of the mass media, this transformation comes to light in relation to the complex possibilities of communication intrinsic to the image itself.

In all of their expressions, traditional or contemporary, images may act as languages, since they may be bearers of iconographic signs, just as, through language, they may be situated in a given context. And yet, where language and other signs interpret sensuous images in relation to their context, images, as publicly interpretable visual phenomena, retain the capacity to overstep the confines of the context in which they emerge—their embeddedness in a specific horizon of contemporaneity—to spontaneously communicate a sensuous meaning that written languages can only indirectly convey.

Traditional iconography in the visual arts, like later images transmitted by mass communications, bring visual icons to public visibility, though traditional works were diffused in limited numbers and to a small audience. In traditional iconography, the sensuous plenitude of the work found its expression not only in interpretable visual signs or suggestive representations, for its legendary ideal lay in the production of *beautiful* images, which deployed the image's intrinsic potency to its fullest extent. In light of the complex role of the image, subsequent transformations in its public function in the era of mass communications may be more closely identified.

The complex role of the image as it is deployed in traditional iconography may be illustrated in terms of a suggestive example: Peter Paul Rubens' Medici Cycle, which was originally displayed in the residence of Marie de' Medici at the Palais du Luxembourg in Paris, and is today in the museum of the Louvre. As Queen of France, Marie de' Medici assumed the regency following the assassination of her husband, Henri IV, and she exercised this function until her son Louis XIII reached majority. In 1621, a little more than a decade after the death of Henri IV, she commissioned Rubens to paint the cycle in order to illustrate her life and those of her husband and their son. The portraits are adorned with the signs of royalty that may be gleaned by all who recognize them; linguistic description may also situate what is depicted in the portraits in the historical context of early seventeenth-century France. And yet the paintings bring an autonomous aesthetic sense to expression that is capable of embodying and generating symbolic meaning. This remarkable potency of the image oversteps the limits of immanent signs that the image may bear and the marks of an external context to which it may be referred. It is this potency of the image that Jacob Burckhardt characterized with particular eloquence in his interpretation of Rubens' Medici Cycle, when he commented that after a certain lapse of time, the contextual significance of such paintings and their political purpose may well become obscure; yet, in spite of this, this work has, in his words, remained *art* (*"es ist noch Kunst geblieben"*). After the quarrels between Marie de' Medici and her enemies subsided, and her enemies' names were all but forgotten, her saga, as Burckhardt pointed out, retains its vitality due to the aesthetic force of Rubens' cycle. This illustrates the uncanny potency of the image in its capacity to convey an aesthetic sense that oversteps the boundaries of any contextually limited significance that it may simultaneously convey. Where the message and the sense of style change over time, the paintings themselves belong, in Burckhardt's opinion, to "an undying genre" (*unsterblichen Geschlechts*).[14] Such convictions concerning the eternal potency of beautiful images were widely shared by late nineteenth-century art theorists, as the comments of Burckhardt's English contemporary, John Ruskin attest, for his theory of art similarly presupposed that through the beautiful, "what is particular to times and temperaments may be distinguished from [what is] eternal."[15]

FIGURE 2. Peter Paul Rubens, *The Felicity of the Regency*, 1623–25, Louvre Museum, Paris. © RMN-Grand Palais (musée du Louvre)/René-Gabriel Ojéda/Thierry Le Mage.

During the century and a half that separates us from Burckhardt and from Ruskin—who had both begun to grasp the changes that mass society and mass communication were bringing to the traditional world that inspired their respective artistic ideals—the mass production of images, their potential dissemination over the entire globe, and the growing profusion of a culture of the image were accompanied by profound changes that they could not have anticipated, not only in art, but in the modes of visual representation more generally. This brings us back to the question, therefore, concerning the transformation that the mass production and communication of images, which have made them ever more prominent in our contemporary world, have brought to our ways of receiving, interpreting, and retaining them in public memory.

A first indication of this transformation may be gleaned from the reflections on modernity by the poet Charles Baudelaire who, as different as he was in temperament and outlook from his Swiss contemporary Jacob Burckhardt or his English contemporary, John Ruskin, shared their quest to discern the unperishing element of art within the ephemeral aspects of its manifestations. If Baudelaire's comments touch on all forms of cultural production, his focus on the visual arts at the same time raises the question concerning the particular potency of the image.

In the age-old quest for the unperishing element in art, which assumed a new urgency in the face of the rapid transformation of the social conditions of life, Baudelaire identified the "modern" with fashion or modishness, which he qualified as "the transitory, the fugitive, the contingent" ("*le transitoire, le fugitif, le contingent*"). The modern, according to Baudelaire's interpretation of painting and the visual image, concerned only part of its significance, for the other part pertained to the "eternal" and the "immutable."[16] His use of the term *modernity*, moreover, was not limited to what we generally consider to be the modern period, for he identified it with the modish and the variable aspects that are manifested in *all* periods. Even antiquity, in this perspective, had its "modern"—that is, temporally limited and contingent—side. Against this, the eternal dimension that it incarnates stands out and transcends the ephemerality of the period in which it emerges. As such comments illustrate, not only traditionalists in the second half of the nineteenth century, but such a resolute modern as Baudelaire could embrace the quest for eternal forms of beauty that images convey with singular vivacity.[17] If we are to characterize in essence a change in ways of interpreting and of being in a common world that has come to the fore in the modes of public visibility, it lies in the weakening of this kind of preoccupation with beauty as an expression of the "eternal" and the "immutable." The evanescence of this ideal corresponded, indeed, to a more general transformation in Western cultural attitudes. Without venturing an all-encompassing judgment of nineteenth-century thought, such important expressions of late nineteenth-century cultural theory permit us to identify a lingering paradigm in Western aesthetics and culture, the holdover of an ancient tradition that found an echo in central doctrines of the nineteenth century that came to expression even as mass society was becoming the predominant human reality. The demise of this paradigm, corresponding to the emergence of artistic criteria that questioned the ascendancy of traditional ideals of beauty in art, corresponded to a heightened exposure to the "ephemeral, the fugitive and the contingent," an intensified sensibility to current events and their flux, bereft of ready possibilities of recourse to moorings in long-term conceptions of stability that, in the mid-nineteenth century, could still inspire the outlook of a modern like Baudelaire. This is not to deny the sporadic recrudescence of the quest for the eternal and immutable in twentieth-century thought, but to pinpoint shifts in the public realm that, as it is shaped through the ubiquitous format of mass communication, correspond to the transformation of more general conditions of public visibility.

This development must be synchronized with a decline in metaphysics and in all-encompassing idealist philosophies of history, as well as the turn to the anthropological underpinnings of human experience that I examined in the introduction. This, in turn, is concomitant with the concern for collective remembrance as a quest for stability and permanence in the public realm that has become a general requisite of contemporary culture.

These preliminary remarks permit us to place in clearer focus the question concerning the specific potency of the image as a form of expression. Even as conceptions of the sensuous plenitude and force of the image, and with them the vocation of the visual arts, shifted their orientation, the capacity of the image to immediately communicate and to insinuate itself into the web of remembered symbols asserted a new vitality both in the visual arts and in the different spheres of visual mass communication. Without directly conveying a sensuous image, language is, of course, also capable of eliciting imagery, especially through the metaphors of poetic expression, which may reach beyond the context of its origin; but language and other contextually bound signs are, without translation, incomprehensible to those who are not familiar with them. When translated, language may indeed reach beyond the cultural confines of its context of origin, yet translation also transforms its meaning as it is adapted to the context in which it is received, rooted in the passive web of embodied symbolic significations retained, within a given horizon of contemporaneity, in the fragmented strata of collective memory. If visual images, too, are open to different kinds of interpretation in accord with the context of their reception, especially in relation to implicit, culturally bound signs they may manifest, they nonetheless retain a capacity for direct communication that words can only indirectly approximate. Images of happy celebration, of squalid poverty, of ruthless violence, are for the most part immediately conveyable beyond the specific context from which they are drawn. Not only the beautiful image in the unique plenitude of its presence, but also the mass-produced image attains an immediacy that reaches across the confines of linguistic contexts; thus, from the earliest days of mass reproduction following the invention of the printing press, images had "the natural advantage of being internationally understood."[18]

Since the pioneering work of authors like Georg Simmel, Paul Valéry, or Walter Benjamin, attention has been drawn to the ways in which mass reproduction has modified our manner of perceiving images. This modification has corresponded to the ever-increasing use of images in all aspects of public and private life—images that, on one hand, are transmitted by ever more diversified types of media and, on the other, encompass disparate kinds of messages that the media continually and ubiquitously bring to public visibility. Following the emergence of the mass media and the technology of mass reproduction, images have assumed an ever more central role. Beginning with the Crimean War of 1854, the American Civil War of the 1860s, and the Franco-Prussian war of 1870–71, war correspondents served as eyewitnesses to events, preparing sketches of them for the mass editions of contemporary newspapers and illustrated journals.[19] The role of images steadily increased in fashion magazines and illustrated weekly journals. In giving the impression that it duplicated immediate perceptual experience, photography lent an essentially new role to the image, and this role was at once reinforced and transformed with the mass dissemination of moving pictures, from celluloid movie and newsreel to televised video news and entertainment programs, and a host of digitalized forms of communication that have accorded to the image and the culture of the image an ever more central role. With each of these technological advances, the representational image comes closer to simulating the lifeworld of everyday experience. And yet, the essential difference between them remains. Images and events that emerge in the field of currency, formatted by the mass media, are necessarily selected from the manifold of direct experience, displaced, condensed, and symbolically reconfigured in the public space opened by the media. News reporting, culminating in the

FIGURE 3. *Battle of Antietam, Maryland—"Burnside's division carrying the bridge over the Antietam Creek, and storming the Rebel position, after a desperate conflict of four hours, Wednesday, 17 September 1862,"* sketch by Edwin Forbes, artist-correspondent for *Frank Leslie's Illustrated Newspaper,* 15, no. 367 (11 October, 1862), 33. Courtesy of the Library of Congress, Prints and Photographs Division, LC-DIG-ppmsca-22526.

eyewitness coverage of "breaking news," is the paradigmatic form of this capacity to simulate original experience in the lifeworld, drawing on the power of images in the ever-changing field of currency.

The altered conditions of public visibility generated by the widespread communication of images in mass-media format appear in a particularly clear light if we consider developments in the parallel ways in which the visual arts convey images before the public eye. In important ways they anticipated the altered conditions of public visibility, participated in their transformation, and were in turn transformed in the process. In many of the forms of expression of modern art, the abandonment of neoclassicism and romanticism has tended to deflect its focus from the direct reproduction of objects and events to favor a heightened concentration on the modes of apprehension themselves in terms of which images are brought to awareness.[20] This highlighted the representation of aspects of the raw immediacy of the perceptual act that are not ordinarily brought to mind. Besides the representation of specific contents of an experiential world, the visual arts may also focus on the act of patterning itself through which the world is experienced, remembered, and communicated. Heightened attention to the immediate modes of perception in Impressionism, simultaneous juxtaposition of a multitude of positions to evoke spatial mobility in Cubism, and expressionist spatialization of emotional dynamics bring to light different manners of patterning a perceptual world. As styles of creation that, in original ways, place us before the sensuous plentitude of visual phenomena, the visual arts brought to expression the altered patterns of perception and remembrance that requirements of adaptation and standardization called forth in the mass production of both objects and images. This transformation of artistic expression elicited by the conditions of mass society and mass communication, closely associated with Cubism, Dada, Futurism or Russian Avant-Garde, Constructivism, and other forms of abstraction, propelled the visual arts beyond iconographic traditions, figurative models, symbolism, and naturalistic representations; parallel to this post-figurative orientation, visual representations also took as their theme the mass media and the format of mass communication. Here the visual arts sought not so much to bring specific objects or events before the public eye, but to highlight the conditions of public visibility themselves and to bring to attention the altered modes of patterning and retaining in memory that are engaged by mass-media communication. Kurt Schwitters and Hannah Höch, El Lissitzky, Francis Picabia and Georges Braque, Marcel Duchamp, Man Ray and Jean Arp, later Robert Rauschenberg and Andy Warhol, to name only a sprinkling of notable examples, opened the way to a profusion of still images in newspaper format, accentuating and intensifying, and thereby placing in an original visual light, the haphazard and anonymous manner of representing information, which selects them in terms of their currency, that I identified in the previous section as a more general characteristic of the mass media per se.

Kurt Schwitters's collages, indeed, often highlighted haphazardness, not only as a mode of the ordinary empirical appearance of things, but also as a format of composition of public accounts presented in newspaper columns. In many of his characteristic assemblages, newspaper articles were presented alone, alongside seemingly unrelated objects or were juxtaposed to highlight the absence of direct relation between their contents. Beauty was not presented in terms of the singular radiance of the individualized portrait, such as the female form in traditional art, but as the anonymous, commercialized

FIGURE 4. Kurt Schwitters, *Carnival*, 1947. Courtesy of the Yale University Museum of Art. © Artists Rights Society (ARS), New York / VG Bild-Kunst, Bonn.

beauty of illustrated weeklies and other kinds of mass circulated publication.[21] If we take, for example, Schwitters' seminal collage *Carnival*, currently exhibited in the Yale University art museum, the smiling female portrait conforms in dress, hair style, and expression to the fashion of the times, as portrayed in mass-produced advertisements. As if to highlight the anonymity both of the image and of the public that beholds it, the eyes of woman's smiling face are blindfolded. Next to this image, and at an oblique angle, another symbolic configuration of the female face appears in the form of a comic-strip parody, alongside of which fragments of undecipherable printed newspaper columns highlight the disjointedness of these different features of mass communication that is a characteristic of the mass-media format more generally.

Robert Rauschenberg's collages, produced in the decades after World War II, present another example of the original way in which visual artists focused on the mass-communication format. Rauschenberg's cycle *Currents*, dating from the early 1970s, to take one of many possible examples from his work, highlighted the haphazard arrangement of newspaper columns, in which the selection of information and images as they are presented to an anonymous mass public is made in virtue of their simultaneity as current events. The collage *Study for Currents no. 27*, dating from 1970, juxtaposes numerous columns from two identifiable newspapers, *The Daily News, New York's Picture Newspaper* and the *Los Angeles Times*, presenting their reports on a variety of themes. At the center of the collage stands a large photo of a beggar on a park bench, in a bent-over position with his hands covering his face, conveying a gesture of apparent desperation; this is straddled by a column detailing the difficulties Ed Sullivan was encountering in getting visas for the Beatles, due to a charge of marijuana possession, by a photo of Pope Paul VI, "sounding a warning on drugs and porno," an announcement of the condemnation of William Kunstler, lawyer of the Chicago Seven group, for contempt of court following his defense of seven men accused of inciting to riot at the 1968 Democratic convention, a Mickey Mouse cartoon, and an advertisement for the film *Bora, Bora* of 1968, bearing the caption "Where every woman can become truly female". All of these images flank one another in a manner that underlines their haphazard arrangement. In commenting on his cycle of *Currents* collages, Rauschenberg referred to the "barrage of information" that, after repeated exposure, "can no longer be ignored."[22] On another level, the information presented in the collage's newspaper columns is not strictly contemporaneous, since most of the reported events occurred in 1968, whereas the final appearance of the Beatles on the Ed Sullivan show was in 1965. These dates are nowhere made clear in the collage itself, and the temporal disparity, where it is recognized, lends an eerie sense to the overall impression it makes, which may be read as a parody on the criterion of novelty as a condition for inclusion of news events in the same field of currency. In the retrospective context of the viewer of the collage, who necessarily beholds it at a later moment, in which the images and accompanying printed information have completely lost their earlier interest as current events, their significance as *news* appears all the more anachronistic. The retrospective gaze lends potency to the work in heightening the sense of decontextualized haphazardness of information presented to an anonymous public, which invites us not only

FIGURE 5. Robert Rauschenberg, *Study for Currents no. 27*, 1970. © Robert Rauschenberg Foundation/Licensed by VAGA, New York, NY.

to absorb the information in the manner of mass consumers, but brings to our awareness the seeming randomness in the way of patterning and lending symbolic form to mass communication of public events, before they fade into the passive recesses of vaguely remembered occurrences.

Over the course of the twentieth century, as art has become adapted to the altered perspective of mass communication, its function has overlapped with the mass media, not only where visual artists have taken the mass media as topics of expression in the form of newspaper, film, and video, but where their works participate directly in the propagation of mass-communicated images themselves. In a host of different domains, from advertising and fashion to sports, social critique, and political propaganda, visual artists have deployed the mass-media format and have, in turn, had a lasting influence on the visual codes adopted by the media for their own purposes. Francis Picabia, Salvador Dali, Sonia and Robert Delaunay, Robert Rauschenberg, and Andy Warhol are among the best known twentieth-century artists who have operated on the border between fashion, art, and advertising, and the latter two have at times added a shade of social commentary to this mixture that has produced and proliferated icons on a global scale. In the format of mass communications they push to its limit the capacity of the image to step beyond contextually embedded significations. Reinforced by aesthetic or other evocative qualities that strike us and resonate in memory, they play on the autonomy of the image in relation to the context in which it emerges.[23]

In their free-floating capacity to move beyond any singular, fixed contextual standpoint, such images assume the role of icons or key images (*Schlüsselbilder*).[24] As publicly reproduced images, disseminated on a global scale, such icons or key images reveal a central trait governing the spatiotemporal pattern and visual logic of the mass-produced image as it is communicated in the public sphere: long after they have relinquished their place as present news in the field of currency, they retain an uncanny capacity, in their autonomous and decontextualized form, to represent events in public memory. Cropped out of the shifting field of currency, they symbolically embody in memory the multiplicity of the whole that is quickly forgotten. As images, they manifest a free-floating autonomy, a "surplus" sense that is capable of overstepping any specific horizon of contemporaneity constituted by the web of symbols interwoven in the segmented strata of memory shared by overlapping living generations. Their potency lies in their ability to communicate a free-floating sensuous symbolism that draws immediate recognition without necessarily conveying a more determinate sense rooted in the original experiential world from which it is drawn. Mixing commercial, artistic, fashion, and other possible motifs, such images, in their ambiguity, are pregnant with different connotations rooted in the corresponding networks of embodied symbols that are retained in collective memory and orient a variety of possible interpretations in the different contexts in which they are disseminated.

Following the return to figurative representation after the wave of abstract expressionism in the 1950s, it is above all the Pop Art movement of the late 1950s and 1960s that focused on motifs drawn from popular culture. The champions of this movement specialized in extracting images from their original context to place them as icons at the crossroads between different sectors of public life, adapting them in paradigmatic ways to the format of mass consumption and communication. In works of the forerunners of this style of the 1940s and 1950s, there is a clear tone of criticism directed against the shallowness of the consumer culture that had emerged after the war, exemplified in such prototypes as Eduardo Paolozzi's *I Was a Rich Man's Plaything* (1947, Tate Gallery) or Richard Hamilton's *Just What Is It That Makes Today's Homes so Different, so Appealing?* (1956, Kunsthalle Tübingen), and a similarly ironic undercurrent is also discernible in the works of Roy Lichtenstein.[25] Lichtenstein himself stressed the connection between his art and mass-media communications. Indeed, he presented his parodies of motifs typical of other artists such as Matisse or Picasso, remodeled in graphic arts style, as commentaries on the fact "that we see everything second or third hand, the way information is disseminated through television."[26] He also underlined the ephemeral quality of the cultural productions he mimed, which he described as "very immediate and of-the-moment meanings which will vanish."[27] Such mimes are best known in his reproductions of comic strip scenes, which were not, as he emphasized, imitations of comics but, as art, modifications of the images he culled from popular culture: where comic strips "depict," his intent was to build "a unified pattern of seeing."[28] Rather than a neutral or disengaged reproduction of mass culture, his art sought involvement with what he took to be "the most brazen and threatening characteristics of our culture, things we hate, but which are also powerful in their impingement on us." And he strove in this manner to make an "ironic comment [. . .] about the commercialization of everything in society."[29]

Andy Warhol, who began his career as a commercial graphic artist, created a particularly influential expression of Pop Art. His icons exhibit in exemplary fashion how motifs taken from art, news reporting, sports, advertising, and fashion are fabricated as icons for mass communication. Campbell's soup cans, newspaper reports of fatal automobile or airplane crashes, thirteen men most wanted by the New York Police, the electric chair, sports heroes such as

FIGURE 6. Roy Lichtenstein, "Masterpiece," 1962. © Estate of Roy Lichtenstein.

the football player O. J. Simpson, boxer Mohammed Ali, or golfer Jack Nick-laus, like the colorful portraits of Marilyn Monroe, are all adapted as icons to the same format of mass communication.

The adaptation of the Pop Art style icon to semicommercial visual productions has tended to depoliticize them and to propagate key images that, through near-mechanical association, resemble commercial logos. The example of the *Guerrillero Heroico* image of Che Guevara illustrates this point nicely. The icon of the Argentine revolutionary that is universally visible on T-Shirts and posters today was originally taken in 1960 by the Cuban photographer Alberto "Korda" Diaz as Che watched a public speech by Fidel Castro in Havana. Korda subsequently gave two copies to Gian Giacomo Feltrinelli, who distributed it in large numbers in Italy in the form of a poster, and the photo later found its way onto the cover of the French magazine *Paris*

FIGURE 7. Andy Warhol, *129 Die in Plane Crash*, 1962. Andy Warhol, Image and Artwork. © 2015 The Andy Warhol Foundation for the Visual Arts, Inc./Licensed by ARS.

Match. Soon after Che's assassination in 1968, the photo of the handsome revolutionary was made into a Pop Art icon by the American-Italian photographer Gerard Malanga, who passed it off in Rome as a Warhol original. When the source was questioned, and Malanga risked criminal fraud charges, he appealed to Warhol who, in exchange for profits from its sale, "authenticated" the work. From its ubiquitous place as an icon for all manner of anti-establishment demonstrations and revolts throughout the world, it was transformed into a symbol of radical chic that inspired fashion designers and was imitated by movie stars. It was later co-opted for all manner of commercial purposes, as illustrated by a well-known advertisement for Smirnoff Vodka.[30]

Warhol's highly successful reproduction of images in mass-media format accorded to the visual arts a very different role than that envisaged earlier by artists like Kurt Schwitters, who set out to make visible what was implicit or hidden in the format of mass communication. The commercial ambiguity of many expressions of Pop Art and, in later years, the subsequent semicommercial productions in the visual arts, propagated the mass-media format without making visible its tacit modes of public communication nor providing elements for reflection on them. It is here that the commercial success of art has led to its co-optation in the service of a mass commercialism oblivious to the symbolic function and contextual ambiguity of its icons.

In many of his silk screen graphics, Andy Warhol had used the photos of professional photographers and cineasts: Marilyn, for example, was extracted from the film *Niagara*, and his adopted work *Che* was culled, as we have seen,

FIGURE 8. *Che, Smirnoff Vodka Advertisement*, 1999.

from the photograph of Korda. He adapted to his own visual codes what had already been composed and professionally developed, bringing out the right texture of grain and the most effective balance of contrast to produce an aesthetically pleasing end result.

Where the visual arts tended toward the post-figurative and abstract, toward minimalism and Pop Art, photography, due to the medium itself, continued to focus on the figurative productions of portrait and landscape and has revived an interest in the beautiful image associated, for example, with photographers like Eugène Atget, Henri Cartier-Bresson, Robert Doisneau, or Ansel Adams. Magazines like *Look*, *Life*, and *Paris Match* utilized the work of some of the best photographers of the period, who imparted an aesthetic quality to their portrayals of current events that has often favored their survival as icons. World War I, the Spanish Civil War, and World War II had already propelled the photojournalist to great prominence and demonstrated the political efficacy and propaganda value of skillfully prepared or falsified images.[31] If the artistic quality of professional photographs also contributed to the profound public impact of pictorial documentation of decisive sociopolitical events, such as Lee Miller's renowned photographs of the last days of World War II and the evacuation of the concentration camps in Germany, soldiers' snapshots also preserved for collective memory images of the horrors of war and of persecution. Such snapshots recorded the haunting images of naked women being subjected to physical abuse during the Lemburg pogrom in 1941 or mass executions on the Eastern front.[32] One need only visit the many museums of World War II in cities like Minsk in Belorussia to see documentary photographs, that are mostly the work of amateurs, of events that would have long since fallen out of living memory had they not been preserved in this manner.

Key images of the horror of later wars were often the work of professional photo-journalists dispatched to the front. The slogan of the current events magazine *Paris Match* until this day is "The weight of words, the shock of photos" ("Le poids des mots, le choc des photos"), and the work of professional photojournalists is normally clear, well-cropped and processed, and, indeed, presented according to norms of composition that are often reminiscent of classical painting. Their straightforward visual language infuses in different ways, in accord with corresponding symbolic codes, the contexts of contemporaneity in which they are received. During the Vietnam War, notably, where journalists had a freedom to photograph the war that has been denied them in later conflicts, such images produced a shock effect that proved to be one of the most politically effective spurs to the antiwar movement on the home front. Professionally produced photos such as Eddie Adams's Pulitzer Prize–winning shot of the summary execution by the south Vietnamese chief of police, Nguyen Ngoc Loan, of a bound young suspect, which was printed on the front page of the *New York Times* in February 1968 or Huynh Cong "Nick" Ut's photo of children running to escape a cloud of burning Napalm, which appeared on the cover of *Time* magazine in June 1972, and also won the Pulitzer Prize, immediately circulated around the globe. They provided key images that, in the public mind and collective recollection, represent the horrors of the Vietnam conflict that are continually reproduced in later accounts of it. The aesthetic characteristics of such professionally produced images, which lends them a spectral quality, only intensifies their effect. The directness of the image and its capacity to portray extreme situations, elicit a sense of vicarious participation, a semblance of eyewitnessing that approximates the sensuous texture of in-the-flesh encounters.[33]

Cropped out of context and reproduced for mass circulation, the decontextualized format of such photos introduces a tacit gap between the original context from which they are drawn and the variety of media spaces toward which they are directed. The sheer horror of an image that calls us to witness

FIGURE 9. Nick Ut, Pulizer Prize–winning photo, *Vietnamese Children*, 1972. © Nick Ut/Associated Press.

a summary execution or the danger faced by frantic fleeing children addresses us in so straightforward a manner that it might seem to make questions concerning the exactness of its place in the world seem superfluous. Nonetheless, in a more general way, this should not lead us to overlook the significance of the gap that lies between the original context from which images are drawn and the variety of media spaces that may receive them and in which they are open to different kinds of interpretation; it is in this gap, indeed, that images may be loaded with a symbolic charge they did not originally imply. In this manner, they may be made to evoke associations that recall other key images, suggesting analogies that are not necessarily warranted by their original context. During the Bosnian war of the 1990s, for example, Bosnian Moslem refugees were photographed by British journalists through a fence of barbed wire at the detention center of Trnopolje in northern Bosnia, and one of the refugees, in the foreground, appeared to be in an emaciated state, as if suffering from starvation. As presented, the scene bore a sinister similarity to the situation of concentration camp internees photographed during World War II and, as if the suggestion was not sufficiently clear, British tabloid newspapers presented alongside this photo 1940s images of inmates of the concentration camp Bergen-Belsen. The shock effect of the photo, invested with an extraneous symbolic charge, proved to be of great political significance, according to its reception in different fields of currency around the globe. Subsequently, independent journalists working for the review *Living Marxism* questioned the veracity of newspaper allusions to the compound as a "concentration camp" and criticized, above all, the comparison that was made with the Nazi camp Bergen-Belsen. They further alleged that the original reports of British journalists at the site deliberately sought to mislead the public, and this allegation led to a lawsuit filed in the United Kingdom against *Living Marxism*. Further analysis in the course of the trial revealed that the camp was not a benign refugee relocation center as the independent journalists had claimed, from which the inmates were free to come and go as they pleased, and allegations of mistreatment of the prisoners, including cases of rape and murder, were subsequently substantiated. In the end, the independent journalists lost the suit. [34] The allegations and counterallegations, which have carried over into Web sites and blogs, give dramatic evidence of the impact of such photographs. As they break loose from their context of emergence, they may be loaded with symbolic signification derived from an extraneous source.

Independently of the problem of falsification or image alteration, such examples of symbolic insinuation could easily be multiplied. They highlight the important fact that the immediacy and rapid turnover of continually

FIGURE 10. *Belsen 92*, *Daily Mirror*, 7 August 1992; photographed at a camp in Trnopolje, Bosnia. © *Daily Mirror*, London.

circulating information within a given field of currency rarely brings to mind the gap itself between this field and the image's precise contextual source. We become aware of this gap above all when we are faced with flagrant cases of abuse. In the exercise of the reflexive function by which they represent and unify the self-awareness of the public world, such images operate in accord with the preconceptions of the collectivity they address. Since key images are tailored to the decontextualized and anonymous format of the field of currency that enables them to circulate spontaneously, divergences in context come to light above all in exceptional circumstances that are most effectively conveyed through the visual arts. As a final example in this section, I recall the Benetton publicity campaign of Oliviero Toscani, which illustrates both the intrinsic dynamic of images that the mass media bring to public visibility and the differences in reception to which such images are subject, above all where they depict violent and controversial topics and are disseminated in mass format on a global scale.

In a publicity campaign, photographer and graphic designer Oliviero Toscani, by means of well-known shock images, promoted Benetton clothing in an effort to direct public awareness toward social issues. His goal was to expose a whole range of social taboos, and he chose as an advertising medium a series of unsettling images: convicted prisoners awaiting execution on death row in the United States, a dying aids victim in the arms of his parents, Albanian refugees struggling to board an overloaded boat, and similar desperate situations in deprived areas of the Third World. They quickly became wide-scale media phenomena that had an impact on a global scale. One of the most revealing of these campaigns was launched in 1994, at the height of the Bosnian war, when Toscani attempted to illustrate the absurdity and the cruelty of the conflict through what he called his "photographic monument to a known soldier." The photo depicted the blood-stained clothing of the young Marinko Gagro, who had been killed in action, over which Toscani placed words typed on a note from his father. Neither his uniform nor the content of his father's message call attention to the specific country or cause for which he fought and highlight above all the human loss his death represented. The thoroughly decontextualized, anonymous manner of portraying the young soldier's death was further reinforced by the ambiguity of its message: a scene of horror that was publicly displayed in the form of an advertisement for clothing. As a key image, this globally exhibited photograph aroused radically different kinds of reactions: banned in Los Angeles and condemned in Sweden, it won a graphics design award in Tokyo. Toscani's image illustrates the free-floating ambiguity that such key images may communicate according to the symbols

FIGURE 11. Oliviero Toscani, *Monument to a Known Soldier—Marinko Gagro*, 1994. © Oliviero Toscani Studio.

they embody in contrasting contexts of group perception and remembrance. Abstracted from the horizon of contemporaneity of their origin and disseminated in the mass-media format, the ambiguity that shrouds them opens them to all manner of interpretation according to the different contexts in which they are received. Toscani himself called attention to this ambiguity, which was underscored by a group of young Sarajevo graphic designers who, in a letter addressed to him, poignantly described this ambiguity: "We will never know if this poster concerned with the conflict in our region is one of the most insolent and cynical reactions or if, on the contrary, it is not one of the most skillful warnings in regard to this deep and atrocious wound perpetrated by modern civilization, which seems to accord an ever greater role to marketing and communication."[35]

III

Over the short space of seven decades, the development and global extension of video in its analogical and digital forms has profoundly modified the way in which the media interact with the public sphere, above all because of the unique capacity of video to simulate the world of everyday experience. If celluloid film introduced the moving image, first mute and in black-and-white, later enhanced through sound and color, film is always prerecorded, and it is less a simulation than a reconfiguration of the spatiotemporal format and logic of the common world of immediate experience. Film may, of course, be used to record experience, as in home movies or experimental films that attempt to mirror, as closely as possible, the immediate events of experience; yet, until the appearance of digital technology, films were arranged in advance, developed through chemical processes, cut, and edited. In classical celluloid film and in digitally configured media prepared for the cinema, narrative methods often adopt literary techniques. The spatiotemporal patterning and logic of literary creations has often inspired film directors who, in the interest of narrative exposition, have become masters of such techniques as flashbacks, condensation of long periods into short episodes, or prolonged exposition of a short period in the interest of highlighting dramatic detail. The literary devices of signs and symbols are often employed in cinema to imply what is not directly shown or to reveal to the viewer what many characters in the film fail to perceive, like the sled in Orson Welles' *Citizen Kane*, which intimates the protagonist's longing for the lost objects of childhood.

Video is characterized above all by its extraordinary versatility, as it incorporates and refashions, or "remediates," techniques employed in film and adapts them to the smaller screen of television.[36] Moreover, the recent development of digital technology has eliminated the need for a traditional material support, whether celluloid or video film. The versatility of video, whether analog or digital, makes it possible to produce through television, computers, tablets, and other devices what film does not do: replicate events in their "live" simultaneity, by simulating the spatiotemporal framework of the lifeworld. I may experience this "live" immediacy of temporal and spatial representation when I perceive an image of myself on a TV screen as I walk by a video camera that captures it in a storefront window. In everyday experience this capacity is illustrated by closed-circuit surveillance cameras, which commonly monitor the interior space and surroundings of banks, stores, or parking garages and may simultaneously scan large areas.[37] The flexibility of video as a medium makes indistinguishable its capacity to portray the deferred immediacy of prerecorded images and live broadcasts that take place in "real time." Since both appear to be immediate, the distinction we make between them is one of circumstance, which is why written indications on the screen are often required to alert us to the fact that what we are seeing is either live or prerecorded and drawn from a video archive. The specific capacity of the video medium lies in its seemingly magical ability, through an interface, to simulate immediate experience according to a spatiotemporal pattern and logic of its own. Simulation creates a "mediated immediacy": it reproduces the here and now of immediate presence in media format. In so doing, it brings the field of currency to its most elaborate form of expression and confirms its autonomous status in relation to the horizon of contemporaneity of collective experience and remembrance in the lifeworld, as it is symbolically embodied by overlapping living generations.

If we relate this video format to the communication of current events, we note an essential difference between what was formerly termed the "pictorial journalism" of the traditional newsreel, "film d'actualité," or "Wochenschau" that, prior to television, was usually projected before feature films or in specialized theaters. They recapitulated the events of the month, week, or day, whereas photos and moving images transmitted in video format, accompanied by the testimony of purported eyewitnesses interviewed by on-the-spot journalists, impart a heightened sense of participation and presence among spectators. In a spatial dimension, film gives a sense of being in a separate reality, one which, if it is convincing, may engage us as if it were our own. The capacity of video to simulate the immediacy of portrayed interaction attenuates the sense of spatial difference. Video may create a sense of spatial proximity enhanced by the fact that it normally takes place in the informal intimacy of household surroundings and belongs to everyday experience, much like direct encounters in the everyday world. A conversation between two individuals participating in a television talk show may occur in a comfortable space that simulates spatial contiguity with the place in which the observer is positioned. The simultaneous portrayal of the studio audience, who may directly participate in the interaction, heightens the effect of spatial proximity and of presence, as if one were a member of the audience. On the other hand, newsrooms are often characterized by more formal, office-like surroundings, and this distinctive newsroom atmosphere symbolically places the audience at a certain distance, reinforcing the official and authoritative character of the news journalists' reports, presented as a form of continually updated testimony. This spatial distance, however, is at the same time diminished by the fact that we make eye contact with the reporter, which simulates participation in a direct act of perception of the other.[38] Television, computers, tablets, and other video media share this uncanny capacity to simulate temporal immediacy and various levels of spatial continuity and distance in relation to the place from which they are observed.

Like film, the video format cuts, crops, frames, and reconfigures the spatial dimensions of everyday experience, yet the size of its screen, which is ordinarily small, further limits its capacity to include background detail of what is portrayed. In this, the video interface abstracts its images still more completely than film from their surroundings in the environing world. As it simulates immediate presence in "real time," it may also record moving images and subsequently rearrange or edit them and play them back at different speeds. In contrast to cinema, which calls for uninterrupted viewing in the dark space of a theater, the difference in format of mass video transmission is accentuated by the commercial interruptions that have become frequent not only on television but also on such web media as *You Tube*, by the possibility of continually changing or turning off and on the programs offered, and by our ability to watch them with reduced attention while performing the mundane activities like eating, chatting, or ironing. Here too, the effect of simulation through the video medium is enhanced by its mode of reception in the familiar everyday temporal activities of the viewer. The specifics of this format are not usually a theme of media presentation and, unless video simulations noticeably clash with normal experience, their simulated character is rarely noticed or later recalled.

Stated in general terms, the novelty of the mass-media video format lies in its unprecedented capacity to resemble the everyday experiential world to the point of leading us to overlook its essential difference from everyday experience. This capacity derives from a refinement and transformation of the specific modes of symbolic embodiment through which the mass-media video format sets the framework for its group reception and retention in collective memory. Whatever its proximity to the everyday world, however, this format of the video media is throughout governed by the broad rules of symbolic configuration that characterize mass communications more generally, which sharply limit their ability to communicate the fullness of experience and of collective remembrance anchored in the lifeworld. The limits imposed by the distance of this format from the lifeworld pertain not only to television but to more recent forms of digital media, whatever nuances they may bring to this format in incorporating and remediating previous technologies. We will examine these nuances more fully in the course of our analysis.

The essential distinction between the video format and the lifeworld of direct experience and remembrance it simulates comes to light in the spatio-temporal and logical pattern that video technology favors. Beyond a simple transposition of reproduced contents, the thoroughgoing transformation in symbolic regime it imposes may be illustrated through examples. In the regime of aesthetic experience, for instance, consider a visit to the quarry Bibémus on the outskirts of Aix-en-Provence in France. Since Roman times, and especially since the flowering of Aix in the seventeenth century, this quarry has served as a source of luminous, ochre-colored stone that was used in the construction of numerous urban edifices until the quarry was closed in the late nineteenth century. The extraordinary quality of the color and texture of the massive rock formations and vegetation, facing the Montagne Sainte-Victoire, inspired the painter Paul Cézanne during the later years of his life, as we can see in his works during this period, when he often slept in a cabin that still stands in the quarry.[39] Live video may capture this site and present a certain impression of its striking qualities, but the spatial dimensions of the massive rock formations in view of the Montagne Sainte-Victoire, the nuances of color and texture of the stone that one can, so to speak, feel with the eyes, remain beyond all capacity of simulation.[40] Video is obliged to transfer these qualities into another symbolic medium that cannot render the vivacity of a direct encounter in the flesh. Cézanne's paintings translate the Bibémus quarry on the canvas in a way that does not "simulate" it, for the canvas is not an interface, but an immediate symbolic medium through which color and texture construe a space of their own. The uniqueness of this space lies not in its capacity to faithfully reproduce a scene but to reveal, in Cézanne's original perspective, nuances of its perceptual possibilities. Where the video medium registers not the natural site of Bibémus itself, but one of Cézanne's paintings of its rock formations, the video image, as precise as its optic functions and as exact as its megapixel color resolution may be, is of a different order than the sensuous plenitude that the painting offers, in which the interplay of color, texture, and spatial proportion are pregnant with an aesthetic symbolism that simulation may only weakly convey.

This is not to deny that television may transmit all manner of programs that deal with artistic themes, which are ordinarily presented in the form of specialized public-interest reports that are most commonly shown on public TV. Often they are presented in a timely manner to publicize temporary art exhibitions. Unless programmed for use in virtual classrooms, they do not address art historians or other specialists in this field, but the general public. Outside of this general-interest format, art is only rarely a topic that interests the mass media, although it may move to the center of public attention following a record sale or a spectacular theft which, as "breaking news" launches it into the field of currency the mass media configure.

In terms of religious experience, to take another example, we may note an analogous gap between the traditional context of the lifeworld and the mass-media format in which it is represented. For believers, the sense of religious

FIGURE 12. Paul Cézanne, *Mont Sainte-Victoire seen from the Bibemus Quarry,* 1897. © The Baltimore Museum of Art: The Cone Collection, formed by Dr. Claribel Cone and Miss Etta Cone of Baltimore, Maryland, BMA 1950.196. Photography by Mitro Hood, Cone Collection, Baltimore Museum of Art.

sanctity is traditionally related to a specific time and place, on given days of the week, month, or year and in accord with set spatial orientations. Churches in the form of a cross, facing toward Jerusalem; synagogues facing the same location, in which services take place comprising a minimum of ten adult males and involving a reading from a Torah that is physically present; and mosques facing Mecca, with services organized among a living assembly according to Koranic rite are all charged with a symbolic sanctity that is not open to simulation. The spatial proximity of the wailing wall that was originally part of the second temple in Jerusalem, invested with a special significance on certain commemorative festivals; the sanctity to all Moslems of the original abode of the Prophet, the shrine of Mecca (where television cameras are forbidden); church services in Vézelay, in Chartres, or Notre-Dame in France, or in a baroque church on the Lake of Constance, in St. Peter's in Rome, or in the Church of the Visitation in Jerusalem exemplify places of worship for their respective religions. The video format of mass communications may simulate the physical dimensions and qualities of such places, but it thereby transposes them into an extraneous symbolic medium with an altered form of immediacy and a reconfigured presence in relation to what they originally embodied. If the video format is not necessarily incompatible with traditional religious services, such as Sunday mass for the aged and infirm that are frequently transmitted on television, this format nonetheless uproots original experience from its traditional context and situates it in a foreign symbolic atmosphere.

Given the limits of the mass-media format, it is not accidental that the most successful religious programs in North America are not occasional broadcasts of church services, but the popular religious programming of fundamentalist television evangelism. Here, religious symbolism is adapted to the decontextualized and anonymous framework, frequently punctuated by interruptions, as it is disseminated by the mass media among vast populations. In this format, traditional religious symbols transmitted on a mass scale are adapted to an ambiguous mix of show business performances, commercialism, and right-wing politics.[41]

Drawn from the fields of aesthetics and religion, these two examples, if they poignantly illustrate the distance between the video format and the life-world it simulates, are admittedly peripheral to the ordinary topics of television viewing. In comparison to these marginal themes, it is above all, as in regard to other forms of mass communication discussed at earlier points of this chapter, the journalistic mode of organization and presentation that, in its coordination with commercial and entertainment spots, plays a paradigmatic role in television programming. It is above all here that we must pursue our investigation of the specific mode of symbolic configuration propagated by the video format that, in its difference from the life-world it simulates, has essentially contributed to the transformation of the public sphere in which group experience and remembrance in a mass context are framed.

Since the beginnings of mass television broadcasting in the 1950s, the essentially journalistic vocation of this medium, which has been its traditional mainstay, reveals to the fullest extent its capacity as a vehicle of mass communication in the public sphere.[42] If it is of recent vintage, this contemporary rise to predominance of the video news and information networks is, however, not fortuitous, nor should it be attributed to merely formal characteristics of organization that it commands. Its predominance must be attributed to a further capacity that concerns us most directly at this point in our analysis: the ability of the video news and information media to inspire belief in their unique proximity to the *reality* of reported actions and events.[43] This belief concerns not only the accuracy of media reports and their fidelity to factual circumstances, but also the superior credibility of the video format in its ability to select, organize, and communicate events and invest them with public significance. In the unprecedented range of its reflexive function, video journalism and accompanying information networks, drawing on vicarious experience retained in collective memory, assert their preeminence as the source of self-awareness of the public world. In view of their uncanny capacity to simulate the lifeworld, the belief they inspire in their unique proximity to reality tends at the same time to dissimulate the disparity between the symbolic configuration imposed by the mass-media video and information format and the lifeworld it seeks to mirror.

The broad influence of this journalistic mode of symbolic configuration and of its claim to proximity to the reality of the lifeworld accounts for the remarkable growth of its public authority in relation to the printed mass media and even to historical works. This authority of the video mass-media format, however, is by no means self-evident. It is, indeed, a recent phenomenon that first imposed itself in the United States and in Western Europe over the course of the 1950s and 1960s. A few words concerning the historical background of the rise to predominance of television journalism, corresponding to the establishment of a public conviction concerning its proximity to reality, will highlight the broader implications of this mode of simulated experience as it is retained in public memory.

In the history of television journalism, video news presentation during the hours and days following the assassination of President John Fitzgerald Kennedy in November, 1963, served as a watershed in the establishment of the authority of this media in its claim to capture the reality of events. The video transmission of the aftermath of the assassination, during which commercial and ordinary programming were suspended and television time was devoted to live coverage of the aftermath of this tragic event and to Kennedy's funeral, places the assumptions of television journalism in a particularly clear light. Of notable interest is the fact that all of the reporters covering the Kennedy visit to Dallas were located in press busses that followed the presidential motorcade. Consequently, the reporters themselves were not eyewitnesses to the assassination itself.[44] Photos and films of this tragic event were recorded by bystanders who happened to be at the scene at the time. After the shots were fired, the presidential limousine sped away, and by the time the reporters realized the gravity of the situation, the president lay dead in the hospital. Although no reporters had directly witnessed the event in the flesh, during subsequent days of live television broadcasting, they could nonetheless assert their authority as witnesses at the scene of events. As Barbie Zelizer has pointed out in her insightful analysis of this theme, their authority was subsequently reinforced by constant repetition during later anniversary commemorations. They had lived through the experience of myriad background details that, pieced together, permitted them to recount events from the standpoint of "eyewitnesses" in Dallas during those fateful days in late November 1963. Having lived through the "here and now" of events that unraveled during the hours and days following the assassination, they could claim a proximity to the scene that, in their eyes and that of television spectators, lent them a privileged position through which they could invite their viewers to vicariously relive the momentous events of the days in Dallas. As Barbie Zelizer notes, "Documenting one's presence at the events of Kennedy's death thus imparted much of the authority for telling the story. [. . .] Attempts to construct presence where there was none, and to imply presence through authoritative retellings, ultimately gave journalists an advantage over other groups of speakers."[45] Most important, television reporters were able to lend their coverage credibility of a different order than that of the historian who, at a distance, weighs different kinds of evidence and contextually embedded explanations to favor a specific interpretation of narrated events. Journalists, as Barbie Zelizer writes, "tried systematically to perpetuate themselves as alternative keepers of the historical record. They fancied themselves as a different kind of chronicler—one who was validated by presence, participation, and proximity, rather than the remote and detached objectivity advocated by traditional historians."[46]

From the early days of television news broadcasting to current around-the-clock news-reporting systems such as CNN, Fox News, or Al Jazeera, the authority of the TV media correspondent and news reporter is anchored in a similar claim to presence on the scene and a similar capacity to deliver eyewitness reports. In accord with its heightened sensitivity to the mutability of current affairs viewed in short-term scope, television journalism places a premium on the spontaneity of on-the-spot accounts that serve as its original sources. This framework, it is true, has often been utilized in important ways by investigative reporters who have exposed problematic situations that would otherwise have remained concealed from the public eye. There is no doubt that such reporting and exposure through Internet blogs have brought to international attention dictatorial political policies and flagrant violations of human rights around the globe where the local authorities sought to conceal them. The video documents filmed on camcorders by members of the armed forces or by onlookers have brought atrocities to the fore that would otherwise have gone unnoticed, and, for example, in the case of the Srebrenica massacre during the Balkan wars in 1995, these visual accounts have provided essential elements to the Hague Tribunal.[47] Moreover, in more recent years globalized television networks, the World Wide Web, and other forms of digital technology have shown a clear potential for breaking the monopoly of narrow national and local structures and the media they control, and of opening isolated regions to external information and communications systems that permit both the expression and dissemination of a plurality of points of view. This potential has been set in relief by a number of political struggles in recent memory, such as the Jasmine Revolution that successfully deposed Tunisian dictator Zine el-Abidine Ben Ali in 2011. The revolt had been prepared by Web sites run by the Tunisian diaspora outside the country and global Arab networks such as Al Jazeera and Al Arabiya added to the momentum by diffusing photos and videos taken by private citizens that placed the dictatorship in a negative light.[48] During the revolution that brought the Ben Ali regime to its knees, the contribution of the World Wide Web, the mobile phone, and social media in organizing protest, and in communicating news of violent confrontations and acts of repression has been abundantly documented.[49] In contrast to Egypt, where digital technology and the social media also played a role in the organization of dissent and the circulation of information, the Tunisian revolution has led to the introduction of a new constitution that has established a system of parliamentary democracy.

This key role of the video media should not lead us, however, to underestimate the essential difference between the mass-media video format and contextually rooted experience in the lifeworld. For, beyond the interpretative perspective of the journalist and the broadcasting system that presents it, the account of "reality" reconfigured in the video mass-media format imposes a fundamental modification, analogous to that I identified in the video configuration of aesthetic and religious phenomena: here too, in abstracting from the environing lifeworld and providing a vicarious sense of presence, the symbolic plenitude of everyday experience is altered and its symbolic significance transformed.[50]

Indeed, if in their paradigmatic role journalistic modes of presentation are singularly propitious to mass dissemination, this is due to the spatiotemporal pattern and logic of discontinuity and of haphazard and anonymous presentation that typifies mass journalism in general. News broadcasts continually change themes as the news team passes from local to national and international affairs, from political to economic and meteorological reports to entertainment, commercials, and public-interest stories, all of which are punctuated according to the split-second exactness required by the format of media programming. None of this leaves room for in-depth investigation or closer interpretation of the context in which events take place and of the near and more distant past through which they might be elucidated. Certainly the media networks also present special-interest news shows and documentaries that focus in greater detail than typical news programs on specific situations. Such shows, which often include interviews and background explanation, are typically adapted to the format of the field of currency in which analysis is presented in an up-to-date perspective.

The video format of television is regularly recreated on the Web and most newspapers and television channels devote special attention to programming on their Web sites. The "hypermedia" format of the Web, as it simultaneously juxtaposes written text, still and moving images that may simultaneously convey commercials, entertainment, news and a multiplicity of other kinds of messages, demonstrates the elasticity of the medium at its most comprehensive level of operation. Certainly, in comparison to video representation in a single field of vision, the phenomenon of hypermediacy has modified the character of video simulation. Indeed, the hypertextual mixtures of written phrases and picture images that appear in disparate windows and segments on the same computer or tablet screen do more than merely simulate direct encounters in the lifeworld. And yet, this important nuance introduced by the hypertextual format has essentially complemented, but has by no means supplanted, video simulation of the lifeworld. Moreover, this format obeys a parallel strategy for creating, in a form shaped by the media, a sense of immediate presence of the world. In comparison to transparent digital simulations, as Jay David Bolter and Richard Grusin have insightfully noted, "digital hypermedia seek the real by multiplying mediation so as to create a feeling of fullness, a satiety of experience which can be taken as reality."[51]

Whether presenting an immediate simulation of the lifeworld or a hypertextual format that mixes windows of simulated representation with texts and other accompanying information, the newer forms of digital technology share with television the aim to mirror social and political reality and to bring it to mass awareness, and thereby to extend what I have referred to as the reflexive function of the mass media. Yet precisely here, the decontextualized mode of presentation of breaking news in the field of currency renders problematic the logic of verification that we employ in everyday experience, by which we test the reality of reported facts by comparing different sources and types of testimony provided by the broader weave of experience in the horizon of contemporaneity. It is the uncanny ability of visual imagery presented by the mass media to resemble what we collectively take to be the real world that ordinarily leads us to overlook the specific character of the reconfigured spatiotemporal pattern and logic of representation of virtual accounts. And, even where we bring this specific mode of reconfiguration to awareness, it is not always possible to detect the operation of external factors influencing the selection and organization of reported events. In the political sphere, on one hand, the condensed and concentrated format of representation facilitates simplification of the real plurality of the public world, where the viewpoint of a predominant group and its elite monopolize the space of public visibility. On the other hand, in countries where the content of television broadcasts is not dictated by the political regime, the survival of news programs, like entertainment and commercial features, depends on ratings by which their popularity is constantly measured. Programming is consequently commanded by the competition to attract the largest possible audience.[52] Here commercial considerations play an ever more central role, which is often not recognized as such, in programming on the World Wide Web interface. In all such cases the *format* itself of mass communication facilitates the kind of influence that such political and commercial factors exercise on the selection of reported events and the way in which they are made publicly visible. In this capacity, they not only limit but may also distort the reflexive function of bringing to mass awareness and retaining in collective memory that the media exercise.[53]

Regarding the altered symbolic sense infused by the media format, public recognition generated by the mass media must be distinguished from collective memory in its contextual depth, shared by generations whose lives overlap in the same horizon of contemporaneity. Publicly retained remembrance engendered by this simulated video format is essentially a memory of association, arising out of what are generally programmed assemblages of images presented through the mediated immediacy of the video interface. Here, beyond the choice that is made concerning the pertinence of events that may be deemed publicly significant, public experience and public remembrance are adapted to the mass-media format, in which the decontextualized, anonymously configured, and continually shifting schema of the field of currency take precedence over the *contextual* logic of experience and remembrance that serves as the principal mode of orientation in a given horizon of contemporaneity. In the field of currency, video presentation may indeed be nuanced, and different sides of a story may be presented, especially in special-interest documentaries. Conflict and crisis, especially where accompanied by visual imagery, lend an eye-grabbing dramatic edge to video accounts. Moreover, the public dissemination of information by the mass media in the flow of the field of currency rarely *contradicts* the logic of contextual analysis, nor does it prevent the subsequent carrying out of contextual research into the background of reported events; however, it does not itself *provide* that background. The logic of the mass-information format, in orienting attention to the up-to-date and in simulating a presence that portrays events as if they were being witnessed in the flesh, or in providing a satiety of hypermediated presence that may be substituted for reality, tends to override the logic of contextual explanation in terms of which group identities in the fragmented horizon of contemporaneity find their source. However much it may be centered on conflict, the mass-media format of television journalism ordinarily homogenizes and standardizes such nuances of perspective, since the short-term format leaves little room for more than cursory contextual analysis of fragmented points of view. In this essential way the format of video communication contrasts with the contextual reasoning directed toward fragmented collective memory retained by disparate groups, whose respective viewpoints draw on the deep strata of sedimented symbolic layers in the framework of a given horizon of contemporaneity. It similarly contrasts with the contextual logic of historical discourse which, when guided by critical historiographical principles, emphasizes the heterogeneity of interpretations and attempts to construct coherent accounts of actions and events in the past in the face of different orders of contextual explanation to which the immediacy of eyewitness accounts is subordinated. The contextual logic of both collective memory and historical discourse carries with it a singular assumption: circumstantial evaluations drawn from the immediacy of a given present do not provide sufficient grounds for understanding the present, for such understanding requires elucidation of the present in relation to a more removed vantage point of the past from which the present has developed. Present attitudes, according to this logic, find their source in a past that, even where neglected, forgotten, or otherwise obscured, retains an essential pertinence for interpreting the concrete reality of the immediately given world.

IV

The live presentation of the aftermath of the Kennedy assassination, which replaced regular television programming for a period of several days, took place at an early point in the development of television journalism, in which the staging of events for political purposes was toned down at a moment of unusual public consensus and national mourning. Over the decades since this time, live presentations of momentous historical events have signaled periods of political change and the abrupt transformation of regimes and political elites. Here television journalism has assumed an active role, not only in reporting events but also in arranging the ways in which they are publicly communicated and interpreted. The novel political power of video and of the mass-communication format came to dramatic expression in the 1990s, following the collapse of the former communist regimes in Eastern Europe. In order to set in relief the implications of the unprecedented role of the video media in configuring the public sphere and in thus infusing collective experience and remembrance, I focus in this final section on the media format as a source of potential aberration in their power, which, as I emphasize in the conclusion of this chapter, comes to clearest expression in their surprising propensity to generate contemporary forms of political mythology.

Television played a decisive and well-known role in the Romanian revolution of 1989, which began with the spontaneous occupation of national TV stations by television staff and supporters of the revolution. One hundred and twenty hours of live broadcasts were recorded of this event and of its immediate aftermath. A documentary film, *Videograms of a Revolution*, gathered hours of these video recordings that portray the euphoria of the initial stages of the revolution in 1989. At a decisive point in the live broadcast on national television, the acclaimed Romanian poet Mircea Dinescu proclaimed, "Now God has once more turned His face toward Romania!" followed by a declaration that was repeated by the crowd: "We are victorious! The TV is with us!"[54] In the course of the documentary, the camera portrays the trial and execution of Nicolae and Elena Ceaucescu on December 25, 1989. In the many hours of video footage, political declarations of former Ceausescu associates and army officials provide a presentiment of what would occur during the months that followed: the fall of the Ceaucescu government and an initial period of transition gave way to the rise to power of a new elite that took control of the media and sought to utilize television as a principal means to legitimate its authority.[55]

A less spontaneous and still more sinister role of the video mass media can be observed in this same period during the decomposition of communist Yugoslavia. Slobodan Milošević and his allies quickly recognized the importance of media legitimacy as a means of gaining and maintaining power. In September 1987, they arranged for live coverage of the decisive Eighth Session of the League of Communists of Serbia, where Milošević made his bid for power. During this session, which witnessed the fall of his former ally, Ivan Stambolić, who was at that time president of Serbia, the live television broadcast publicly confirmed his rise to power.

As primarily political in character, such events demonstrate the power of television communications and of the video media as a means of consecrating political elites and controlling the flow of information diffused in the public sphere. Yet, beyond the purpose of political legitimation and control, the extraordinary versatility of this medium lends it a potency that extends far beyond traditional political categories. This versatility and symbolic potency, along with the correlative ambiguity inherent in the mode of simulation adapted to mass television communication account for the unprecedented influence it has wielded in recent years.

Versatility, symbolic potency, ambiguity: these aspects of the mass-media video format come to light above all through the mixing of heterogeneous messages where, in the rapidly changing field of currency, programming is intended to appeal broadly to mass audiences in their anonymous generality. Newscasts that focus on political or social issues appear in the same decontextualized and haphazard format, and often in the same program, as sports, entertainment, and commercials, which are designed to grab and retain public attention on a mass scale. They fuse different functions into publicly recognizable icons through which simulated experience is generated and retained in public memory. In this framework, the conflation of political, commercial, and show-business factors in the modes of mass-media representation only heightens the potential ambiguity that characterizes mass-produced still images. Moving images, in their ability to simulate direct experience, may combine with particular effectiveness different kinds of messages that, abstracted from their original context and interjected into a given field of currency, are charged with a free-floating iconic sense. In bringing to public visibility personalities from a variety of sectors, the video media are capable of lending them, irrespective of their differences, a common aura of celebrity. In the confines of the field of currency, celebrity conferred by public visibility in the mass media is the common denominator that unites them as a group and distinguishes them from their spectators.

In our contemporary globalized societies, sports, show business, high finance, and politics are all typical paths to celebrity, which in media format are often interchangeable in their functions. This phenomenon is well known in contemporary Europe, as illustrated in particular by the example of Silvio Berlusconi in Italy, who became a powerful media figure in the early 1970s, concentrating his private television broadcasting companies into nationwide networks: Canale 5, Italia 1, and Rete 4. In the mid-1980s he acquired the Italian football club, A. C. Milano, and became a key Italian political figure, serving as prime minister three times between 1994 and 2011, before being convicted of tax fraud in 2013. In similar fashion, Bernard Tapie in France combined his influence as owner of the Olympique de Marseille football club with a political role as minister of urban affairs in the socialist government during the second mandate of François Mitterrand, from which he was forced to resign in the wake of corruption charges in the early 1990s. Tapie has also been a television personality and an actor in the cinema, and his continued involvement in high finance has led to much debate. Berlusconi and Tapie, however, are only two of many examples who illustrate that the mass appeal of association with spectator sports—whether as influential owner or player—is a source of media presence and public notoriety that is readily translated into political power. Arnold Schwarzenegger, a champion body-builder turned cinema celebrity and later governor of California, or world-champion boxer Vitali Klitschko, who became a leader in the Ukrainian political opposition during the protest movement of 2013–14 and mayor of Kiev in 2014, illustrate the emergence of this phenomenon in recent decades on a global scale.

Here I by no means wish to deny, as I noted in the previous section, that the newer forms of media, from the camcorder and mobile telephone camera to the World Wide Web and Twitter messages, may provide independent sources of information that may complement established media coverage or contravene the monopolistic hold of state-controlled networks. If the promise of this decentralizing trend cannot be denied, the predominant sociopolitical impetus of the mass-media video format has been mobilized above all by groups that are prominent in the public sphere, from the larger networks, financial institutions, and political parties to popular sports clubs. They readily become both the propagators and the vehicles of popular mythologies that reinforce their influence. It is here that the video format, whether in the framework of traditional television or of hypermediated websites, plays an unprecedented role in the sociopolitical arena by investing public figures not only with political influence but with what might be identified as a mythical aura.

The combined and varied functions of these figures, spanning the disparate realms of sports, finance, entertainment, and politics, invests celebrity with an iconic status that flourishes in the light of mass-media visibility. The aura of celebrity associated with the multiplicity and ambiguity of these functions marks the distance of the icon from the concrete everyday horizon of contemporaneity with which it interacts. This distance lends the icon a mythological potency that parallels the notion of the everyday mythologies described by Roland Barthes, in their abstraction from the "group of human relations in their real social structure."[56] In order to explore the mythical implications of the aura of celebrity conferred through public visibility in the mass media,

I conclude this chapter by focusing on two examples, drawn from different geographical regions, that each gained global notoriety in the 1990s. The mythologies that they constitute place in evidence the problematic side of the journalistic format of mass-media publicity in a globalized world. They each illustrate the symbolic potency conferred by media notoriety that, beyond the horizon of the shared, everyday lifeworld, sets its objects in an autonomous field of public recognition and remembrance.

The first example, drawn from the former Yugoslavia, places this symbolic potency in a particularly clear light. In this case, the process of conflation of different symbolic functions transpired through the television media, for what began as televised football entertainment set the scene for the emergence of nationalist ideologies. In a general sense, it graphically illustrates how the popularity and prestige of spectator sports in our contemporary globalized world open the way to influence in a variety of areas, which may involve sports club owners, managers of high finance, media representatives, and very often, as recent experience amply demonstrates, political figures at the highest levels of command.

During the gradual decomposition of Yugoslavia in the late 1980s and early 1990s, sports players, sports fans, and club owners adopted ever more multivalent roles that fused together sports, show business, politics, finance, and paramilitary organizations. Both the Croatian and the Serbian teams and their followers, in the stands and on TV, provided clear indications of this tendency. The Zagreb-based *Dinamo* team and the Serbian *Crvena Zvezda*, or Red Star, football club, whose matches were continually transmitted by the media, were early vehicles of nationalist sentiment that became increasingly vehement as the Yugoslav state neared collapse. As historian Ivan Čolović has noted, these matches furnished opportunities for militant Croat *Dinamo* supporters to publicly brandish Ustashe symbols mobilized by the fascist dictatorship during World War II and the *Crvena Zvezda* spectators to publicly recycle songs, slogans, and banners that drew on the Serbian Chetnik folklore from the same period.[57] In their ambiguity, sports matches not only provided media events and commercial publicity of the first order, but their political role became increasingly significant. As Čolović illustrates, even in the period of Yugoslav communism, political leaders played a central part in the direction of *Crvena Zvezda*, but this political direction took on a wholly different character as national antagonisms emerged at the end of 1980s.[58] Here, as the Serbian case demonstrates, hooligan spectators at football matches formed the core of the paramilitary forces led by the notorious Željko Ražnatović, or "Arkan," whose ultranationalist "Tigers" were held responsible for war crimes in the ensuing conflict in Bosnia. Ražnatović was the owner of the Obilić football team in Serbia, named after the hero of the battle of Kosovo, which the Serbs had waged against the Ottoman invaders in 1389. Ražnatović at the same time assumed an important political function as leader of the Serbian Unity Party. As the Milošević government centralized the predominant sectors of the mass media, purged a large number of journalists, and placed the media under strict government control, the earlier ambiguity of sports matches gave way to armed conflict, during which a policy of media manipulation instrumentalized them as organs of the official ideology. The simultaneous reinforcement of government control of the mass media was also brought about by the Tudjman government in Croatia, and the alignments of the different mass-media systems in the Balkans, corresponding to the positions of their respective sports teams, closely reflected their ideological leanings in a period of war.[59]

The reinforcement of national ideology through government control of the mass media limited the trans-ethnic appeal they assumed in the earlier Yugoslavian context and realigned them more explicitly in terms of national perspectives and political mythologies that re-elaborated the legacy of a more distant past. Consider in this light the example of the Serbian media icons represented by the sports club owner and paramilitary chief Ražnatović and his wife, turbo-folk singer Ceca. Presented live on national Serbian television in 1995, during a period that coincided with the brutal ethnic murders allegedly committed by him and his forces in Bosnia, the carefully prepared work of image-production and promotion encapsulates in particularly blatant form the ways in which such icons are fabricated for mass consumption in the public sphere. Married in the uniform of a Serbian World War I officer, his appearance evoked the memory of patriotism in more favorable conflicts, while Ceca's flowing white dress, which was reportedly modeled on Scarlett O'Hara's attire in the film *Gone with the Wind*, underlined her stated desire to make of her wedding a fairy tale. The live transmission of the religious ceremony and of the festivities that followed over a period of many hours, during which Ceca herself performed, highlighted its multifunctional character, mixing military, political, and religious rites and symbols that were presented to the television spectators in an entertaining show-business format. On the day following the wedding, the national newspapers devoted extensive coverage to the event and, as if to reinforce the political mythology that surrounded it, an editorialist in the journal *Duga* likened Ceca to the maiden in Serbian medieval epic poetry, the so-called Kosovka Djevojka, who sought her betrothed among the dead and injured following the loss of the fourteenth-century battle of Kosovo.[60]

In spite of its political significance in the context of the Balkan wars, the success of the icon was by no means limited to Serbia, and it showed a remarkable plasticity in its capacity to cross national borders and adapt itself to very different kinds of contexts in which it was brought to public visibility. On Saturday, March 1, 2003, a little more than three years after Ražnatović's assassination in front of the same Belgrade hotel where the couple's marriage festivities had occurred, the conservative and highly influential French magazine *Le Figaro Magazine* published an article on Ceca, accompanied by a series of still photos. Titled "Ceca, Madonna of the Balkans," the article underlined her flamboyant personality and her show-business acumen, while downplaying her function as a folk icon and the political role her husband had accorded to her in the Serbian Unity Party. The photos remodeled the icon by presenting her as a faithful wife (only one of the four photos shows her with Ražnatović), a good mother, a highly successful businesswoman, a pop star, and, following the death of her husband, the owner and inspirer of the Obilić football club. Several years after the NATO strikes that led to Milosevic's downfall and the conclusion of the Kosovo war, and following her husband's indictment for war crimes by the international tribunal in The Hague, just prior to his assassination, Ceca could emerge in a new, decontextualized field of currency. The political mythology with which she had been associated could fade, especially in a non-Balkan context, to the point that she could appear, as stated at the conclusion of the French article, as the "Cinderella of Today."[61] Here, the full ambiguity of such icons became apparent: beyond the specific horizon of contemporaneity in which they originated, the different facets of the image were tailored to different symbolic networks. In a decontextualized field of currency, the imagery of the mass media could reconfigure the icon's ambiguous meaning while lending selected aspects of its implicit sense a spontaneous force and obscuring the deeper significance of other aspects, which only contextual analysis might critically evaluate. In the mass-media format relayed by the illustrated magazine, the absence of any deeper contextual analysis also privileged the semi-mythical status of the celebrity, in which her previous ideological function receded before the ambiguity of symbolic roles that, according to the situation, her "key image" might fulfill. Here the different features of the mass-media format, news, entertainment, or commercial, are all blended together to serve a multiplicity of uses that fuel celebrity in the view of the mass public.

If the problematic side of this new and ever more familiar situation has become increasingly evident in recent years, my second example illustrates its implications from another perspective—that of the 1995 murder trial of former football star and actor O. J. Simpson, who was accused of killing his wife and her friend. The broadcast of Simpson's trial became one of the most popular media events of that year. In a completely different context than the Balkan wars, it illustrates in a similar manner the heterogeneous and ambiguous facets associated with icons that are brought to public visibility in the format of mass-media communications.

Moreover, this example is particularly illustrative because of the way in which the controversial use of television in the courtroom, simulating eyewitness presence at the trial, became a central issue in the proceedings themselves, for the television coverage was criticized by many legal experts for distorting the function of the venerable institution of judicial procedure in the courtroom. In accordance with the provision for freedom of the press provided by the First Amendment to the Constitution of the United States, newspaper reporters are admitted to trials. Nonetheless, out of the fear that photography and, in particular, live television coverage, might influence the performance of lawyers, witnesses, and defendants, they were traditionally excluded from public courtrooms. Indeed, in the earlier years of television, the Canons of Judicial Ethics prohibited the broadcasting or televising of courtroom proceedings. More recently, however, many states have allowed judges to admit photographers and television cameras if the judge determines that there is no conflict between their presence and the rights of the parties represented in the trial. To the present day, the use of television in the federal courts is extremely limited, and it is banned altogether from proceedings of the United States Supreme Court, although the so-called *Sunshine in the Courtroom* bill that would reverse this practice, introduced in different forms since 2007, is currently before the Congress of the United States. One of the main objections to the bill has been formulated in Senate hearings by Congressman Lamar Smith, member of the House Judiciary Committee, who fears that television cameras in federal courtrooms might "trivialize and commercialize" the proceedings.[62]

At the time of the Simpson trial in 1995, television cameras had also been banned from courtrooms in many European countries, such as France. According to legislation enacted by French Minister of Justice Robert Badinter in that same year, television cameras may be authorized in important trials that are of historical importance, and under this law the trial of Nazi war criminal Klaus Barbie was transmitted by video and published for sale as a DVD. In view of the gravity of the crimes of an aged defendant, the fact that his acts had been committed more than forty years before the trial, and the concerted effort on behalf of the Badinter ministry to avoid sensationalism, media coverage of the trial was kept within the limits of a journalistic and pedagogical exercise.

The murder trial of O. J. Simpson in California illustrated the extent to which televised trials might bring out ambiguous and even incongruous facets favored by the format of mass-media communications. As a football hero and actor, who for many years had also been known for his role in the commercial promotion of Hertz car rentals on TV, Simpson had long become a familiar figure in mass-media productions and had achieved a quasi-mythical status in the public eye, and it was precisely his celebrity that lent the trial its sensational aura for months on end. Nonetheless, where Simpson's previous aura of celebrity as a sports hero and media personality had abstracted the semi-mythical person from the everyday experience of a mass public and lent his previous appearances before the public eye a decontextualized and depersonalized iconic status, in at least one regard the murder charge brought Simpson's image resolutely into the sphere of concrete experience for the different groups that viewed the trial on television. As much as the image of the hero had conformed to the anonymous and decontextualized format of the mass media, the symbolism of a black man on trial for the murder of his white wife and her friend burst beyond the abstract iconic status of the celebrity presented in the field of currency to confront the fragmented perspectives in the horizon of contemporaneity of different groups of media spectators. The strong emotions and virulent debate that the trial unleashed were rooted in fragmented collective remembrance in regard to the recent past which, for blacks, embodied specific symbolic significance in view of recent episodes of police brutality in Los Angeles, such as the beating by police of a black man, Rodney King. It was fueled for blacks by long-standing, collectively shared memory, reinforced by a "borrowed" memory bequeathed by an historical past, reaching beyond the pale of living recollection. Moreover, the situation was greatly complicated by the details of the case itself: on one hand, the prosecution produced a disturbing quantity of incriminating circumstantial evidence; on the other hand, there were clear signs that the police had tampered with the evidence. These discrepancies unleashed passions and broad dissensus among black and white television viewers. Simpson's acquittal by a predominantly black jury reflected this dissensus, in which a large majority of the white population presumed his guilt, whereas a large majority of black Americans concluded that guilt had not been sufficiently established by the trial.[63]

In spite of this polarization of the mass audience in relation to concrete issues such as race, Simpson's celebrity still lent the trial the ambiguous status of a television spectacle. The anonymous, decontextualized framework of mass communications, presented in the format of daily updates in a constantly shifting field of currency, favored the blurring of the lines between the incongruous spheres of serious legal proceedings, sensational news journalism, and TV entertainment.

In a way that legal experts have since acknowledged, video perception of the trial by TV spectators molded their awareness in ways that were different from the perception of the members of the jury, who were constantly present at the trial. In explaining the innocent verdict reached by the jury, which was open to sharp criticism by the general public (more often, it is true, among the white than among the black population), the legal counsel to ABC television, Peter Arnella, accounted for this discrepancy in terms of a difference between the context of the courtroom and its simulated reconstitution on the television screen: "They're not in the courtroom; they don't see what the jurors see. [. . .] You don't see the nonverbal behavior of witnesses in the same way as you see it on a television camera. [. . .] You don't see some of the photographs."[64] Here, indeed, mass-media coverage transposed the direct experience of participants in the courtroom into a simulated format that obeyed an extraneous spatiotemporal pattern and logic through which public experience and collective remembrance of the event were configured.

In bringing the trial before broad public attention for a sustained period of time, the televised proceedings influenced the performances of judge, witnesses, and lawyers alike, and legal experts frequently voiced the opinion that this had a significant impact on the outcome of the trial itself. As in many such instances, the fact of being thrust before the public eye conflated the roles of the participants in the trial themselves, such as chief prosecutor Marcia Clark, who subsequently abandoned the legal profession to become a TV entertainer. Indeed, she later accepted a lucrative position as actor/reporter for the television series *Entertainment Tonight* and participated in other television tabloid presentations of famous trials. Here as elsewhere, the light of celebrity conferred by frequent appearances in the mass media conflated in an ambiguous manner different, largely incongruous symbolic spheres.

Such examples highlight the essential gap that lies between the mass-media video format that permits its spectators, more fully than any other medium, to vicariously experience and remember the events shown as if they had been episodes of direct encounter and the horizon of contemporaneity interweaving the symbolically embodied experience and remembrance of overlapping generations. If the two levels do not exist as separate realms and are in continual interaction, the subtle differences between them are of vital significance for identifying the characteristics of the contemporary public world. In the public sphere, the gap that separates them is of decisive importance, because the light of public familiarity, in its decontextualized and anonymous distance from the lifeworld, opens the way to the insinuation of secondary mythologies. Indeed media celebrity, the fact of being a familiar household image in the public eye, is the potent mythology of our times. It is quickly translated into super-ordinary powers that associate the most divergent kinds of incongruous functions and interchangeable virtues. And here the aura of celebrity reveals the principal paradox that the mass-media format has bequeathed to public experience and public memory in our times: the more convincingly its symbolic format is able to simulate experience in the horizon of contemporaneity, the more readily we may forget the gap that separates it from the lifeworld it is meant to encompass.

CHAPTER 6

The Contextualized Past: Collective Memory and Historical Understanding

In the preceding chapters, my focus on the theme of collective memory has dealt with it both as a faculty deployed at various levels of human comprehension and coexistence and as an anthropologically centered topic of inquiry. At different points in my analysis, I have called attention to the relation between collective memory and the historical past. As I have interpreted it, the historical past lies beyond the pale of collective memory, which, in the primary sense of the term, arises in the interwoven and symbolically embodied strata of experience shared by living generations.

In the introduction to this work, I presented the historical background of this manner of distinguishing between collective memory and the historical past in relation to a century-long development of theoretical approaches to this theme elaborated by Hegel and by the subsequent critical theorists of historical understanding, Dilthey, Droysen, and Croce. I noted that Hegel initially centered his analysis on the radical historicity in ways of understanding truth and being, and on the margin of incommensurability that this historicity traces between the horizon of a given present and the historical past that lies beyond living memory. Nonetheless, in spite of the radical discontinuities that punctuate the changes in historical epochs, Hegel presupposed that a rational grasp of the past in the present makes possible the comprehension of its essential meaning. This, as we have seen, he conceived in terms of a capacity to penetrate the past in a synthetic act of reminiscence (*Erinnerung*). The critical theorists of the late nineteenth and early twentieth centuries elaborated on his insight into the ways in which the quest to make sense of the historical past is necessarily anchored in the here and now of present preoccupations incorporated in the language and gestures, the direct recollections, preoccupations, and expectations of living individuals and groups caught up in the multiplicity of their current circumstances. Critical theories of history extended and deepened this insight into the historical variability of human understanding to the point of questioning its compatibility with the all-encompassing rationalist metaphysics that Hegel had imposed upon history as a process. They each adopted an open-ended, anthropological principal of unity underlying the expressions of human historical diversity and making possible present understanding of the essential meaning of the remote past. As I noted in the introduction, critical thinkers like Dilthey, Droysen, and Croce, in interpreting the act of historical comprehension as a work of remembrance, also paid an implicit tribute to Hegelian assumptions. In the wake of Halbwachs, the distinction I am drawing between collective memory and the historical past seeks to radicalize their insight into the historicity of human modes of understanding and of being.

In the framework of our present investigation of collective memory and human historicity, we are faced with a realm of group finitude that cannot be accounted for on the basis of the *singular* finitude of the members of a given collectivity. This realm of group contingency is situated at a fundamental level that, contrary to the singular finitude of mortal beings through which Martin Heidegger and his school sought to interpret the possibility of group existence, corresponds to unique modes of being arising from the symbolic networks that underlie group cohesion and, through shifts in its structure, sets the phenomenon of human historicity in relief.

Although in the perspective of *Being and Time*, to which I briefly referred in the introduction, Heidegger dealt with the topic of the "sign" (*Zeichen*) and the "reference" (*Verweisung*), symbols and symbolic interaction were hardly prominent themes in this or in other of his writings, which accounts for the paucity of his investigations of the intersubjective realm and his neglect of the specific modes of group finitude set in relief by collective memory and the dynamics of symbolic interaction.[1] He therefore presented only a bare outline of human historicity considered as a direct transposition onto a collectivity of shared being-toward-death that brings singular human individuals together in view of a common fate. As Heidegger wrote: "Authentic being-toward-death, in other words the finitude of temporality, is the hidden ground of historicity."[2]

My interpretation of the fundamental status of group finitude leads me to draw a very different conclusion. Indeed, human historicity is first and foremost set in relief by the passage of the collective memory of living generations into the historical past beyond its range. The cohesion of group perspectives and the finitude of their scope arises not in virtue of an ultimately singular finitude, but from the intermediary symbolic space underlying group cohesion. All expressions in this symbolic interspace emerge in the limited perspective through which human beings communicate and coexist in a common world. As I see it, the task of elucidating this limited perspective is of particular importance in our contemporary period, in which the phenomenon of collective memory has become an increasingly central preoccupation, and in which historical studies often purport to deal with remembrance not only in and of the contemporary period, but of the remote historical past.

The fundamental demarcation I have proposed in the preceding chapters therefore distinguishes between understanding of actions and events that are open to recall in the fragmented perspectives of the memory of living groups, and past contexts that are anchored in the web of symbolic structures and idioms that are no longer available to living remembrance. According to this interpretation, the temporal patterns of shared experience specific to the human world are manifested in two adjoining spheres, those of the historically recalled past and of living memory that collectivities retain. Overlapping and undergirding these spheres lie the latent propensities and long-term dispositions of a shared *êthos*, but after the disappearance of all living remembrance of the past, this layer of latency and of passive proclivities becomes ever less palpable as it gradually fades beyond the pale of awareness. These passive recesses may at times be brought to awareness, where they lie within the reach of memory of living generations, but they tend to fade into a more opaque and imperceptible form of latency the farther they recede into the historical past. In view of the historicity, contingency, and discontinuity of human groups, of the radical shifts between successive horizons of contemporaneity, the ongoing continuity of the *êthos*, deposited in the passive recesses of shared symbolic forms, is more often a source of ideological claims and political mythologies than of empirically ascertainable comprehension. It is in light of this limit that our anthropologically centered investigation must designate the line of demarcation between the two spheres of collective memory and the historical past.

I

If we set aside the traces of the past bequeathed by prehistory, from the Paleolithic vestiges of tool use and burial to the Neolithic revolution in the domestication of animals and sedentary agriculture, the field of historical representation may be extended, as is customarily done, as far back as there are interpretable traces or written records or chronicles open to verification. In view of the general schema of historical time, historical periods may be demarcated in terms of longer or shorter intervals. In this sense, Fernand Braudel distinguished what he termed the short duration or *"courte durée"* of historical periodization from long and intermediate duration (*longue, moyenne durée*), which lend formal temporal structure to any and all periods under historical investigation.[3] It is significant for my analysis of the periodization of collective memory and the historical past that all long- and medium-range historical duration stands outside the bounds of shared memory retained by living generations; only relatively recent years overlap with the temporal sphere of what, for any given contemporary period, might be termed "collective memory."

According to these general schemata of historical time, however, historical interpretation is by no means limited to the remote past of the *longue* and *moyenne durée*, and may also legitimately focus on recent events that are retained by living rememberers. Whole disciplines, under the rubric of contemporary history, *"Zeitgeschichte"* or *"L'histoire du temps présent,"* focus on contemporary history in this sense, which draw on recorded oral testimony and other traces of the recent past. In this time-span of the historical present, we may also situate Reinhart Koselleck's "space of experience," to which I referred in the preceding chapter. Here the boundary between collective remembrance and historical representation is thin, and the overlap between the two domains is most extensive. In such cases, as I have noted in previous chapters, historical method codifies and critically assesses what, in the sphere of collective remembrance, remains for the most part spontaneous and unsystematic. Nonetheless, this difference points toward a more fundamental consideration that comes to light as soon as we identify collective remembrance and historical interpretation not only as parallel fields of endeavor that retrospectively engage symbolically embodied past experience, but also as different *spheres* of collective awareness. Here we observe that if collective memory in its primary forms is spontaneous and unsystematic, whereas historical interpretation aims toward coherence and codification, this is because it is spread in its immediacy over a field of shared experience that historical accounts generally presuppose and, in any given situation, take for granted. Where collective memory, above all in its passive recesses, infuses group experience without necessarily occasioning explicit notice or reflection, the historian, far from naively adopting the predominant preconceptions of her present context, seeks to bring them to explicit awareness in order to explore their specific difference from the attitudes at work in the past under investigation. This possibility is, of course, always limited, for the historian is never able to step outside the margins of his respective present, whose thick levels are embedded in the passive spheres of personal and group awareness. To a limited extent, however, it is possible to bring these margins to awareness against the backdrop of the past in its specific differences from a later present that reflects on it.

This consideration raises an unavoidable problem: the very spontaneity and diffuseness of collective memory—which does not *primarily* function as a deliberative activity but as a precondition of experience, emerging out of its passive, symbolically embodied reaches—account for its tacit evanescence once living rememberers have disappeared. Remembrance in the pregnant sense involves the concrete context in which remembered experience was set, and this is why we cannot be said to "remember" the historical past in anything but a secondary and derivative manner. On this basis, I question more recent attempts to break down the distinction Halbwachs initially drew between collective memory and the historical past by stipulating that all knowledge bequeathed by the past, whether remote or recent, is a form of collective memory.[4] To my mind, this overlooks the central dilemma posed by the remoteness of the historical past. Collective memory, indeed, concerns not only an abstract capacity to recall given past events and circumstances or elements encompassed in a vast cultural heritage. As I have stressed in different parts of this work, collectively significant modifications concern not only data, facts, or circumstances, but primarily the temporal horizon itself, involving unperceived shifts in the passive, symbolically embodied recesses in which this horizon is anchored. To claim that we collectively "remember" the historical past may carry a certain rhetorical suggestiveness, but it leads to confusion when it is taken as a theoretical axiom. Where the discourse of collective memory is applied to remote history in more than a metaphorical way, there is a danger of obscuring the margin of incommensurability between the horizon of contemporaneity of a given present and the historical past that lies beyond living remembrance. Where it is assumed that the historical past is retrieved as "collective memory," its opaque dimensions that are not available to present reminiscence risk being overshadowed. Indeed, this distinction between the present scope of memory and the remote past lies at the source of what may be termed the *historical sense*, understood as the capacity to apprehend nuances that distinguish particular sensibilities and the specific logic that predominate in a given present—and that are couched in the idioms and categories of living, contemporaneous memory—from a past to which they are alien. The historical sense presupposes that the opacity of the past is not only due to the incomplete state of knowledge or to the complexity and fragmentary state of its sources, but to the alterity of its remote setting, which reveals itself in piecemeal form and can only be deciphered through painstaking immersion in its unfamiliar contours.[5] It is for this reason that I question the methodological presupposition according to which the concept of collective memory may be indifferently applied to all forms of group recollection of living generations and to historical representations of the remote past that only documents and other traces attest.

In its recent expressions, the theoretical conviction that all kinds of approaches to the past may be grouped under the rubric of collective memory is problematic for a further reason. According to this conviction, which has been most consistently defended by Aleida and Jan Assmann, not only living memory and the historical past, but the whole of a cultural heritage that is collectively retained and serves to define group identities comprises collective memory in the broad sense they accord to it. From their standpoint, collective memory assumes two different forms: first, as "communicative memory" shared by living generations over a period roughly spanning eighty to one hundred years, which more or less corresponds to Halbwachs's conception of collective memory; second, as "cultural memory," encompassing not only the historical past but legends, rites, myths, literary creations, and all manner of fictive narratives that the past has bequeathed.[6] Beyond the scope of communicative memory as it arises from the recent past, the question may be raised whether the concept of "cultural memory," as the Assmanns understand it and as it has permeated current discourse more generally, might not be so broadly interpreted that it risks leading to conceptual confusion. Indeed, the term *culture* itself admits of a variety of meanings: besides the notion of oral and written cultural expression that they evoke, the broad concept of culture also comprises, for example, "high" or "popular" culture, human cultural production as opposed to natural phenomena, and "culture" understood as an ethnological category. In the Assmanns' vocabulary and in much current usage, where the term *culture* is not explicitly limited to any of these references, it tends to reoccupy the terrain of what previously went under the rubric of *tradition*. Jan Assmann himself acknowledges this when he defines it in terms of long-standing social bonds that are invested with a quasi-sacred aura and are transmitted by specialized agents, including "shamans, bards, griots, priests, teachers, artists, scribes, scholars, mandarins, and others."[7] In Assmann's view, "cultural memory" is called to account for a past heritage in a contemporary period where formerly accepted concepts of tradition no longer seem viable. The redefinition that he and Aleida Assmann propose of tradition in terms of cultural memory also intends to encompass repressed and unconscious aspects of past group experience, interpreted from the perspective of Freudian psychology, which earlier concepts of tradition tended to exclude. As the word *tradition* formerly referred to a broad spectrum of domains, from literary and mythical legacies to methods of historical scholarship, so the single category of *cultural memory* comprises all forms of cultural production and is further expanded to encompass unconscious psychological dynamics.[8] In the final analysis, this inflation of the concept of tradition to fit the data of cultural memory proposes a tool of analysis so general that the only salient criterion for qualifying this data lies in its correspondence to productions, acts, or events a group remembers or represses over time. As I interpret it, this amalgam leads to confusion, especially where Jan Assmann concludes that in the undifferentiated perspective of cultural memory, the question concerning the factual basis of remembered events becomes inessential. As he writes, "Here any distinction between myth and history is eliminated." Indeed, according to his interpretation, cultural memory tends to transfigure historical facts, "thereby turning them into myth."[9]

Assmann's point of view is helpful in reminding us that myths, legends, and collective fantasies often have greater vivacity and longevity than the remembrance of factual events, and also that mythical beliefs lend orientation to historical actions. Once this point is acknowledged, however, a conceptual strategy that conflates myth and history raises what seem to me to be insurmountable difficulties. If, in a metaphorical sense, all of the collectively remembered heritage may be ascribed to the realm of "cultural memory," the question nonetheless arises whether this dilation of the concept of memory does not risk obscuring what I have equated with collective memory's finite province. In its more specific sense, collective memory of the living past is primarily spontaneous, diffuse, and fragmented, yet this may well include a *cognitive* moment of group self-awareness.[10] This cognitive moment corresponds to a spectrum of beliefs that, at different levels, draw on representations of what is taken to be the *reality* of the factual past. On one hand, we may refer to the manner in which collectivities distinguish, to varying degrees and from various perspectives, those aspects of the remembered past that are taken to be anchored in factual reality or, in accord with other forms of belief (e.g., religious faiths, ethical codes, or political creeds), may draw on what is accepted to be a remote factual basis that, in a given present, engages what is invested with a superior spiritual, ethical, or political significance. On the other hand, collectivities generally differentiate these beliefs from events, both of the recent and distant past, that are merely reputed to have happened or from legends that are broadly acknowledged to be fictions. Such cognitive distinctions between different levels of factual belief and disbelief are, of course, not always a reliable index for testing the reality of remembered group experience since, as I have noted, collectively retained beliefs are subject to manipulation and may be influenced by fanciful illusions and political myths. Ideally, where it is a question of occurrences retained in the memory of living generations, critical scrutiny may be called upon to reinforce this cognitive moment, subjecting reports to the review of evidence and to logical investigation with the aim of establishing the veracity of what has been recounted. In the final analysis, Halbwachs's original conception of collective memory has the advantage of covering the field of what Assmann terms "communicative memory," while opening a space for the diversity of temporal contexts in which the memory of living generations gives way to the different temporal perspective of history. In the framework of this concrete temporal plurality, the possibility of distinguishing between fanciful illusions, mythical beliefs, and factual occurrences depends upon collective assumptions concerning the real contours of a contextually anchored past.

In the case of historical understanding, critical analysis must go a step further, for it depends not only on recorded testimony or documents, but on the exercise of the historical sense that, in its capacity to bring to awareness preconceptions and biases at work in the immediate lifeworld, ideally strives for a measure of impartiality in its understanding of the historical past and of its relation to the present. On this basis, historical understanding, indeed, may claim not simply to retrieve what still resonates in the living memory of contemporaries, nor even a motley collection of traces of past historical events, but to recover a measure of what may be termed the "reality" of the remote past. Where, however, all forms of a past heritage, from historical narrative to fictive creations, are indifferently assimilated to the sphere of collective memory, the question remains concerning the possibility of adequately accounting not only for the cognitive capacity of collective memory but, beyond this, for the critical exercise of historical understanding in its claim to retrieve some aspect of past reality.

The topic of the "reality" of the historical past brings us to the heart of the problem that concerns us in our present discussion: any meaningful distinction between collective memory and the historical past assumes that discontinuities in the temporal horizons that separate them have a real basis. Reality in this sense corresponds not only to events that actually occurred or to circumstances that truly existed, for it concerns the capacity to accord a real foundation to a past temporal horizon, comprising a network of symbolic idioms and nuances that distinguish it from the context of a given present.

Since the 1960s and 1970s, a radical challenge to the historian's claim to retrieve a measure of "reality" of the historical past has come to the fore in both literary theory and in historiography. From the historiographical premise that all understanding is necessarily rooted in the sensibility and the logic, the language and the idioms of the present, this orientation concludes that the remote past in the diffuseness of its factual reality remains essentially opaque and impenetrable to current interpretation. While thus limiting the scope of historical understanding to the linguistic and symbolic horizon of the present world, this skeptical attitude takes historical representation to be a figment of the historian's imagination that, in overlooking the radical opacity of the past, projects upon it a sensibility and a discourse that it confuses with its reality. In limiting the thrust of historical understanding to representations derived from the historian's present, this skeptical theory, without evincing any particular concern for the topic of collective memory, nonetheless undercuts any meaningful distinction that might be drawn between interpretation within the confines of the contemporary world in which collective memory is rooted and understanding of the remote historical past. This skeptical doubt, in questioning the possibility of apprehending what lies beyond the context of the present and the recent past, homogenizes the diversity of temporal nuances and collapses the depth of temporal perspectives that a differentiation between collective memory and the historical past presupposes. Here we must grapple not with a theory of collective memory, but of history.

In the following section I analyze this skeptical position, above all as it has been propounded in the literary criticism of Roland Barthes and the historiographical writings of Hayden White. They each have the merit of placing in evidence analogies between the literary qualities of historiography and works of fiction, and the implausibility of earlier positivist assumptions, which overlooked or downplayed the role of selection and organization of narrative in the historian's work, and thus the unmistakable resemblance of historical emplotment to the writing of fiction. As I interpret them, the conclusions that these authors respectively drew from this insight are, however, too extreme, since each of them equated the writing of history, depicted as a projection of modes of present representation onto the remote past, as a form of fiction. Might one not, however, legitimately draw a different conclusion from their premises? If we accept the idea of an analogy between historiography and works of fiction, might we not account for this analogy not only in terms of the literary qualities of the historian's craft, but also of the eminently *historical* elements that contribute to the evocative force of exemplary works of fiction? Might it be that the historical aspect of fiction lies not only in the fanciful relations it creates between past facts and events, but in the historical sense it imaginatively engages? Here, as I will argue, in bringing to light the contours of the historical past in its difference from contemporary horizons delineated in collective memory, fiction may indeed provide an exemplary illustration of the real contours of historical time that distinguish past from present. In the concluding sections of this chapter I address these questions in relation to different examples drawn from works of fiction and, by this means, reinforce and substantiate my argument concerning the essential difference between collective memory and the historical past attested by shifts in the temporal horizons that are fundamental indicators of past reality.

II

In this first part of my analysis, I briefly examine how comparative analogies drawn between historical works and works of fiction have fueled historical skepticism. According to analogies that skeptical interpretations make be-tween historical and literary narratives, historical works, in spite of their claim to resuscitate the past, are no more faithful to its reality than the fictional rep-resentations of literature. In assimilating historical narrative to the products of the historian's imagination, this assumption erases any essential difference be-tween the historian's present imaginings and his or her representation of the historical past; however, critical analysis of this skeptical assumption enables us later to reestimate the real distance of a given present, configured both by remembered experience and by imaginary creations, from the historical past that precedes it.

Comparative analogies between literature and historical representation that are meant to cast doubt on the historian's claim are by no means of re-cent origin. In the eighteenth century, for example, the period in which the modern novel emerged, such comparisons became frequent vehicles for what had traditionally been termed historical pyrrhonism. Consider in this light the opinion of Denis Diderot, in his eulogy for the English novelist Samuel Richardson: "Oh Richardson!," he wrote, "I will dare to say that the truest of histories is full of lies and that your novel is full of truths."[11] Jean-Jacques Rousseau, in espousing a similar attitude, advised in his work, *Émile*, against the inclusion of the writings of modern historians in his program of education, for he accused them of having little relation to the reality of the past: "I see little difference between these novels and your histories," he wrote, "except that the novelist draws principally on his own imagination while the historian depends more upon that of someone else."[12] In entirely different philosophical frameworks, based on more elaborate epistemological justification, comparisons between historical works and works of fiction as a means of bolstering skeptical doubt concerning the historian's claim have found important expression in writings from Arthur Schopenhauer's reflections on history in *The World as Will and Representation* (*Die Welt as Wille und Vorstellung*) and Nietzsche's proclamations in the second of the *Untimely Meditations* to Theodor Lessing's *History as Making Sense of the Senseless* (*Geschichte als Sinngebung des Sinnlosen*).[13]

More recent years have witnessed the emergence of an analogous skepticism in the different framework of semiotics and literary criticism, beginning with the seminal writings of Roland Barthes in the 1960s and 1970s. Without engaging in the kind of rigorous analysis of the epistemological conditions of historical understanding characteristic of earlier philosophical investigation, Barthes' reflections began from Nietzsche's premise that facts are essentially linguistic constructs: "The fact never has anything but a linguistic existence."[14] On the basis of this theory of the constitutive role of language in the production of what is taken to be factual reality, Barthes developed his comparison between the historical work and the novel into a radical expression of historiographical skepticism. In the opening paragraph of his seminal essay on the relation of fiction and history, "The Discourse of History," Barthes raised the decisive question that has come to haunt historiography ever since: "Since the Greeks, the narration of past events is generally subject in our culture to the sanction of historical 'science,' put forth with the imperious guarantee of being real, and justified by the principles of 'rational' demonstration. But is this narration truly different, due to some specific feature or to some indubitable relation, from imaginary narrative articulated in the epic drama, novel, or play?"[15] Historical works, according to Barthes's argument, are narrative constructions that are couched in the linguistic style or rhetorical mode they adopt. Attempts to retrieve the historical past, like the creations of fiction, have little basis in the "reality" of the past, since their narrative constructions are ultimately expressions of the present context in which they are anchored. Motivated by concerns of the present, as so many expressions of its current ideology, historical representations, as Barthes and his school have argued, are essentially fictions, and it is on this basis that historical works are fundamentally comparable to the narratives found in novels. As Barthes has written, "Historical discourse is essentially an ideological elaboration or, to be more precise, one which is *imaginary*, if it is true that the imaginary is the language by which the enunciator of discourse (a purely linguistic entity) 'fills in' the subject of the enunciation (a psychological or ideological entity)."[16]

Here we find the essential argument for historical skepticism in our times, which has gained wide influence since its expression in Barthes's writings. What counterargument might we advance, therefore, in response to the skeptical current that Barthes's writings incarnate, permitting us to assume that, beyond fictional constructions couched in the discourse of the present and providing a vehicle for its ideological elaboration, the quest to reconstitute the historical past might find a counterpart in the depths of past "reality"? Without delving into the technicalities of Barthes's linguistic investigations, or into a detailed examination of the influence of his presuppositions on subsequent historiographical theory, a succinct examination of Barthes's direct references to historiographical practice will suffice to bring into focus what I take to be a principal limit of contemporary historical skepticism more generally.

It is consistent with Barthes's critical perspective that his analysis of historiographical practice took as its focus the formative period of modern historiography, which, as he notes, is also that of the modern novel. In this regard, he chose as an exemplary expression the work of Jules Michelet, whose talent for achieving dramatic effects served Barthes's purpose well, since Michelet's narrative techniques showed a marked affinity with literary creation, above all with the novel. Michelet's account of the French Revolution in his multivolume *Histoire de France*, which was of particular interest to Barthes, dealt with events witnessed by generations directly prior to Michelet's own time, who were still close to contemporary idioms and symbols and stood in proximity to the recollections of living persons. For dramatic effect, as the semiotician convincingly argues, Michelet introduced linguistic devices and fictive elements, which sustained the illusion that the narrative was anchored in historical "reality."[17] To the grandchildren of the revolutionaries who were Michelet's contemporaries, the means of portraying recent events that had shaken European civilization to its foundations provided a particularly vivid way of rendering the pathos of the recent past, and it is above all here, as Barthes illustrated, that the historian's dramatic discourse resembled that employed in the contemporary novel.

If the techniques of historical narrative and the reach of the historical imagination were limited to the creation of such dramatic simulations, the skepticism of Barthes and of his school might seem warranted. But is this all that the quest to retrieve the historical past might accomplish? Might it be, on the contrary, that beyond the devices used to create a plausible plot, a pal-pable—if often only implicitly discernible—"reality" pulses beneath the his-torical narrative? Since Barthes, in his critical writings, has focused on literary techniques in historiography, he has avoided making any essential distinction between more or less rigorous methods of historical representation, which might have obliged him to nuance his manner of lumping together fictive ele-ments in historical writing, and painstaking efforts to retrieve and compare available sources that, in their contextual interrelation, might lead the histo-rian to impute to them a measure of "reality." For him, all historiography is ultimately based upon imaginary reconstruction tacitly expressing the current situation of the narrator.

The deeper implications of this position become visible as soon as we ex-amine the unspoken presupposition governing the assumption that "fiction" and "historical representation" are analogous in their essence. This presup-position comes to light if we consider Barthes's interpretation of the *imagi-nary*. For Barthes, the imaginary, as fictive, is spontaneously contrasted with the real. Historical imagination is essentially employed in the production of fictive representations; however, in limiting its grasp in this way, Barthes's method betrays its dependence on an abstract preconception that he adopted without critical examination. This abstract preconception issues from a long tradition of reflection on the faculty of imagination, according to which its ob-jects are opposed to truths of reason as the guarantors of reality or "Being."[18] And here skeptical theory, in my opinion, by limiting historical imagination to the role of emplotment of "facts" in the fictive sphere of the narrative, fails to apprehend its fundamental significance for historical understanding. This ex-cessively limited theory of the imagination, indeed, risks confining historical reflection within a hermetically sealed circle, in which the historian's present imposes rigid constraints from which no interpretation is capable of escaping. If we have recourse only to imaginary narratives issuing from the ideological representations of a contemporary world, then the past exists only insofar as it has been covered over with the projections of the present. In this opera-tion, representations of the historical past and literary fiction would equally express wholly contemporary concerns.

In more recent years Hayden White, in the framework of a theory of the historical imagination, has further elaborated the skeptical implications of Barthes's conception of the analogy between historiography and fiction. In his critical essays, White has provided an insightful discussion of Barthes's ideas and other contemporary theories of history, and, even as he acknowl-edged that Barthes's conception of history relied on a "vast mass of highly problematical theories of language, discourse, consciousness, and ideology,"[19] he took Barthes's Nietzschean formulation—"The fact never has anything but a linguistic existence"—as the motto for the volume of critical essays in which his discussion of Barthes is included.[20] Where White, in the essay "The Historical Text as a Literary Artifact," interpreted this to mean that historical narratives are essentially "verbal fictions, the contents of which are as much *invented* as *found*," and the contexts of which "are themselves products of the fictive capability of the historians who have studied these contexts," historiography is very nearly assimilated to literary fiction. From this perspective, the function of the historical imagination, much as in the theory of Roland Barthes, is essentially limited to the task of spinning out imaginary tales.[21]

The limitations that White imposes on the historical imagination in face of the distant past account for his conception of the *present*-orientedness of the historian's task. This task, indeed, lies in the "*re*familiarization" of vestiges of the past in the present, "by showing how their developments conformed to one or another of the story types that we conventionally invoke to make sense of our own life-histories." Here literature and historiography share a common goal securely oriented in terms of present concerns. According to White's revealing comment in this essay, we recognize the two genres of fiction and history both to be "the forms by which consciousness both constitutes and colonizes the world to inhabit it comfortably."[22]

This leads us to the decisive point: if all understanding, and the imagination that guides it, are so radically rooted in the present that they are incapable of penetrating the contextual thickness of past "reality," what capacity might permit us to apprehend, in its distinction from a "real" past, the precise contours of the present *as present*? Skeptical interpretation, by limiting imagination to the emplotment of "facts" in the fictive sphere of the narrative, skirts by its broader capacity, which is not only to tell stories, but to demarcate the concrete temporal framework of experience through which historical understanding is made possible. In accord with this capacity, imagination discerns temporal nuances that distinguish the remembered past of contemporary experience from the historical past. In this function, it endows historical judgment with an ability to surmount its absorption in present preoccupations and in concerns arising from the immediate past to illuminate aspects of the historical past lying beyond all living memory. This capacity of the imagination, which is at once deliberative and empathetic, is, of course, essentially limited. It is necessarily "*standortsgebunden*," linked to the contextual standpoint from which it emerges; yet history is not for that reason a spontaneously generated *product* of the imagination. Imagination in its full scope, placed in the service of what I have termed the "historical sense," permits us to distinguish between the timely plausibilities of contemporary existence and past possibilities that have lapsed into the sphere of the unfashionable and the anachronistic. And the mark of the "reality" of the historical past lies primarily in its anachronistic contextual coherence in relation to the present, lodged in the language, symbols, and gestures that, beyond the pale of living memory, it is the task of historical discernment, guided by the imagination, to reinterpret. Against the mirror of that dimension of the past that is incommensurable with the present, the timely aspect of current persuasions and predominant fashions may be revealed in its contingency and ephemerality.

Barthes and his school have brought to light with great perspicacity the fictive elements that the historian's linguistic devices unwittingly transpose into historical narrative. And there is truth in his pronouncement, and in its reformulation in the work of Hayden White, that the rigidity of traditional distinctions between works of fiction and those of history does not hold. But if this is the case, then it is not only due to fictive elements that enter into historical narrative, but also for the inverse reason: in specific instances, the novel may draw on the historical sense that, although employed toward a different aim, inspires the historian's efforts. It may thus reveal the capacity of the imagination to illuminate symbolic structures that delineate the "reality" of an historical context.[23] It is here too that the past's real contextual difference from the present reveals a primary distinction between the horizon of contemporaneity in which collective memory is rooted and the historical past lying beyond it. In the concluding sections that follow, I explore this assumption more closely through a series of illustrations drawn from the classical historical novel of the nineteenth century, as well as from twentieth-century novels that stand closer to our own period.

III

The observation has often been made that the historical novel was inspired by a heightened sensitivity to stylistic, linguistic, and other forms of symbolic expression that, amid all heterogeneity in its manifestations, brought to the fore the concrete texture of an historical epoch. This heightened sensitivity, in turn, was not only directed toward the historical past, but nourished reflection on the historical uniqueness and contingency of the present itself in its difference from previous forms of human historical existence.[24] In an early nineteenth-century context that had recently been rent by unprecedented dislocation of the traditional social, political, and religious moorings of the

European order, the heightened sensitivity to the historical dimensions of human experience came to light not only in terms of an awakening of interest in the remote reaches of the past, but of a widespread conviction concerning the importance of a quest for its singular texture, set in relief in its difference from the present.

The fiction of Walter Scott is of particular significance for my analysis, due to its international acclaim, to the paradigmatic role it played in the early development of the historical novel as a genre, and also to Scott's insightful commentary on his conception of historical interpretation. In briefly examining Scott's originality, I highlight his conception of remembrance shared among generations and, on this basis, examine his effort to designate a kernel of historical reality that reveals itself in the midst of his eminently fictive narratives.[25] I consider both his commentary on previous romances and novels of the early and mid-eighteenth century, presented in his journals and miscellaneous essays, and his comments in the prefaces to the Waverly Novels, in which he explained his purpose in elaborating the new form of artistic expression for which he became famous.

Scott dealt with novelists who were his eminent predecessors in the volumes of his *Biographical Memoirs*, written in the 1820s, during which he was elaborating the voluminous series of his Waverly Novels. His comments on Samuel Richardson are particularly revealing in this light, for he credited Richardson with having produced a new, modern style of novel that broke with the romances of earlier periods, dominated by what Scott qualified as "the old French taste, containing the protracted amours of princes and princesses, told in a language cold, extravagant, and metaphysically absurd." Beyond the artificial situations of the classic romance, Richardson was able to "paint mankind" in a most effective manner, "as it exists in the ordinary walks of life."[26]

If Richardson's talent was immediately appreciated on the British Isles, his success was even greater on the Continent, and the praises heaped upon him by Rousseau and Diderot were clear signs of an "enthusiasm of the passions" that Scott considered to be all too typical of both their artistic works and their criticism.[27] In England, as he noted, the critics had signaled this tendency toward bombastic enthusiasm in the French reception of Richardson, typified by Diderot's declaration, which Scott cited in a footnote: "'O Richardson! I dare pronounce that the most veritable history is full of fictions, and thy romances are full of truths.'"[28] Scott's appraisal of Richardson, by contrast, as the *Biographical Memoirs* amply illustrate, did not shrink from critical remarks. He questioned the extensive detail that accompanied much of his eminent predecessor's narratives, above all where the "tediousness" of a "combination of minutely traced events, with an ample commentary on each" was thought necessary for the development of the narrative.[29]

Scott's comments on Richardson have a bearing on his own conception of the novel, which, in the aftermath of the French Revolution and the Napoleonic Wars, he sought to anchor in a portrayal of past manners and customs that had been so rudely challenged by events on the Continent. If, in his estimation, an earlier European reading public might have accepted the exorbitant flights of fantasy and the most implausible anachronisms typical above all of the French school, which, for example, introduced in "the early Republic of Rome the sentiments and manners of the court of Louis XIV,"[30] the taste of the contemporary world required a more faithful historical record; yet this style of portrayal should not for that reason be encumbered by a fastidious insistence on minute detail. Here, the experience of his first attempts at historical romance taught him the pitfalls of "tedious" forms of narrative, not only in the development of character and plot proposed by earlier English romances, but above all in the treatment of antiquarian detail in the dramatic portrayal of historical personages. In the years prior to the composition of the Waverly Novels, during which Scott attempted to find an appropriate narrative style, he came to understand the dangers that tedious antiquarian illustrations might involve. In his general preface to the *Waverly Novels*, included in the 1829 edition of the first of them, *Waverly*, initially published anonymously in 1814, Scott recounted how, prior to composing this work, he had been commissioned to complete for posthumous publication the unfinished romance of a recently deceased "artist and antiquary," Joseph Strutt.[31] This work, entitled *Queenhoo Hall*, sought to illustrate the "manners, customs and language" of the people of England during the fifteenth-century reign of Henry VI. Yet, because the romance was weighted down by myriad antiquarian ingredients expressed in a language that was "too ancient," it was not easily comprehended by the general reading public and, in spite of Scott's early editorial efforts, proved to be a flop. He subsequently resolved to produce a more engaging mode of historical expression, capable of drawing inspiration from historical events while at the same time arousing and maintaining interest among the reading public.

Scott's aim, nevertheless, was not to write history but historical romance: "Our purpose," as he bluntly stated at an important juncture in *Waverly* "is not to tread on the province of history."[32] And his insistence on grounding his narrative in factual circumstances and contingent historical realities fulfilled the requirements of romance, for the use of historical manners and customs of the past intended to enhance the psychological plausibility in the explanation of human affairs. Several generations prior to Scott, his fellow Scotsman David Hume, whose works on English history Scott admired, presented a philosophical theory of fiction and of history that highlighted the dramatic effect of historical illustration and, in its psychological emphasis, roughly anticipated the strategy that the historical novel as a genre would exploit to the fullest extent. In his *Treatise of Human Nature* Hume had dealt with the essential difference between passions inspired by pure fiction and those which arise from "memory and judgment," which are the primary sources of historical narrative. As powerful as the former may prove, a different feeling is aroused by historical accounts, because they are accompanied by the *belief* that they once existed. "There is something weak and imperfect," Hume wrote, "amidst all that seeming vehemence of thought and sentiment which attends the fictions of poetry." And this is why poets tend to borrow from historical narrative as a means of making "a deeper impression on the fancy and affections."[33]

In Scott's work, the psychological and dramatic effect of historically grounded narrative was extended through its fictional vehicle in an original direction. It is noteworthy that in his own descriptions of his novelistic creations, he often borrowed metaphors from painting, which he referred to as the romance's "sister art,"[34] for his quest to use historical illustrations in order to produce psychological effect brought him into the proximity of a constellation of assumptions that were voiced in his period in the domain of historical painting and portraiture. Although he himself did not comment on this, his intention to steer between the bombastic artificiality and manifest anachronism of traditional romance and the antiquarian tediousness of contemporary historical novels bore a marked resemblance to the theories of the greatest historical painter of Richardson's generation, Joshua Reynolds, whom, as Scott noted, had been the novelist's friend and acquaintance.[35] In the journal of Scott's voyage with his son to Waterloo and Paris, Reynolds's estimation of Rubens's paintings in Antwerp are cited with great admiration.[36] In his *Discourses on Painting*, Reynolds had questioned the traditional predominance of the fanciful themes of mythological representation, and he also disparaged the facile anachronisms that had been so common in religious painting. At the same time, if the historical painter was to portray the perspective of his times, this did not mean that historical painting must serve as the historian's handmaiden. Historians themselves, indeed, took obvious liberties in the interest of producing coherent and agreeable narratives, and the painter must be allowed still greater liberty in this domain. Yet the painter must bear in mind the importance of arousing a sense of plausibility that diminishes where factual reality is clearly falsified.[37] And, among Reynolds's contemporaries in France, a parallel interest in historical painting arose, and the theoretical treatment of this genre among authors such as Marc-Antoine Laugier, Jean-Bernard Le Blanc, or Étienne La Font de Saint-Yenne similarly insisted on the importance of the psychological effect that fidelity to historical detail might produce.[38] In France, too, the interest in historical painting steadily increased up through the French Revolution and the Napoleonic period.

In a manner reminiscent of the predominant theoretical orientations in the historical painting of his period, Scott himself, in his dedicatory epistle to *Ivanhoe*, drew a noteworthy comparison between the writer of romance and the painter. Like the painter, according to his assumption, the novelist produces his best effects where he shuns an overemphasis on detail while at the same time presenting a historically plausible representation, avoiding any "ornament inconsistent with the climate or country of his landscape."[39]

In regard to the pictorial themes of the visual arts, Scott particularly admired the satirical and realistic paintings of Reynolds's contemporary William Hogarth, whose depiction of popular and moralistic motifs Scott lauded in his *Journal*. Indeed, at a time when Scott's financial situation took a drastic turn for the worse, he found humorous words to say in comparing his plight with that portrayed in Hogarth's famous caricature "The Distressed Poet."[40] Here Scott was animated by an interest not only in the historical action of kings and aristocrats but also, like Hogarth before him, in the social and moral circumstances of the modest classes. If the upper classes nonetheless retained their predominant role in Scott's historical romances, his depiction of the situation and attitudes of commoners at the same time reinforced his broader attempt to present a plausible portrayal of past manners and mentalities. The peasantry of his own country, above all, was according to Scott "the last to feel the influence of that general polish which assimilates to each other the manners of different nations," and typically marshals the "antique force" and "simplicity of language."[41]

Scott's new genre of historical romance revealed its full potency in the first of the series of novels, *Waverly*. After the failure of his early attempt at revising the work of Strutt, he decided to deal in his own historical romance with a more recent and more familiar tale, a "Highland story and more modern events."[42] Scott chose as the subtitle for *Waverly* "'Tis sixty years since," which situated it in a recent period. Where in later *Waverly* novels, Scott often set his romances in more remote contexts, *Waverly* and the following two novels of the series, *Guy Mannering* and *The Antiquary*, formed a group of their own, for they were each set in a context that could be both related to significant public events and at the same time recalled to the memory of living generations. As he stated in the "Advertisement" to *The Antiquary*, *Waverly* "embraced the age of our fathers, *Guy Mannering* that of our own youth, and the *Antiquary* the last ten years of the 18th century."[43] This strategy set up the temporal parameters intermixing the visual imagery "painted" by living memory—or what was skillfully portrayed to be such—with historically significant events; it thereby established the paradigmatic relation between the vivacious portrayal of remembered images of a personally experienced context and historical events that endow this context with public interest and significance. In illustrating historically memorable events through the singular vivacity of what took on the appearance of recollected contexts, Walter Scott elaborated the original vehicle of the historical novel.[44]

In the first three Waverly Novels and particularly in his commentary on *Waverly* itself, Scott highlighted this *remembered* quality of the setting of the novel and of the manners and customs portrayed in it. Hence, in his postscript to *Waverly*, Scott recounted that although he was not a Highlander, he had spent much time as a child in the highland country described in the romance.[45] And he insisted that the narrative of battles and skirmishes recounted in the novel was based on the reports of reliable "eye-witnesses," just as his written "portraits" presented his personal testimony to "remnants" of the "individual habits of the period" in question.[46]

In this series, *Waverly* occupied a special place for another reason: beyond the personal setting of Scott's childhood, he focused on the remembered context of the broader region that had undergone radical transformation. "There is no European nation," as he wrote, which "within the course of half a century, or a little more, has undergone so complete a change as the kingdom of Scotland."[47] And, in the postscript to this first work, he stated his aim to call immediate attention to this great watershed in Scottish life that followed the failure of the Highlanders' 1745 Jacobite revolt against the rule of the English Hanoverian dynasty. Where the Highlanders had sought to maintain their independent way of life and traditional customs, the union of the two countries and the eradication of the Jacobite party marked the end of an era in Scottish life.

And here lay the specific historical interest of the first of the Waverly Novels: in his general preface to the series, Scott underlined the marked historical discontinuity in relation to the present to which *Waverly* gave testimony, and which, in spite of this temporal dislocation, the remembrance of living generations could still bring within reach. The temporal setting was thus distant enough to appear discordant with the perspective of contemporary society, yet near enough to make its precise contours available to the living memory of an ageing generation. However much fiction was involved in the events portrayed, the great psychological impact and the historical interest of this first of the Waverly Novels lends it a quality distinguishing it from later novels set in a remote past.[48] Above and beyond the psychological use of historical circumstances as a means of entertainment for his readers, Scott's choice of a time-span in this first of his historical novels recalls a contextual setting that the younger generations were already beginning to forget. And here, beyond the goal of arousing a psychological impact, he sought to call attention to the *implicit* dimension of this change, which, "though steadily and rapidly progressive" has not for that reason been apprehended. Like those who "drift down the stream of a deep and smooth river," as he wrote, "we are not aware of the progress we have made until we fix our eye on the now distant point from which we have been drifted." Only those older generations who might still recollect the last twenty or twenty-five years of the eighteenth century would be able to recognize the nature of the changes. And Scott's avowed purpose here was to "preserve some idea of the ancient manners" that he himself could recall beyond the scope of their present oblivion. Certainly, the characters themselves are fictive, and their interactions quaintly romanticized, but this did not prevent Scott from drawing the somewhat paradoxical conclusion that in *Waverly* "the most romantic parts of this narrative are precisely those which have a foundation in fact."[49]

What Scott here attested as the basis of his first historical novel is the essential difference between the manners and habits, indeed the context itself, that are retained in the collective memory of living generations who have experienced them and the historical past which, following a period of rapid change, recedes into oblivion for younger generations. His method was particularly effective in dealing both with the recent Scottish past and, as works such as *Old Mortality* attest, with the not-yet-remote period of the seventeenth-century English civil war. While they lay beyond living memory, such periods were close enough to the contemporary period described in the early Waverly Novels to lend themselves to portrayal in a romance of the bygone Scottish manners and mentality. By contrast, if we follow Scott's own assumptions, any attempt to reconstruct the manners and habits and, in general, the deeper contours of a more remote context that had long been unavailable to living memory encounters insurmountable difficulties and must be painstakingly reconstructed on the basis of available sources. Given the fictitious nature of the drama in the first of the Waverly Novels, a close inspection might well detect historical inconsistencies and anachronisms in their respective narratives. Yet the temporal setting of the novels in a period in which Scott himself had lived lends his narratives a timeliness that overshadows such discrepancies for a later reader and is the immediate source of their overall psychological effect.

If in many of the later Waverly Novels, Scott chose to anchor his narratives in more remote historical periods, his method of portrayal was nonetheless substantially the same as that adopted in the first three novels of the series. As in his treatment of more contemporary settings, his depiction of remote historical events in the later novels drew on the available documentary evidence and on the works of well-known historians, while producing the psychological impression, through the dramatic narratives of fictive characters, that the events were recounted as if they had been drawn from the recollection of direct experience. In presenting past historical events in this manner, Scott's method was least plausible where it dealt with historical periods far removed from the scope of living memory. Here the entertaining results of historical romance depended on the psychological impact of a vicarious reliving of the past that could not avoid the artificiality that its means of portrayal required. In such illustrations, the anachronistic character not only of language and costume, but of the world lying beyond the purview of living memory, lends to it the artificial and implausible character that Scott's critics did not fail to notice.

In spite of the success of many of these later Waverly Novels, this method of anchoring narratives in reliable historical accounts while developing the drama in relation to artificially created language and manners opened him up to similar charges of anachronism that he had leveled against the earlier romances of the eighteenth century. As much as he might refer to sources such as the thirteenth-century Wardour manuscript in *Ivanhoe* or, in *Quentin Durward*, to works of Philippe de Commynes, the fifteenth-century historian and direct witnesses of the momentous struggles between the King of France and the Duke of Burgundy, Scott acknowledged that the "severer of the antiquaries" would detect great artificiality and obvious discrepancies in the language and costumes that he lent to his characters, as in other aspects of his narrative. Scott nonetheless defended his technique at different points in his writings, and most forcefully perhaps in the preface to *Ivanhoe*. Here he frankly admitted that he might have "confused the manners of two or three centuries," but he considered this to be of little consequence since errors of this kind, if noticed by the antiquaries, "escaped the general class of readers."[50] What was uppermost in Scott's intention in these illustrations of the remote past was not historical accuracy, but the psychological impact aroused in the reader by the belief that the romance was anchored in the authentic historical record.

Among contemporary historians themselves, however, evaluations of the

impact for historical understanding of Scott's romances were not entirely negative. The celebrated French historian, Augustin Thierry, whose researches
on the history of the Middle Ages were stimulated by Scott's historical romances, freely admitted that they were not to be considered as "authoritative
historical works." And yet Thierry also highlighted one aspect of the works,
concerning both Scott's treatment of remote and more recent periods, that
proved to be of great importance as a spur to a more comprehensive historical study of the setting of past history. Where, indeed, classic historians
such as David Hume had often skirted by the deeper social issues in their
dry treatment, for example, of the medieval Norman conquest of Britain and
considered it to be a "mere change of government" and an affair of kings and
aristocrats, Walter Scott enlarged his focus to include broader sectors of the
population. In spite of the fictive nature of his dramas, he was able to inspire
historians who were subsequently convinced that "the territory, the wealth,
the indigenous persons themselves were objects of scrutiny, as well as the royalty."[51] In the attention he devoted to deeper social factors that had been involved in historical change, Walter Scott touched on aspects of the historical
past that previous historians had neglected.

Against Thierry's positive evaluation of Scott, however, the young Leopold von Ranke, to cite another contemporary example, explicitly opposed
his own conception of historiography to what he viewed as the liberties taken
by Scott with the manuscripts of Philippe de Commynes in his depiction of
fifteenth-century French history in *Quentin Durward*.[52] And, a number of
decades later, Hippolyte Taine, after admitting that Scott had sparked his initial interest in history, passed what has perhaps been the most durable critical judgment on Scott's portrayal of the remote historical past: " How [. . .]
could these great Catholic and mystical dreams, these acts of gigantic audacity, or these impurities of carnal art enter the mind of this bourgeois gentle-
man? Walter Scott stops at the threshold of the soul and the waiting-room of
history. He chooses in the Renaissance and the Middle Ages only the suitable
and the agreeable, erases naive language, unbridled sentimentality and bestial
ferocity."[53]

In his preface to the medieval romance *Ivanhoe*, Scott returned to the topic
of historical discontinuity and to the problem it posed for his manner of treat-
ing distant historical settings. After admitting, as I have noted, that he might
have confused the details of "two or three centuries," he discounted the empirical intuitions of his own historical sense as expressed in the afterward to
Waverly and simply grounded his self-defense in metaphysical assumptions
concerning human nature, which, in spite of outward veneer, was taken to be

identical throughout the centuries. The passions, as he wrote, "the sources from which sentiments and manners spring," are in all of their modifications "generally the same in all ranks and conditions, all countries and ages." One may therefore freely transpose them from one epoch to another, for they are as "proper to the present time as to those in which he has laid his time of action."[54]

In light of the artificial and anachronistic character, however, of Scott's general representations of the remote past, which would indicate an historical mutability of the ground of human experience that renders problematic such a conflation of different epochs, Scott's metaphysical assumptions in the preface to *Ivanhoe* would hardly seem warranted. The more nuanced historical sense manifested in the afterward to *Waverly* is of particular significance for my present discussion, for it favors a more plausible interpretation of human historicity in admitting an essential distinction between the past available to collective remembrance and the unfamiliar contours of the historical past beyond its grasp. If Scott's later romances produced an acute sense of anachronism in their treatment of the remote historical past, where he assimilated it to the more familiar language and categories of the present, this sense of anachronism is revealing, for it indicates a capacity standing at the basis of historical judgment itself. It is, indeed, through the exercise of the historical sense that artificiality of representation and implausibility arising from the blurring of the distinction between historical contexts are discerned. This exercise stands at the basis of any capacity to differentiate between a fanciful projection of the sensibilities of a given present onto the remote past from historical constructions that, however partial and incomplete, are nonetheless capable of critically reflecting on the disparity in contextual horizons. Conceived in this manner, the active exercise of the historical sense depends not only on attention to documentary sources and to "facts," but above all on the ability to liberate historical judgment from the self-evident assumptions of the present in which the historian is working. The distinction Scott himself continually made between romance and history implicitly recognized a proximity of historical research to the "reality" of the historical past that I seek to delineate.

Following his fanciful excursions into the remote historical past in a number of the later Waverly Novels, Scott, in his final years, turned to the writing of contemporary history. In this last period he devoted his efforts to the composition of the multivolume work *Life of Napoleon Buonaparte*, in which he sketched a broad portrait of the period beginning just before the great Revolution and extending up until Napoleon's exile and death. He plunged with relish into available documentary sources, frequenting archives and investigating the geographical sites of battlefields. Here too it was as an indirect witness of the French Revolution, the Consulate, and Empire that he traced the history of the contemporary period "now remembered by only the most advanced part of the present generation."[55] And, in presenting himself as a witness and portrayer of his times, Scott aimed to retain a vivid recollection of it for posterity. It is perhaps not surprising that it was this eminently ocular quality of the work that Goethe praised in a letter to one of Scott's friends, quoted in Scott's *Journal*, in which the German writer recounted the impact on him of the *Life of Napoleon Buonaparte*, which Scott had sent him:

> I received [Scott's] *Life of Napoleon*, and have read it this winter. [. . .] To me it is full of meaning to observe how the first novelist of the century took upon himself a task and business, so apparently foreign to him, and passed under review with rapid stroke those important events of which it had been our fate to be eye-witnesses. [. . .]
>
> The book was in yet another respect of the greatest importance to me, in that it brought back to my remembrance events through which I had lived. [. . .] The work has become to me as it were a golden net, wherewith I can recover from out of the waves of Lethe the shadowy pictures of my past life."[56]

I V

First published in 1831, Victor Hugo's *Notre-Dame de Paris* provided an epoch-making French contribution to the genesis of the historical novel as a genre. This work clearly presented itself as a romance and thereby took liberties with the available sources that set it apart from the typical historical works of the period, even those that came closest to reproducing the novelist's quest for dramatic effect, such as Jules Michelet's *Histoire de France*. In this work, Victor Hugo played on an ambiguity that constitutes a principle mode of operation through which the historical novel attains its effect: the narrator relates events of the late fifteenth century with a directness and detail that could only be given by one who has experienced them, while at the same time claiming to present the historical account of distant events drawn from testimonies and documents. Hence, while the plot and most of the characters of the novel are entirely fictitious, they are at the same time portrayed in their interaction with other characters who are modeled on actual personages of the past, such as the late medieval dramatist Pierre Gringoire or Louis XI, King of France. While relating a wholly fictive tale, the narrator refers to himself in the novel as "just an historian,"[57] whose account draws upon the earlier records of "other" historians, such as the fifteenth-century *Mémoires* of Philippe de Commynes or Henri Sauval's *Antiquités de Paris,* which had been composed in the mid-seventeenth century. The ambiguous mix of fiction and history sustains the dramatic effect by creating for the readers the temporal illusion that they are uncovering a distant prefiguration of the contemporary Paris they inhabit, while in fact the narrative recasts what is most distant, particular, and opaque in the past—beginning with the language, gestures, and other forms of symbolic interaction typical of the fifteenth century—in order to make this remote past accessible to contemporary understanding and sensibility.

In its quest for dramatic emplotment the historical novel is thus anything but "historical," for it presents what is supposedly "past," while continually assimilating it to the present, portraying as historical what in fact is fiction, not only in terms of the characters it invents, but of imaginary reconstruction of the contextual structure of the period in which it is situated. This earlier age is brought up to date, while made to look archaic through the selection of isolated relics and piecemeal accounts: the staging of a passion play of Pierre Gringoire with which the novel opens, the detailed topographical descriptions of medieval Paris, the grave illness of King Louis XI. All of these elements simulate a past that, in its essential features, remains fictive. This only highlights the principal artifice introduced by the novel: the remembered past, which in a strict sense is available only to personal and group experience in a contemporaneous world, is extended backward as if to encompass in memory a context that, having long ago disappeared, lies beyond what any living memory might grasp.

This dramatic effect is achieved from the very beginning of the novel by Victor Hugo's remarkable narrative technique. The narrator explains to the reader in the preface of 1831 that during a visit to Notre-Dame several years earlier, he had noticed an old inscription in an obscure niche of the church, the ancient Greek word *anagke,* or "fate," written in Greek capital letters and in medieval Gothic style. He asked himself what troubled spirit might have written this word in his intention to leave a last trace, the "stigmata" of his troubles, before disappearing from the face of the earth. Since his previous perception of this faint trace, the narrator notes that it has entirely disappeared. It symbolizes for him the fate of medieval churches like Notre-Dame, which are doomed to disappear due to disinterest, neglect, and a quest for modernization: "The priest whitewashes, the architect scrapes, and the people arrive to demolish them."[58] Nonetheless, the word itself remains firmly implanted in the narrator's *memory*, even after all traces have disappeared, and it is the desire to retrieve what has been effaced among the vestiges of the distant past that, as Victor Hugo explains, has motivated the creation of the work itself.

The impact of the novel is, however, not limited to the dramatic effect that is produced by the impression of rediscovering a long-lost past, and by the creation of a fictional impression that we are experiencing this past as if it were being retrieved in memory. Its strength lies not only in this *fictive* capacity, but also in its sensitivity to the concrete nuances of historical time. This sensitivity, or what may be termed the historical sense, comes to light in *Notre-Dame de Paris*, where Victor Hugo departs from his dramatic narrative to reflect on the scope of the metamorphosis and thus on the discontinuity between past and present that separates this medieval heritage from later centuries that behold it. Here the author centers reflective imagination on profound changes in the predominant sensibilities and mentalities that rendered gothic symbolism in all of its forms unattractive and even incomprehensible to the later tastes that replaced it. In a poignant description of the ways in which a given "present" relates to its past, in this case an epoch extending over a period of centuries up until the French Revolution, Victor Hugo evokes the loss of a capacity in later times to appreciate the significance and the beauty of the archaic forms of expression of the medieval past. The fashions of each successive present destroyed what they could neither understand nor appreciate, and proved in this far more devastating than revolutions themselves. As Victor Hugo writes,

> Fashion has done more mischief than revolutions. It has cut to the quick— it has attacked the very bone and framework of the art. It has mangled dislocated, killed the edifice—in its form as well as in its meaning, in its consistency as well as its beauty. And then it has remade, which, at least, neither Time nor revolutions had pretended to do. It has audaciously fitted into the wounds of Gothic architecture its wretched gewgaws of a day—its marble ribands—its metal pompoons—a very leprosy of ovolos, volutes, and *entournements*, of draperies, garlands, and fringes, of stone flames, brazen clouds, fleshy Cupids, chubby cherubim, which we find beginning to devour the face of art in the oratory of Catherine de Médicis, and making it expire two centuries after, tortured and convulsed, in the boudoir of Madame Dubarry."[59]

Such sensitivity to the past, which aims to grasp the ways in which its contextual sense may lapse into an absence beyond the possibilities of appreciation or of comprehension of succeeding ages is, of course, not the chief province of fiction—even if it is vividly evoked in *Notre-Dame de Paris*—but of historical works. This motif, indeed, furnished a source of intense reflection among contemporary historians culminating several decades later in Hippolyte Taine's description of the "esprit classique" in his work *Les origines de la France contemporaine*. The "esprit classique," as he wrote, which reached its apogee in seventeenth- and eighteenth-century France, reduced the multiplicity of sensibilities at work in the distant past to a set of clear-cut models that were comprehensible to contemporary polite society. In generalizing its own sensibility, the "esprit classique" assumed that human nature is fundamentally the same in all periods: "It has no historical sentiment," as Taine wrote; "it acknowledges that humanity is everywhere the same."[60] This justified a manifest indifference toward the singular texture of the past and, in particular, toward vestiges of the medieval world that, due to fundamental changes in sensibility and comprehension, it could no longer comprehend.

It might be argued that the fascination for the Middle Ages that gripped historians and novelists of Hugo's period was itself no more than a fashion that supplanted the classicism that was in vogue in a previous age. And, in doing so, fashionable assumptions became the vehicle of polemical intentions current in their period, fueling above all the radical criticism of the world that had culminated in what they perceived to be the revolutionary cataclysm. Such representations of the past were patent expressions of ideological presuppositions. And yet, does the perception that the historical imagination of this period, as in all periods, was enmeshed in the contemporary orientations of the world in which it arose permit us to conclude that all such forms of historical reflection were no more than *functions* of that world, of its predominant rhetorical devices or of one or another of the ideological intentions lodged in its discourse?

What seems to me to resist any attempt at reduction to the vantage point of a given present is the incommensurability of the past, as it is temporally configured, with later times; this incommensurability is manifested through symbolic expressions that are not immediately available to later reconstruction, but require imaginative deliberation and conceptual discernment to bring out their implicit sense. Literary creations can suggestively intimate the implicit singularity of the historical past; it is the work of historical investigation to explicate the symbolic texture that imparts to it its deeper contextual significance. The "reality" of the historical past lies in its transcendence of all representations of the present world, and of all ideological intentions that seek to mobilize it, continually enjoining us to rethink its meaning in each successive present. However biased and incomplete even the most impartial attempt to recover the vestiges of a past beyond living memory may be, its significance, far from limited to the status of a fictive invention of the present, reveals itself not only where it is capable of illuminating what has preceded current times, but where it enables us to place the fluctuating horizons of our own present in perspective.

It would be possible, indeed, to pursue this point through the analysis of any number of historical novels or realist portrayals of the past that, as they emerged over the course of the nineteenth century, provided original experiments in the imaginative retrieval of the concrete horizon encompassing the symbolic embodiments of the past. Where in the quest for dramatic effect and readily comprehensible narratives, representations of the remote past easily fell prey to anachronism, such romances were at times also animated by the attempt to avoid such pitfalls through scholarly research. Alessandro Manzoni's *The Betrothed* (*Promessi Sposi*), set in seventeenth-century Piedmont, focused on a historical past that, like the one in Scott's *Old Mortality*, was remote enough to reach beyond the scope of living memory, yet close enough to be able to plausibly mobilize language and other symbols that retained their comprehensibility in the contemporary period of their reception. Manzoni's narrative of the separation of an engaged couple, Lucia and Renzo, and their subsequent attempts to find each other, was enriched not only by reliance on well-known historians but also by research he undertook in the archives of Milan. Here he uncovered material for his narrative of the years of the great plague of Milan in which important segments of the drama were set. Sensitivity to linguistic nuances and to their transformations, as to the differences in regional dialect, contributed essential elements to Manzoni's attempt to revive the texture of the past in which the novel was set.

Following the vogue of the historical novel and of the different currents of realism and naturalism, the transformation of stylistic and narrative modes of fictive representation of the early twentieth century permits us to explore in a different constellation the capacity of the novel to illuminate what might be termed the real contours of the historical past. Like the emergence in painting of post-figurative representation of the brute data of perceptual experience and of the interpenetration and juxtaposition of different spatiotemporal aspects and planes, innovations in the novel set in relief the stream of intimate apprehension as it draws on and is absorbed in the departed time of the past. In this work too the question of "reality" concerns less the depiction of isolated elements or "facts," than of the shifting horizon from which they draw their meaning. Here we may place in relief the mode of portrayal of this horizon, articulated in terms of concrete temporal patterns of human interaction and communication as they are symbolically embodied and remembered. Among the many examples that might be chosen, Marcel Proust's novel *A la recherche du temps perdu* provides a noteworthy paradigm for this investigation.

v

In chapter 3 I briefly evoked Proust's conception of forgotten memories that, out of the lost time of the past, may make a sudden and involuntary reappearance at often unexpected moments. Proust's conception of involuntary memory, as I stipulated, brings to the fore a dimension of personal identity in which the latent, the forgotten, the obscure episodes of experience play an essential role in defining selfhood. Far from being limited to the personal sphere, involuntary memory at the same time resuscitates a network of relations with others.

At this concluding stage of my investigation, I am concerned less with the specific dynamics of involuntary memory than with the broader structure of the passive and tacit spheres of experience that all forms of memory, both voluntary and involuntary, bring to expression. By means of examples, I set in relief Proust's subtle conception of these shared passive and tacit spheres, which he brings to visibility against the shifting horizon of time. Proust, moreover, portrays not only transformations in the modes of human interaction and communication that, in the flux of temporal horizons, often remain unperceived; he brings *reflection* on the temporal conditions of group perception and group remembrance into the foreground of the narrative itself. Here he illustrates the transformation of group perception and remembrance among successive generations that transpires in the tacit dimension of an underlying contextual "reality" to which experiencing and remembering groups pay little if any heed.

My first example concerns transformations in collective perception of the visual symbolism of painting. In his *Essais et articles*, as in his novel *A la recherche du temps perdu*, Proust dealt extensively with painting and with changes in the way it is judged by the broader public, composed mainly of painters themselves, critics, aristocrats, and the wealthier members of the bourgeoisie. In Proust's writings, the public reception of the works of two of the best known nineteenth-century painters, Jean-Auguste Dominique Ingres and the younger and less conventional Edouard Manet, played a particularly prominent role. Ingres was held in high esteem by his contemporaries and was the preferred artist of Napoleon Bonaparte and later of his nephew, Napoleon III. Ingres's celebrity was based on his representations of classical themes such as his *Apotheosis of Homer* or *La Source*, which portrayed a nude woman carrying a vase, evoking a preferred motif of classical antiquity. The contemporary art critic and writer Théophile Gautier considered that the painting *The Apotheosis of Homer*, excepting certain modern figures set in the painting's foreground, "might have been included among the ancient masterpieces in the pinacoteca of the Propylaea."[61] And Hippolyte Taine, who otherwise showed little enthusiasm for Napoleon III and for what was considered to be officially sanctioned art of the period, nonetheless expressed great admiration for Ingres's work: "Raphael," as he wrote, "does not have a

FIGURE 13. Jean Auguste Dominique Ingres, *La Source*, 1820–1856, Orsay Museum, Paris. © RMN-Grand Palais (Musée d'Orsay)/Hervé Lewandowski.

FIGURE 14. Jean Auguste Dominique Ingres, *Apotheosis of Homer*, 1827, Louvre Museum, Paris. © RMN-Grand Palais (musée du Louvre)/René-Gabriel Ojéda.

more faithful student."[62] At a later moment, when Ingres's work had begun to seem pretentious and backward in modernist circles, Proust, in a brief text included among his *Essais et articles*, emphasized that all such judgments need to be qualified, since even a contemporary like Edgar Degas, who was hardly out of step with the fashions of his times, considered Ingres to be one of the great artists in the history of painting.[63]

By contrast, Proust called attention to the much less favorable attitude that the public accorded to the paintings of the younger Manet, especially in the initial period of his work. He underlined the disparity between Manet's perception of his painting as an original expression of classical styles and the more general public reaction to his work, which was often vehemently critical of his unconventionalism. Even Manet's mother, as Proust reminded his reader, had mixed reactions to his talent. Proust alluded to Jacques-Émile Blanche's reminiscence in *Propos de Peintre*, to which he wrote the preface, according to which she praised her son's ability to faithfully copy a painting by Tintoretto, but found it necessary to add that his own paintings would be different, were it not for the circles he frequented.[64] The exhibition of his

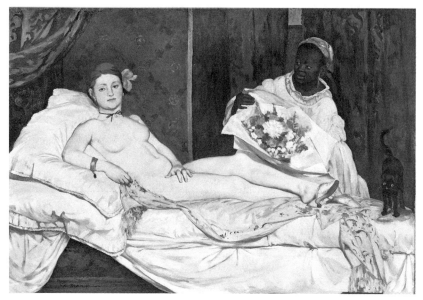

FIGURE 15. Edouard Manet, *Olympia*, 1863, Orsay Museum, Paris. © RMN-Grand Palais (Musée d'Orsay)/Hervé Lewandowski.

painting *Olympia* provided an occasion for a famous public scandal at the salon of 1865 and, as Proust noted, an outlet for acrimonious attacks on his work. The reasons for this public reaction have often been noted by later art historians: the nude woman represented in *Olympia*, far from alluding to classical themes and exulting traditional forms of beauty, portrays a well-known contemporary model, Victorine Meurent, lying on her couch and staring directly at the painting's beholder, while her maid brings her a bouquet of flowers ostensibly sent to her by a client. The public scandal that the painting aroused several years after the general acclaim accorded to Ingres's *La Source* attested Manet's break with traditional conventions of his period that the Impressionist movement would confirm more generally.

It is in this light that the juxtaposition of the two painters at various points in *Le côté des Guermantes*, the third in the series comprising *A la recherche du temps perdu*, sets in subtle relief changes in the temporal context of the period—what I have termed its "horizon of contemporaneity." The narrator of *Le côté des Guermantes* dwells upon the initial negative reaction of the public to Manet's *Olympia*. After a certain number of years, however, this initial reaction was followed by a gradual transformation as the public became habituated to the innovative mode of representation introduced by the Impressionist movement, which it even began to find attractive. In this paradoxical situation, as the narrator of the novel noted, the seemingly unbridgeable distance between what the public took to be a chef-d'oeuvre of Ingres and the *Olympia* of Manet, which it thought would "always remain a horror," diminished to the point where "the two canvases seemed like twins."[65] And, in a letter written in 1920, Proust affirmed that the greatness of Manet was to be found precisely in his unconventional originality: "I believe one only resembles the masters when one does differently (for example the 'scandal' of Manet's *Olympia*)."[66]

Proust attests here an important shift in temporal horizon that, in regard to artistic styles, marked a metamorphosis in public sensibility. What is noteworthy, above all, as Proust remarked, is the fact that this change was barely acknowledged or was even unnoticed by most of the people who underwent it. Proust emphasizes this point in relating the shift in group perception of art to the most recent developments in painting in the years after the Impressionist movement began to win wide acceptance. The young narrator of the novel, while attending a large dinner party to which he is invited at the home of the Duke and Duchess of Guermantes, obtains a long-awaited opportunity to see the paintings of a contemporary artist—the fictive painter Elstir—whose originality the protagonist greatly admires and most of the snobbish aristocrats in the milieu of the Duke and Duchess vehemently reject. The young protagonist comments that they remain oblivious to the variability of their own tastes and, more generally, of those of their social milieu. The appeasement of their earlier hostility toward Manet's innovations has in no way led them to reflect on subtle changes in temporal context, even where they are remembered, although, as Proust adds, the eldest members of the generation, who had witnessed this change, might well have recognized its implications for their present artistic judgments.[67]

Changes in concrete temporal context that lead the public to gradually accept what it had previously rejected are often tacit occurrences. In a broader sense, shifts in the horizon in which the manners of perceiving and of interacting occur often go unnoticed. It is this obliviousness to the finitude and contingency of a temporal context that Proust qualified as the incapacity to adopt the "perspective of Time" ("*la perspective du Temps*").[68] Where it is brought to awareness, however, this perspective permits us to appreciate the contingency of our own standpoint, in which the conventional character of attitudes we share with contemporary groups comes to light.

Given these transformations in the horizons of shared experience and remembrance among living groups, how much more radical are the subtle shifts that mark the temporal contexts separating living generations, especially in periods of radical dislocation following World War I! Among the examples in Proust's work that might be evoked to illustrate such metamorphoses, the Dreyfus affair provides a poignant illustration. In his references to this affair in the later volumes of *A la recherche du temps perdu*, Proust interweaves fictive narrative with real historical events and, using a technique reminiscent of the historical novel, portrays them as if they were being experienced and remembered. As a political event, the Dreyfus affair provided a dramatic catalyst that sharply divided fin de siècle French society, pitting those sympathetic to the army's accusation that Dreyfus was a spy, who were often aristocrats and members of the political right, against the liberal bourgeoisie, who, with Émile Zola and Georges Clemenceau, were convinced of his innocence. One of the main protagonists of the novel, the Jew Charles Swann, who is an elegant member of high society, begins to descend the social ladder due to his marriage to a woman of doubtful reputation, Odette de Crécy. His loss of social status is completed when he espouses the pro-Dreyfus position of his coreligionaries and falls into disgrace among his aristocratic contemporaries—represented above all by his former intimate friends, the fashionable Duc and Duchesse de Guermantes and their circle.[69] His wife Odette, on the other hand, after first being snubbed by fashionable society, begins to rise on the social scale when she becomes the mistress of the Duc de Guermantes and frequents anti-Dreyfusard and anti-Semitic aristocratic circles into which she is assimilated following her husband's death. Proust highlights the irony of this situation in his depiction of the emergence of a new generation of aristocrats after World War I, who dismiss, or simply forget, the passionate anti-Dreyfusard stance so often espoused by their parents and grandparents. The new generation manifests a modish and naive hindsight that made fashionable the unquestioned embrace of pro-Dreyfus attitudes. Hence, where the older generations considered Dreyfus and his supporters to be traitors, Proust writes, "Twenty-five years later, after ideas had had the time to settle and Dreyfusism to assume a certain historical elegance, the sons of these same young nobles, waltz dancers and Bolsheviks, would declare to the 'intellectuals' who questioned them, that surely, had they lived then, they would have been for Dreyfus, without knowing much more about what the affair had been than the countess Edmond de Pourtalès or the marquise de Galliffet, those other splendors already extinguished on the day of their birth."[70]

In his depiction of the social impact of the Dreyfus affair and of its evolution, Proust presents a telling illustration of the ways in which group perceptions and patterns of collective remembrance and forgetting tend to be fragmented along the lines of social class and ethnic group. At its deeper lev-

els, however, Proust's depiction of temporal context—the "horizon of contemporaneity"—affects living generations as a whole and marks their outward
appearance, demeanor, and modes of expression in ways that cut across all
differences in social group. And, in taking as his example the historical past
beyond living memory, Proust points out that such affinities shared by contemporaries in the same historical period may in many instances be more
evident to later perception than any distinctions in social class that separated
them during their lifetime. Proust writes in this vein,

> The perfect conformity in appearance between a petit bourgeois of Com-
> bray of his age and the duke of Bouillon reminded me [. . .] that social
> and even individual differences dissolve at a distance in the uniformity of
> a period. The truth is that the resemblance of clothing and also the rever-
> beration through the face of the spirit of an epoch assume in the individual
> a place that is so much more important than his or her caste, which plays a
> significant role only in the vanity of the person concerned and in the imagi-
> nation of others. To comprehend that a great nobleman of Louis-Philippe's
> period is less different from a bourgeois of his period than from a great
> nobleman of the time of Louis XIV, it is not necessary to go through the
> galleries of the Louvre."[71]

Evidently, Proust draws his examples from the wealthier strata of society,
extending from the aristocracy to the upper and lower bourgeoisie. And yet,
what is important here is not only his remark concerning the immediate relation of the different strata of society as a whole, including their modes of
appearance and expression, but also the distinct singularity of the epoch in
which they lived. This difference between periods that appears in terms of
intricate characteristics shared by contemporary generations underlies the essential discontinuity between concrete temporal horizons, which become all
the more opaque and difficult to penetrate the farther they retreat beyond the
capacities of remembrance of living contemporaries. Proust's preoccupation
with such temporal discontinuities is similarly reflected in the attention he
devotes to memorialists of the past. In this vein, he evokes not only Madame
de Sévigné's autobiographical revelations in her seventeenth-century correspondence with her daughter or the roughly contemporary memoirs of the
duke de Saint-Simon, but also the more recent memoirs of the Comtesse de
Boigne, who is mentioned both in his essays and in *A la recherche du temps
perdu*. In this novel, she provides a model for the fictive character, Madame
de Villeparisis, who is a high-born and socially unappreciated friend of the

protagonist's grandmother. Born in the last years of the ancien régime, the Comtesse de Boigne had frequented the royal family at Versailles in her early youth. Her nephew, for whom she wrote her memoirs, had often been a guest at the home of Proust's parents and had told them stories his aunt had related, allowing Proust to establish a form of contact with a distant past. Certainly Proust was skeptical of the point of view Madame de Boigne depicted, and he questioned the accuracy of many of her statements.[72] Yet his perception of her nephew, "with his own eyes" (*"avec les yeux de la chair"*), permitted a vicarious participation in the life of an earlier period, including the revolutionary events directly witnessed by those "who had seen Marie-Antoinette pass by." Proust was careful to stress that through "skillfully manipulated transitions," such scenes took on the "relief of reality (*"le relief de la réalité"*) that he could vicariously recreate.[73]

Proust's fascination with memoirs of the past, spurred by his profound sensitivity to social metamorphosis, animated his singular quest: in the face of radical change, the narratives of persons who had a living contact with direct recollections of the past generated the impression that historical discontinuity might be surmounted. Yet, as Proust himself realized, this was only an impression. For, even within the limits of the past encompassed by direct experience and personal memory, human existence is continually haunted by "lost time." Lost time is engendered not by the mere passage of days and years, nor even by the relentless process of ageing, but above all by radical transformations in individual sensibilities that are interwoven in a collective context formed by the shifting temporal horizon of succeeding generations. From this vantage point, Proust's novel engages an exercise of the historical sense: it reveals changes in finite human modes of understanding and of being which, in light of the shifting symbolic horizon of interaction and of communication with the passage of each generation, casts in its wake a deepening shroud over the past's singular texture. The obscurity of "lost time" in the brief period in which his efforts at remembrance are set, and which comes most immediately to light through involuntary recollection, underlines the opacity of the more remote historical past beyond the memory of living generations. And yet, according to my interpretation, opacity is tantamount neither to un-nuanced shading nor to wholly irremediable blindness. In its sensitivity to discontinuity and to the metamorphosis in temporal horizon, the historical sense makes it possible to set timely assumptions of our own present in relief and to distinguish them from aspects of the past to which they are foreign. Proust's reflections on the lost time of the past, deployed in the medium of fictive representations, elucidate this sense through vivid illustrations.

In the previous sections of this chapter, my examination of fictive narratives in literature has centered on representations of the historical past developed in different forms of the novel. In the wake of historical dislocation and discontinuity, the different examples I have chosen set in relief, in different periods, a variety of ways of exploring shifts in concrete temporal horizon underlying the historical variability of group perceptions and collective remembrance. The subtle mesh of fictive narrative and historical event is capable of eliciting the impression that historically significant past events might reappear as if they were being recalled to memory. In the novels I have examined, the potency of this impression is due not only to the imaginary status of the narrative, nor to constraints imposed upon it by the quest for a faithful representation of facts; its vivacity depends upon the plausibility of the singular contours of a past context that the narrative sets in relief. If historical novels as a genre and, in a later period, Proust's literary creation, may in a certain measure illuminate what might be termed the "real texture" of the historical past, this is because their respective ways of exploring the temporal variations in group perception and group remembrance highlight concrete and often tacit metamorphoses in the temporal horizon underlying the historicity of human experience.

The different examples I have chosen thus far have been centered around the two periods extending between the upheaval of the French Revolution and the Revolution of 1848 and between the fin de siècle and the immediate aftermath of World War I, during which Proust elaborated his work *A la recherche du temps perdu*. In the final section, I complement this examination by extending it to the contemporary period. This permits exploration of the fictive representation of a specific facet of the relation between collective memory and the historical past that has come to play a particularly prominent role in contemporary interpretation. Here I am concerned with collective remembrance and the representations of recent history that highlight their essentially *burdensome* quality.

In the second of his *Untimely Meditations* to which I alluded in the introduction, Nietzsche presented his seminal ruminations on this burdensome quality of memory and of history which, in their hypertrophied modern form, had become a hindrance to the fulfillment of vital needs and to original creation. Written in a period in which material development and nationalist aspirations had fueled the ideals of progress and expansion among elites and among broad sectors of Western society, Nietzsche's warning was decidedly untimely. The catastrophe of World War I, followed by the rise of totalitarian

dictatorships and the advent of World War II, and culminating in the programmed industrial genocide of the Shoah and in the mass murders that have
followed in later decades, have brought to the fore intense reflection, both
among survivors and later generations, on the problematic status of the past in
its relation to the present. However diversified the perspectives on this topic
may be, its prominence in recent sociocultural and intellectual life attests that
the dread it inspires in collective remembrance and recent historical study
has not ceased to haunt our current period and to mark its singular character.
If, indeed, the circumstances that brought about this hiatus now belong to
history, their very existence as past reality raises the question concerning the
fragility inherent in modern mass existence that, in view of the unpredictable
contingency of human affairs, stands like a specter over our increasingly inter-
dependent and globalized situation.[74] In view of the loss of vast communities
and of whole cultural heritages since the beginning of World War II, it is ques-
tionable whether a psychological process of "working through" the burden of
the past in the hope of mastering its traumatic legacy might lead to a new form
of "contented memory" (*mémoire heureuse*).[75]

My purpose in this final section is not to speculate on such possibilities but
to explore from another angle the specific question concerning the reality of
the historical past that fictive narration may reveal. This question takes on a
new significance in view of the temporal position of the early twenty-first century in relation to the recent past: we live at the turning point where the great
hiatus wrought by the destruction of large segments of the European population—Jewish communities and other exterminated minorities, vast civil
populations, and the combatants themselves—has begun to retreat beyond
the purview of the living memory of the survivors into the depths of history.
And the passage of the collective memory of living generations into history
modifies our perception of this radical caesura within our present horizon
of contemporaneity, even while our renewed preoccupation with this period
attests the intensity of the burden it has bequeathed.

Out of the many contemporary fictional representations of the dread of
collective memory and of the terror of history, I dwell on the seminal example
provided by W. G. Sebald's novel, *Austerlitz*. In this novel, Sebald deals in
a particularly evocative manner with the complex interrelation of the different levels of personal, small-group, and large-scale remembrance of collective
memory and the historical past. The novel recounts the story of a young child,
Jacques Austerlitz who, at the age of four and a half, in the period between the
Nazi invasion of Czechoslovakia and the outbreak of World War II, is sent by
his mother on one of the last authorized trains of the *Kindertransport* from

Prague to Wales. Upon his arrival in Wales, he is sheltered by a Calvinist minister and his wife, who never reveal to him the details of his past. After giving him a new name, they conceal from him his original identity. Following the lead of his foster parents, the child himself, as he is growing up, adopts the practice of avoiding all attempts to recall his early life and, over the years, he succeeds in repressing his memory of it. It is upon completing secondary school, when he has to sign official papers in order to accept a scholarship award, that he learns the name he was given at birth. In the following years, he begins to experience marked psychological troubles that continually haunt him and make it difficult for him to lead a productive life. Gradually, as "scraps of memory" began to "drift through the outlying regions of [his] mind," he is led to search for the forgotten past that he is not able to obliterate.[76] Through a series of fortuitous discoveries, among them the disused ladies' waiting room in London's Liverpool Station where, many years earlier, he had waited for his foster parents when he first arrived in England, he is brought to discover his past. This experience provides the decisive triggering event through which memories begin to return—memories, as Austerlitz exclaims, "behind and within which many things much further back in the past seemed to lie, all interlocking like the labyrinthine vaults I saw in the dusty grey light, and which seemed to go on and on forever."[77] He is able to discover his country of origin and, through the help of a former neighbor following his return to Prague, he is brought to face the traumatic events of his early past, including the separation from his parents, who were subsequently murdered during the war.

Two aspects of this fictive narrative, which adapts techniques of the historical novel to a contemporary theme, are of particular interest for our discussion. The first concerns the interrelation of the personal past with that of the protagonist's larger social and historical setting. Throughout his youth Austerlitz avoids not only uncomfortable questions concerning his origin but also concerning religion, social status, and group identity: "It never occurred to me," as he states, "to wonder about my true origins, [. . .] nor did I ever feel that I belonged to a certain social class, professional group, or religious confession."[78] Moreover, although he becomes a specialist of European architectural history, he continually deflects his attention from the recent history of Europe, such as that of twentieth-century Germany, the Vichy regime, the Nazi occupation of Europe, and its consequences. As he grows older, this obliges him to confine his thought within an ever more specialized space of attention, leading him, as he states, to "recollect as little as possible, avoiding everything which related in any way to my unknown past."[79] Here the intertwining of an individual and a collective past, of personal and group memory with the collective recollection and historical past retained in omnipresent public awareness gradually makes it impossible for him to avoid facing his own personal identity and the social and historical milieu with which it is intermeshed.

At another level of interpretation, the protagonist's discovery of his personal past and, in relation to this, of frightful aspects of the collective past that have marked his development, reach beyond the framework of a personal psychological problem to encompass awareness of the broader implications of the collective repression of dreadful memories, above all in regard to the recent past. Through the metaphor of architecture that Sebald elaborates toward the end of the novel, he introduces the idea that municipal zoning and urban renewal are effective vehicles for the tacit collective repression of the dreadful memories of the past. Illustrating his description by means of evocative photographic images, he develops this idea in relation to the recent transfer of the old French national library to a new location. The old Bibliothèque Nationale in Paris, on the rue de Richelieu, was situated in the vibrant center of the city, near the stock market and financial center, the Opera, and the galleries and passages in neighboring streets, the French Theatre, and the splendid rectangular edifice and public garden of the Palais Royal. Constructed during the reign of Napoleon III in the 1860s, the elegant reading rooms of the old Bibliothèque Nationale were frequented by numerous generations of intellectuals who came from all points of the globe, and it served as a center of intellectual life in France throughout the twentieth century. In the 1990s, in view of the shortage of space in the old Bibliothèque Nationale, the Mitterrand government decided to construct four gigantic modern towers to replace it, which were located in a more or less disaffected part of the city behind the dilapidated Austerlitz train station, which the government and the urban planners sought to develop. As Sebald insists in his vivid and highly critical description, the result of this transfer was to sever intellectual activity in the library from the historic center of Paris and from its social, economic, and cultural life, and to move it to a secluded and sterile modern setting. More important still, the site chosen for the new Bibliothèque Nationale de France was previously occupied by a vast network of warehouses that, like numerous other sites recently renovated by urban planners, had served purposes associated with traumatic episodes of the past. These vast warehouses, as Sebald reminds us, were the sites where the precious belongings of many thousands of Jewish families were stored after they had been driven from their homes, which, like the belongings themselves, were expropriated by the German and

French authorities before the families were sent to meet their deaths in Eastern Europe. From this large network of warehouses, more than seven thousand trains crammed with confiscated goods transferred them from the Austerlitz station to the German Reich.

It is here, by means of metaphors drawn from architecture and urban renewal, that Sebald brings home a principal motif of the novel as a whole: attempts to obliterate the past, he subtly suggests, are no more feasible on the collective level than they are in regard to the personal past. Far from presenting a solution to the problem, the attempt to exclude dreadful memories of the past, whether on an individual or on a collective level, can only be an invitation to the kind of cramped sterility and rootless amnesia that the fictive protagonist Jacques Austerlitz encounters, which prevent him from surmounting the burden of the past he seeks to avoid.

A plausible objection might readily be raised against this point of view. However much the requirements for urban renewal may have coincided with the effacing of traces of the past, have we nonetheless not developed a culture which, far from forgetting the past, promotes ongoing commemoration, while favoring the proliferation of archives, museums, and monuments, indeed of national libraries themselves, in an ongoing effort to retain the past's most minute traces? Are these publicly sponsored attempts not born of a desire to prevent amnesia by recalling painful legacies of the past?

Here, it seems to me, we may reach beyond Sebald's fictional metaphors and respond that institutionalized attempts to retrieve and retain what living memory of the past has experienced and physical traces attest are lent a sense of urgency as memory begins to fade, above all following a period of obstruction and neglect of the dreadful memories that the past has bequeathed. If, in light of the enormity of the Shoah and the profound hiatus it occasioned, it has reemerged into the forefront of historical attention after several decades of indifference, this only highlighted long-standing neglect or repression of other kinds of painful memories, experienced by different groups over the course of past decades and centuries. From this perspective, it is perhaps not surprising that preoccupation with dreadful memories of the recent past should simultaneously call to the fore the difficult experiences encountered in different and more remote periods. Indeed, the painful legacy of the practice of enslavement to which African populations fell victim, though it had different ends than the quest for a "final solution," was long shunned as a theme of public discussion, in part due to forms of discrimination to which, until recent decades, their descendants were subjected. After centuries of near oblivion and relative public unconcern, such painful themes of the historical past and of more recent memory have fueled current preoccupation with obstructed memory and with commemoration and have lent a new significance to historical research.

In the final analysis, Sebald's narrative in *Austerlitz* suggests that the real density of the collective past persists in the present, even where awareness of it has been obstructed. This is indeed a manner of response, reaching perhaps beyond Sebald's own intentions, to skepticism regarding the ongoing reality of the historical past, toward which the historian claims to direct her analysis. At the very least, it provides matter for further reflection concerning the assumption inspired by Nietzsche and propagated in fashionable theories during the decades directly following World War II that the facts of the past "never have more than a linguistic existence" and that, ultimately, they are figments of the historian's imagination.

The Province of Collective Memory and Its Theoretical Promise

In the different chapters of this book we have traversed an extensive territory encompassing a number of areas of investigation. Each of them has aimed to contribute to the elaboration of a philosophical basis for the concept of collective memory and to delimit the scope of this concept in relation to the historical past. In this concluding section of my work, I will propose an overview of the principal elements I have investigated in view of the broader aim that a theory of collective memory entails.

I

As I conceive of it, the specific province of collective memory may be placed in evidence through an assessment of its relation to memory as a general human faculty interwoven with a totality of capacities of perceiving and imagining, thinking and willing. In this general function, memory may be examined from a variety of viewpoints, presented for example by psychology, biology, cognitive science, literature, or other disciplines. Nonetheless, in spite of this variety of approaches that are currently available for its study, I have granted a privilege to investigation of historical variations in its interpretation over the course of centuries among the predominant traditions that have attempted to define its significance and scope since Greek antiquity. According to my argument, variations in the predominant philosophical approaches to memory in given historical periods are not merely fortuitous speculations, but owe their persuasive force to the fundamental convictions they convey concerning the sense of human existence and of human interaction in the sociopolitical sphere.

Viewed in historical perspective, the phenomenon of collective memory appears in a singular light. On one hand, collective remembrance, as it has been embodied in age-old practices, is as old as human communal existence and the symbolic realms that forge its cohesion. These practices were elaborated in a great variety of ways in accord with oral traditions that, over the course of time, were substantially modified following the development of traditions in written and codified form. Be this as it may, in spite of its ancient sources, the theoretical focus on this phenomenon, and the term *collective memory* as we use it in contemporary discourse, are of recent vintage, and they bear the traces of the historical situation in which they arose. This recent emergence of theoretical interest in collective memory has directed my attention in this work to the specific sociopolitical functions it fulfills in the contemporary world.

The rise of theoretical preoccupation with collective memory coincided with the decline of more traditional ways of accounting for collective cohesion in the sociopolitical sphere. Its conceptual visibility corresponded to the weakening of the conviction that immutable metaphysical ideas or, in a more modern perspective, all-encompassing philosophies of history or ideologies might definitively account for human identity and sociopolitical existence. Whereas in the relatively stable framework of premodern societies, the continuity of collective existence was postulated in terms of fixed metaphysical principles, in a later period theories of the cohesion of the social order were sustained by assumptions concerning the intelligibility of human historical development. Following the ever more general experience of radical discontinuity and dislocation that gained momentum in the decades before and after World War I, such assumptions began to lose all plausibility. The radical historicity and contingency that became ever more visible in the passage of succeeding generations fueled a climate of "crisis"—what was often perceived as a crisis of relativism or historicism—that brought the experience of discontinuity and dislocation to clear theoretical expression. At this precise juncture, theoretical attention began to turn toward the phenomenon of collective memory and to its role as a source of social cohesion and continuity. In light of this generalized perception of radical discontinuity at the different levels of group and public life, the concept of collective memory began to reoccupy the place left vacant by the decline of traditional ideas of human identity. In more recent decades it has been increasingly invoked to frame the discourse of cohesion and continuity of the sociopolitical realm. It is in this contemporary situation that the concept of collective memory calls for an appropriate theoretical foundation.

I I

In our contemporary context, the difficulty of elaborating a theoretical foundation for the concept of collective memory becomes immediately apparent, above all where it is extended beyond small groups or associations to encompass the vast sphere of public existence in mass society. This difficulty comes to light when we acknowledge that memory in its original sense always transpires in the personal sphere of individual rememberers and that, at a fundamental level, it involves direct encounters among individuals and groups in the context of a lifeworld. All secondary or indirect sources of remembrance presuppose this original form of experience. Nevertheless, direct experience and remembrance of *publicly* significant events, beyond the scope of small groups and associations, are normally possible only for a tiny minority of eyewitnesses. Remembrance of events endowed with public significance is almost always based on indirect reports or accounts diffused among the vast strata of contemporary mass societies. This indirect quality of public remembrance underlies the paradoxical disparity that I have situated between remembered experience in the original sense and collective remembrance of actions and events in the public sphere. In view of the gap between original remembrance and the indirect quality of what is retained in the diffuse representations of vast collectivities, the concept of collective memory might itself seem dubious. It might even be claimed that collective memory, since it rarely corresponds to any direct and original form of remembered experience, is essentially a figment of the social imagination.

From the standpoint I have adopted in this book, a convincing theoretical resolution of this problem depends on an adequate conception of the multiple facets of the imagination. The imagination, as we have seen, far from limited to the production of fantasy or fiction, configures the patterns of symbolic interaction through which remembered experience is made communicable among vast groups. This theory of the imagination at the same time calls for a reevaluation of the complex role of the symbol. It attributes to the symbol not only the narrow function of representing through images what cannot be presented in direct apprehension—for instance, the state or the supersensuous quality of the sacred—but accords to it the broad function of lending general spatiotemporal and logical pattern to experience. In this function, symbols confer a communicable sense to what is apprehended and remembered in the original sphere, and they do so in a manner that lends it coherence in the larger weave of what we acknowledge to be publicly intelligible reality.

This manner of interpreting the symbol has at the same time called for a deeper exploration of the temporal articulations of collective memory. Here we encounter a realm of collective remembrance that is not confined to voluntary acts nor to the express aim of bequeathing remembered experience to posterity. At different levels and in different forms, the active exercise of group remembrance draws on a passive basis. The passive preconditions of collective remembrance comprise a many-layered network of collectively communicable symbolic configurations, interwoven over time in the shared context of contemporaneous living generations, which I have identified as a common "horizon of contemporaneity." However fragmented the memories shared among different groups may be, communication among them depends upon the web of spontaneously graspable symbols that defines the contours of their contemporaneity and sets it apart from the historical past outside all living memory. Beyond the demise of single individuals and groups, the disappearance of living generations signals the evanescence of the horizon of contemporaneity in which their symbolic interaction transpired. Following the disappearance of this theater of group interaction, the legibility of the symbolic structures embedded in it begins to weaken. Even where the broad intelligibility of general linguistic and other symbolic categories is retained over centuries, the more specific nuances groups invest in them, constituting the living context and intrinsic sense of their coexistence, are subject to remarkable and often barely palpable variability as collective memory recedes into the historical past. In a situation of radical discontinuity, the passage of each successive generation marks a drift in the symbolic framework of communication and interaction. Such an abrupt change in context, calling forth mostly imperceptible displacements of its passive reaches, casts in its wake a deepening shroud over the essential significance of the symbolic patterns that constitute the past's singular texture.

In our contemporary world, the emergence of increasingly anonymous and fragmented conditions of public existence indicates the distance of our present horizon of contemporaneity from the historical past. Corresponding to this development, transformations in the public sphere over the past century have been channeled by the novel technical evolution of the mass media. Their ever-growing predominance as organs of public information has tended to accentuate the disparity between the lifeworld of original experience and remembrance and the public space that the mass media configure. Here, as I have illustrated, the gap between remembered experience in the immediate lifeworld and the information the mass media disseminate appears not only as a difference between experienced events and their representation, but as a reframing of events in terms of an autonomous symbolic order constituted by the virtual spatiotemporal pattern and logic of mass communications. As I have argued, this autonomous symbolic order draws its potency from an uncanny ability to simulate direct experience while *dissimulating* the gap that separates it from the immediate lifeworld in which it originates. In this framework, as we have seen, the format of mass communications has become a principle contemporary source of public visibility, indeed of an iconic status which, as it is publicly conveyed and remembered, is readily translated into novel contemporary forms of public influence. The mass-media format, which enables the spontaneous communication and global impact of information, gives testimony to essential transformations in the modes of organization of the public sphere. Here the mass media have served both as a mirror and a vehicle of discontinuity in regard to past forms of public life.

III

In a public world rent by successive waves of discontinuity and dislocation, the broad preoccupation with collective memory—expressed in the form of commemorations, theoretical preoccupations, or the creation of museums and archives—orients a quest for cohesion and continuity. The contemporary period of increasing public concern with collective remembrance is paradoxically also one in which the limits of collective memory become increasingly palpable. The concern for remembrance has brought ever more clearly into view a specific finitude that is intrinsic to group perspectives. Indeed, as I interpret it, the phenomenon of collective memory reveals a fundamental order of collective finitude that cannot be elucidated, as Martin Heidegger and his school have held, in virtue of the singular existence of mortal beings who choose a way of being in the face of future death. And, if it is not accountable through the singularity of mortal beings, the specific regime of collective finitude does not participate in a super-individual medium in which remembrance might surmount the limited perspective of human historical existence. Group coexistence and remembrance in a common world reveal their finitude in the network of shared language, gestures, styles, and other symbols that are continually subject to modification over time. This comes nowhere more clearly to light than in the collective incapacity, through *memory*, to rise beyond its contemporaneous symbolic horizon to plumb the remote depths of the historical past.

My attempt to demarcate the finite bounds in which living group experience and remembrance are inscribed has led me to emphasize what I take to be the eminently critical aim that a theory of collective memory entails. This critical aim is directed against assumptions that overlook the specific regime of remembered finitude and erase the boundary between collective memory and the historical past. It is engaged above all where the reach of collective memory is extended beyond its finite limits to encompass the remote historical past. In this regard, the delineation of the bounds of collective memory serves to highlight the illusory quality of beliefs according to which the historical past might be retrieved as if it were available to living memory and placed at the disposal of the present. It is this belief, as we have seen, that has fueled the widespread political mythology according to which a shared past might potentially resurge, so to speak, from the "earth and the dead" and confer on living groups ancient and venerable powers. In designating the singularity of the remote past and its irreducible alterity in view of the present, my aim is to deflate mythical claims concerning the scope of collective memory and to distinguish it from the historical past lying beyond it.

The possibility of making the distinction between collective memory and the historical past does not only depend on elucidation of the finite regime of collective memory but, at the same time, of the real temporal context of the historical past that, in spite of its remoteness, the historian claims to retrieve. Here it is the skeptical doubt leveled against the historian's claim that must be critically appraised. This doubt appeals to the unavoidable distance between language and the reality of events and, on this basis, disputes the possibility that the historian's attempts to fit past events into a plausible narrative might encounter something of past reality. This doubt undermines the possibility of distinguishing between critical methods of reconstruction on a factual basis and fictions or mythological elaborations.

My attempt to defend the legitimacy of the historian's claim has relied less on historical works themselves than on novels. Even if the historian's narrative is admittedly partial and subject to organization in terms of his or her particular viewpoint, my use of the novel in no way disputes the importance of factual analysis for historical accounts. Novels, however, may well illustrate that what we term the "reality" of the past corresponds not only to an assemblage of verifiable details, but also to patterns of contextual nuance implicit in the past's symbolic structure. Here, by mirroring subtle and often barely perceptible modifications in contextual pattern, novels may sound the finite depths of collective memory and reveal the dynamics of its passage into the historical past.

The doubt voiced by historical pyrrhonism reduces the historian's representations to the merely imaginative projection of the historian's present constructions onto a past to which they are ineluctably foreign. The claim to historical knowledge is in these terms no more than an illusory expression of present concerns and, in this manner, pyrrhonism undercuts any meaningful distinction that might be made between collective memory retained by present generations and the historical past. By contrast, my insistence on the essential difference between the temporal orders of memory and of history is animated by the conviction that skeptical assumptions concerning the irreducible opacity of the historical past risk engendering a self-fulfilling prophecy. Where, indeed, such assumptions are soberly entertained and all hope of finding meaning in a real past is abandoned, the only remaining criterion is that of the timely standard of the present. Where the past in its essential alterity no longer provides a backdrop for critical evaluation of the present and current attitudes provide the sole measure for reality, it is above all the present that risks growing opaque to itself.

NOTES

INTRODUCTION

1. Historians and sociologists who work on this theme have often referred to this contemporary preoccupation with collective memory as a "memory boom" that signals a specific feature of our current civilization; see, for example, Jan Assmann, *Cultural Memory and Early Civilization*, vii–xii; Andreas Huyssen, "Present Pasts: Media, Politics, Amnesia"; Wulf Kannsteiner, "Finding Meaning in Memory"; Kerwin Lee Klein, "On the Emergence of Memory in Historical Discourse"; Pierre Nora, "L'avènement mondial de la mémoire"; Jeffrey K. Olick, "Collective Memory"; Jay Winter, *Remembering War*, 1–17. For a useful anthology of classic studies of collective memory, see Jeffrey K. Olick, Vered Vinitzky-Seroussi, and Daniel Levy, *The Collective Memory Reader*.

2. Plato, *Phaedo* 76d–77a, in *Works*, 1:266–69.

3. Ibid., 76e, 266–67.

4. G. W. Leibniz, *Nouveaux essais sur l'entendement humain*, 41–42. Unless otherwise indicated, all translations from foreign-language works are my own.

5. A more direct source of the Leibnizian theory of reminiscence was probably the philosophy of St. Augustine. Although he drew on the Platonic theory of the eternity of the soul and of the ideas recollected by reminiscence, St. Augustine criticized, due to its incompatibility with Christian doctrine, the Platonic presupposition of the pre-existence of souls before birth. Leibniz adopted a similar argument in the *New Essays Concerning Human Understanding*; see his *Nouveaux essais*, 75. See, in this regard, St. Augustine, *De Trinitate*, in *Œuvres*, vol. 16, bk. 12, 256.

6. On Aristotle's theory of memory in this treatise, see especially the translation and commentary by Richard Sorabji in *Aristotle on Memory*.

7. Leibniz, *Nouveaux essais*, 42.

8. Locke did not distinguish between the functions of memory and reminiscence but regrouped all of the mnemonic operations under the general heading of memory.

9. Aristotle, *De Anima* 430a, 134–35.

10. John Locke, *An Essay Concerning Human Understanding*, 302.

11. Henri Bergson, *Matière et Mémoire*, 148.

12. Ibid., 87.

13. Ibid., 89.

14. G. W. F. Hegel, *Phänomenologie des Geistes*, 3:591.

15. On Hegel's conception of memory in *The Phenomenology of Spirit*, see Donald Phillip Verene, *Hegel's Recollection*; and, more recently, Angelica Nuzzo, *Memory, History, Justice in Hegel*.

16. Hegel, *Phänomenologie des Geistes*, 590–51. "Erinnerung" signifies both memory and interiorization.

17. Hegel explicitly cited Herder's words in his *Vorlesungen über die Geschichte der Philosophie*, vol. 1, in *Werke*, 18:21.

18. Ernest Renan, *L'avenir de la science: Pensées de 1848*, 172–73.

19. Ernest Renan, *Qu'est-ce qu'une nation? et autres essais politiques*, 54.

20. Droysen, Johann Gustav, *Historik: Vorlesungen über Enzyklopädie und Methodologie der Geschichte*, 31.

21. Ibid., 325.

22. Wilhelm Dilthey, *Der Aufbau der geschichtlichen Welt in den Geisteswissenschaften*, 7:213–16.

23. Ibid., 7:277.

24. Benedetto Croce, *Aesthetic as a Science of Expression and General Linguistic*, 28–29.

25. Dilthey, *Aufbau der geschichtlichen Welt*, 7:215–16.

26. Croce, *Aesthetic*, 29.

27. Benedetto Croce, *Theory and History of Historiography*, 25.

28. In identifying what he took to be a Platonic motif at the heart of Hegel's philosophy of history, Croce raised a point that equally concerned his own historical theory: "And since the philosophy of history is transcendental in its internal structure, it is not surprising that it showed itself to be such in all the very varied forms it assumed. [. . .] Hegel, a great destroyer of Platonism, yet remained to a considerable extent engaged in it, so tenacious is that enemy which every thinker carries in himself and which he should tear from his heart, yet cannot resist" (ibid., 281–82). In his early lectures on the phenomenology of religion, Martin Heidegger discerned this Platonic motif in contemporary historical theory, which he considered to be a subtle reformulation of the ancient quest for stability and permanence in the midst of historical flux. See Martin Heidegger, "Einleitung in die Phänomenologie der Religion" (1920–21), 39–50.

29. Droysen, *Historik*, 327.

30. Ibid., *Historik*, 63.

31. Friedrich Nietzsche, *Vom Nutzen und Nachteil der Historie für das Leben*, pt. 1, 268.

32. Ibid., 251.

33. Ibid., 305.

34. Ibid., 288–90. Paraphrasing Schiller, Nietzsche compared modern historical methods with the superficial understanding that is unable to see "certain things that a child nevertheless sees and is unable to hear what a child nevertheless hears; these things are, however, what is most important" (ibid., 276).

35. Ibid., 292.

36. Ibid., 268, 299

37. Here is one example: "I presuppose that in all that is organic there is memory and a kind of spirit: the apparatus is so fine that it would not seem to exist" (Friedrich Nietzsche, *Nachgelassene Fragmente: Frühjahr—Herbst 1884*, 403). On this point, see Gregory Moore, *Nietzsche, Biology, and Metaphor*.

38. Nietzsche was familiar with Francis Galton's theories of inherited characteristics and, for example, cites his work *Hereditary Genius: Its Laws and Consequences* in a letter sent to August Strindberg on December 7, 1888; see Friedrich Nietzsche, *Aus dem Nachlass der Achzigerjahre: Briefe (1861–89)*, 929. Gregory Moore has pointed out similarities between Nietzsche's conception of organic memory and those propounded by contemporaries, such as Ewald Hering, in *Über das Gedächtnis als eine allgemeine Funktion der organischen Materie* (1870); Ernst Haeckel, beginning with his *Theorie der Zellseele* (1866); or Samuel Butler, in his work *Unconscious Memory* (1880); see Moore, *Nietzsche, Biology, and Metaphor*, 34–42.

39. Friedrich Nietzsche, *Jenseits von Gut und Böse*, 228–29.

40. Friedrich Nietzsche, *Zur Genealogie der Moral*, pt. 2, 313. On the question of Nietzsche's theory of biological adaptation in relation to social control, see Christian J. Emden, *Friedrich Nietzsche and the Politics of History*, 275–77.

41. See Freud's comments on Hering and Butler in appendix A to his essay "The Unconscious" (1915), 205.

42. Sigmund Freud, "On Narcissism: An Introduction" (1914), 78–79.

43. Sigmund Freud, "Screen Memories," 303–22.

44. Sigmund Freud, "Remembering, Repeating, Working Through" (1914), 145–56.

45. Sigmund Freud, *The Interpretation of Dreams*, pt. 1 (1900), 141–44.

46. Sigmund Freud, "Group Psychology and the Analysis of the Ego" (1921), 69–70.

47. Ibid., 122–28.

48. Sigmund Freud, *The Future of an Illusion*, 42.

49. Sigmund Freud, "On Narcissism: An Introduction," 78.

50. Sigmund Freud, *Moses and Monotheism* (1937–39), 100.

51. Ibid., 99–100.

52. "The group (*die Masse*) appears to us as a revival of the primal horde." Freud, "Group Psychology," 123.

53. According to Helmuth Plessner's apt terminology, this is the "sphere of communal familiarity" ("*Sphäre gemeinschaftlicher Vertrautheit*"); see Helmuth Plessner, "Grenzen der Gemeinschaft: Eine Kritik des sozialen Radikalismus (1924)," 55–56; see, in this light, Volker Gerhardt, *Öffentlichkeit: Die politische Form des Bewusstseins*, 202–7.

54. Martin Heidegger, *Sein und Zeit*, 125.

55. Ibid., 126.

56. Ibid., 127.

57. Paul Valéry, "La conquête de l'ubiquité." Walter Benjamin cited this text as an epigraph to his essay "The Work of Art in the Age of Mechanical Reproduction," 217.

58. Fernand Léger, "Les réalisations picturales actuelles" (Contemporary achievements in painting), 20–21; Piet Mondrian, "La nouvelle plastique dans la peinture," 20.

59. Walter Benjamin, "The Storyteller," 87.

60. Ibid., 98.

61. Maurice Halbwachs, *The Psychology of Social Class*, 22.

62. Maurice Halbwachs, *La mémoire collective*, 128–29.

63. Ibid., 129.

64. Ibid., 70.

65. Ibid., 83–91.

66. See, in this regard, Paul Ricœur's remarks on Halbwachs in *Memory, History, Forgetting*, 120–24; Jeffrey K. Olick has pointed out the tension in Halbwachs's thought between a collective memory that exists only in the minds of remembering individuals and the collectively shared symbolic representations in which individual memories are anchored; see his "Collective Memory: The Two Cultures," 335–36.

67. Halbwachs, *La mémoire collective*, 129.

68. Ibid., 130.

69. Hippolyte Taine, *Essais de critique et d'histoire*, 237.

70. Hippolyte Taine, *Histoire de la littérature anglaise*, 4:277.

71. Halbwachs, *La mémoire collective*, 131.

CHAPTER 1

1. Edmund Husserl, *Zur Phänomenologie der Intersubjektivität*, 278–79; Klaus Held, *Lebendige Gegenwart*.

2. Chateaubriand's account of the aim of his work is found in a manuscript preserved in the archives of Combourg, France; see the introduction by Maurice Levaillant in François-René de Chateaubriand, *Mémoires d'outre-tombe*, 1:x–xi (1951).

3. Chateaubriand, *Mémoires d'outre-tombe*, 1:221–22 (1951).

4. Niklas Luhmann, *Die Realität der Massenmedien*; Jane Feuer, "The Concept of Live Television," 13–16.

5. For an account of debate on this question, see the commentary by Jean-Claude Berchet in the footnotes of the Garnier (1989) edition of *Mémoires d'outre-tombe*, 1:739–40, where the editor suggests that Chateaubriand probably did encounter Washington, although he perhaps simplified the sequence of events in harmony with the structure of his narrative.

6. In this regard, a useful distinction has recently been made between what has been termed "eyewitness" and "flesh-witness" narratives. This distinction accounts for the difference between events witnessed by parties who are not themselves involved in recorded interaction and "flesh-witness" narratives by those who directly participate in the events. The concept of "flesh-witnessing" is particularly important in accounting for the difficulty of translating direct experience of traumatic events into readily representable categories. See the issue of *Partial Answers* on eyewitness narratives, and especially the articles by Yuval Noah Harari, "Scholars, Eyewitnesses, and Flesh-Witnesses of War"; and Sarah Liu, "The Illiterate Reader," 213–28, and 319–42, respectively. On trauma, memory, and the perplexities of verbal expression, see also the insightful work of Richard Kearney, *On Stories*, 15–76.

7. See, in this regard, Renaud Dulong, *Le témoin oculaire*. On the concept of the witness, see C. A. J. Coady, *Testimony*.

8. Benedict Anderson, *Imagined Communities*, 6.

9. Friedrich Nietzsche, *Die Geburt der Tragödie, Kritische Gesamtausgabe*, vol. 3, pt. 1, 142.

10. Friedrich Nietzsche, *Vom Nutzen und Nachteil der Historie für das Leben*, pt. 1, 292.

11. In *De Anima* (434a) Aristotle already clearly distinguished between a sensuous imagination (*aesthetike phantasia*) common to humans and other animals, and a deliberative imagination (*bouleutike phantasia*), which only humans possess; see Aristotle, *De Anima*, 3.154–55. For Goethe, imagination takes on a further sense as a capacity to distinguish the "truth of reality" or, as he remarked in a comment to Eckermann, "an imagination for the truth of the real" ("*Phantasie für die Wahrheit des Realen*"); see Goethe, *Eckermann Gespräche mit Goethe*,154. See in this vein Ernst Cassirer's interpretation of Goethe and the imagination in *An Essay on Man*, 204–6.

12. My approach to the symbol is in part inspired by the thought of Ernst Cassirer. What I have borrowed from him concerns less the theory of symbolic forms that he presented in the three volumes of his *Philosophy of Symbolic Forms* than what he conceived to be the "primordial forms of synthesis" (*Urformen der Synthesis*)— space, time, and number—for which symbols provide the ordering principle. See Ernst Cassirer, *Philosophie der symbolischen Formen*, 3:17. In a different philosophical framework, Nelson Goodman made at least implicit use of the symbol in what I take to be both its narrower and broader senses. For Goodman, symbols may stand for

things or elements other than themselves. Yet the symbol is not limited to this role for, at another level, it exercises what he aptly termed a more general, "world-making" function. A "world," as he wrote, "may be made up of atoms or qualities, of ordinary objects of certain kinds or of other kinds, of riotous Soutine-like or geometric Braque-like patterns." See Nelson Goodman, "Routes of Reference," 130. It would reach beyond my present discussion of the symbol to investigate the nuances that distinguish Cassirer's theory of symbolic forms from Goodman's analytical approach to the symbol. I note only that Goodman, in his initial discussion of the symbol in his book *Ways of World-Making*, elucidated his concept of the symbol's world-making function with explicit reference to the work of Ernst Cassirer. See *Ways of World-Making*, 1.

13. Edward S. Casey's concepts of "implacement" and "displacement" set in relief this aspect of the phenomenology of spatial apprehension as it is presupposed in everyday experience. See his *Getting Back into Place*, 3–39.

14. Edmund Husserl, *Die Bernauer Manuskripte über das Zeitbewusstsein (1917/18)*, 327–54; see also Edmund Husserl, *Erfahrung und Urteil*, 184–207.

15. Chateaubriand, *Mémoires d'outre-tombe*, 1:223 (1951).

CHAPTER 2

1. Martin Luther King Jr., "I Have a Dream," 224.

2. Ibid., 223.

3. In his *Lectures on Aesthetics* Hegel underlined the role of clothing, which lends significance to pure nudity. It is through clothing that an individual is situated in his or her temporal context. See Hegel, *Vorlesungen über die Ästhetik*, 2:406, 409. In a later period Roland Barthes highlighted this Hegelian idea in *Système de la mode*, where he quoted Hegel's *Aesthetics*: "As purely given to the senses, the body is unable to signify: clothing assures the passage from the sensuous to sense" (288n). In his elucidation of the phenomenon of fashion, Roland Barthes has analyzed clothing in terms of a system of signs that, in a similar way, concerns "a great number of cultural objects." "As functional as it may be," he perceptively writes, "real clothing always contains the element of a signal" (ibid., 294).

4. It is in this sense that Halbwachs refers to a "dissolution of continuity" ("*solution de continuité*"), to which I referred in the introduction; see Maurice Halbwachs, *La mémoire collective*, 130.

5. Chateaubriand, *Mémoires d'outre-tombe*, 1:181–82 (1951).

6. In the face of the unforeseeable and at times astonishing events of history, Hans Blumenberg has elaborated his conception of the "impoverished capacity of fantasy" (*Leistungsarmut der Phantasie*). Fantasy is impoverished because it is tied to the perspective of a given "historical place." Blumenberg writes in this regard, "The impoverished capacity of fantasy confirms nothing else than that, in its specific historical place, under the spell of blindness, it is able to accomplish only a reinforcement of existing circumstances" (*Arbeit am Mythos*, 179).

7. King Jr., "I Have a Dream," 226.

8. On this theme, see Drew D. Hansen, *The Dream: Martin Luther King, Jr. and the Speech That Inspired a Nation*, 214–29.

9. The theme of "fragmented memory" has been explored in the stimulating analysis of Doron Mendels, *Memory in Jewish, Pagan and Christian Societies of the Graeco-Roman World*, 30–47.

CHAPTER 3

1. John Locke, *An Essay Concerning Human Understanding*, 302.

2. Ibid., 311.

3. "Who can tell me," as Hume wrote in *A Treatise of Human Nature*, "what were his thoughts and actions on the 1st of January 1715, the 11th of March 1719, and the 3rd of August 1733? [. . .] Memory does not so much produce as discover personal identity" (David Hume, *A Treatise of Human Nature*, 309–10).

4. G. W. Leibniz, *Nouveaux essais concernant l'entendement humain*, 220.

5. Ibid., 219.

6. Ibid., 219. The speaker here is Theophile, who, in the *New Essays concerning Human Understanding*, represents the viewpoint of Leibniz.

7. Marcel Proust, *A la recherche du temps perdu*, 3:146.

8. Ibid., 3:488.

9. Marcel Proust, *Contre Sainte-Beuve*, 559.

10. Proust, *A la recherche du temps perdu*, 1:47–48.

11. Walter Benjamin, "On Some Motifs in Baudelaire," 159.

12. Hannah Arendt stressed the point that the web of interrelated facts ultimately stands beyond the reach of ideological interests that attempt to manipulate them: "That facts are not secure in the hands of power is obvious, but the point here is that power, by its very nature, can never produce a substitute for the secure stability of factual reality, which, because it is past, has grown into a dimension beyond our reach. Facts assert themselves by being stubborn, and their fragility is oddly combined with great resiliency—the same irreversibility that is the hallmark of all human action" (*Between Past and Future*, 258–59).

13. Niklas Luhmann, *Die Realität der Massenmedien*, 11.

14. See the remarks of Alexis de Tocqueville in *De la démocratie en Amérique*, (2:122):

I am very well convinced that even among democratic nations, the genius, the vices, or the virtues of certain individuals retard or accelerate the natural current of a people's history; but causes of this secondary or fortuitous nature are infinitely more various, more concealed, more complex, less powerful, and consequently less easy to trace in periods of equality than in ages of aristocracy, when the task of the historian is simply to detach from the mass of general events the particular influences of one man or of a few men. In the former case the historian is soon wearied by the work; his mind loses itself in this labyrinth; and, in his inability clearly to discern or conspicuously to point out the influence of individuals, he denies their existence. He prefers talking about the characteristics of race, the physical conformation of the country, or the genius of civilization, which abridges his own labors, and far better satisfies his reader at less cost.

1. Paul Ricœur, *Freud and Philosophy*, 9–10.

2. Ibid., 514–43.

3. Paul Ricœur, *Time and Narrative*, 1:54.

4. Paul Ricœur, *Memory, History, Forgetting*, 102–9, 120–24.

5. Edmund Husserl, *Cartesian Meditations*, 128–29.

6. Ricœur, *Memory, History, Forgetting*, 118–19.

7. Ricœur, *Freud and Philosophy*, 439; Paul Ricœur, *Oneself as Another*, 16–23.

8. Ricœur, *Memory, History, Forgetting*, 119.

9. Tzvetan Todorov, *Les abus de la mémoire*, 56.

10. Paul Ricœur, *Memory, History, Forgetting*, 85–86. In the twenty-second Marc Bloch Lecture held at the Sorbonne in June, 2000, Ricœur reiterated his opinion that it was no longer fruitful to refer to a "debt of memory" in regard to the Jewish victims of the Shoah, and he favored in its place the idea of a working-through of the trauma of the past; see Paul Ricœur, "L'écriture de l'histoire et la representation du passé." For a critical response to this idea, see Rainer Rochlitz, "La mémoire privatisée," and "Mémoire et pardon," in *Le Vif de la critique*, 3:257–71, as well as Sarah Gensburger and Marie-Claire Lavabre, "Entre 'devoir de mémoire' et 'abus de mémoire,'" 75–98.

11. Gerard M. Edelman, *The Remembered Present*, 8.

12. Ibid., 248.

13. Wilfred Quine, *Quiddities*, 132–33.

14. Donald Davidson, *Essays on Actions and Events*, 214.

15. Husserl's *Prolegomena to Pure Logic* presents in my opinion the most convincing argument in favor of this conception of the intrinsic validity of truth. See Edmund Husserl, *Prolegomena zur reinen Logik*, vol. 1.

16. Pierre Nora, "Entre mémoire et histoire," xvii.

17. Ibid., xix.

18. In evoking the work of contemporary social scientists, Aleida Assmann has contested this conclusion concerning the demise of collective memory, given the particularly important role it has assumed both in the practices and theoretical work of our times. See her *Erinnerungsräume*, 15.

19. Nora, "Entre mémoire et histoire," xvii.

20. Pierre Nora, "Introduction," 13. On Nora's methodology, see Frank Ankersmit, *Sublime Historical Experience*, 262.

21. Christiane Taubira, "Mémoire, histoire et droit."

22. The petition "Liberté pour l'histoire" appeared in the French newspaper

Libération on December 13, 2005. Less than a month later, it had been signed by more than four hundred university instructors and professors. See also Pierre Nora, "Liberté pour l'histoire!"

23. Pierre Nora, "Malaise dans l'identité historique," 15.

24. Ibid., 20.

25. Ibid.

CHAPTER 4

1. Daniel Defoe, *The Life and Strange Surprizing Adventures of Robinson Crusoe, of York, Mariner*, 64–65.

2. The passive environment is "pre-given." As Husserl has stated in his elucidation of the concept of passivity, it is there "without any contribution, without the attentiveness of the comprehending glance, without any awakening of interest." Moreover, the distinction between activity and passivity, as Husserl explains, "is never a rigid one" (Edmund Husserl, *Erfahrung und Urteil*, 119).

3. Languages are in this sense what Leibniz eloquently termed "the most ancient monuments of peoples" (Leibniz, *Nouveaux essais*, 264).

4. Aristotle, *Politics* 1269a, 130–31.

5. Niccolò Macchiavelli, *The Prince*, 18.

6. Erwin Panofsky, *Gothic Architecture and Scholasticism*, 20–21.

7. Marcel Mauss, "Les techniques du corps" (1934), 368.

8. Ibid., 368–69. Norbert Elias, whose sociological theory also focused on the concept of the habitus, similarly conceived it as the expression of typical and habitual social patterns. He centered his investigation on the ways in which gradual transformations in habitual attitudes and practices gave rise over the centuries to the process of formation of what we term "modern civilization." See his *Über den Prozess der Zivilisation*.

9. In formulating his theory of the habitus in the chapter "Structures, Habitus, and Practise" of the early work, *Outline of a Theory of Practice*, Bourdieu quoted a passage on the social unconscious appropriated from the past that is found at the beginning (p. 16) of Durkheim's book *L'évolution pédagogique en France des origines à la Renaissance*: "In each of us, in varying proportions, there is part of yesterday's man; it is yesterday's man who inevitably predominates in us, since the present amounts to little compared with the long past in the course of which we were formed and from which we result. Yet we do not sense this man of the past, because he is inveterate in us; he makes up the unconscious part of ourselves. Consequently we are led to take no account of him, no more than we take account of his legitimate demands" (Pierre Bourdieu, *Outline of a Theory of Practice*, 78–79).

10. Bourdieu, *Outline of a Theory of Practice*, 82–83

11. Ibid., 78–95; on the theme of the body as a repository of dispositions that correspond to long-term expressions of collective memory, see Paul Connerton, *How*

Societies Remember, and the recent work of Didier Fassin, *When Bodies Remember: Experiences and Politics of AIDS in South Africa*.

12. Recent analyses of the *Calendrier Républicain* and its social impact can be found in James Friguglietti, "The Social and Religious Consequences of the French Revolutionary Calendar"; Bronislaw Baczko, "Le calendrier républicain,", 67–196; Reinhart Koselleck, "Anmerkungen zum Revolutionskalender und zur 'neuen Zeit,'" 61–64; Eviatar Zerubavel, *Hidden Rhythms*, 82–96.

13. Philippe François Nazaire Fabre d'Églantine, *L'Evangile des Républicains pré-cédé du Rapport fait par le citoyen Fabre d'Eglantine, sur le nouveau Calendrier dé-crété par la Convention Nationale*, 8.

14. François Victor Alphonse Aulard, *Le culte de la raison et le culte de l'Être su-prême (1793–1794)*, 33–34.

15. Cited in François Victor Alphonse Aulard, *Histoire politique de la Révolution Française*, 667.

16. Ibid.; see also Hippolyte Taine, *Le Gouvernement Révolutionnaire*, 89.

17. In "The Social and Religious Consequences of the French Revolutionary Cal-endar," James Friguglietti provides a detailed analysis of the modifications in the ap-plication of the measures of the Republican Calendar during the different periods of the French Revolution and the reign of Napoleon Bonaparte.

18. Jules Michelet, *Histoire de la Révolution Française*, 8:188.

19. Fabre d'Églantine, *L'Evangile des Républicains*, 9.

20. Ibid., 34–35. As Eviatar Zerubavel has noted, "Since names invoke images—thus affecting both imagination and memory—there was no reason why the collec-tive memory of an entire society could not be controlled and manipulated through the use of particular names. It was this particular educational function of names that guided Fabre d'Eglantine in designing the new nomenclature of time for the people of France" (*Hidden Rhythms*, 92).

21. Madame de Sévigné to Madame de Grignan, Letter 368, February 5, 1674, in Sévigné, *Correspondance (mars 1646–juillet 1675)*, 1:691.

22. Ivo Andrić, *The Bridge on the Drina*, 24; translation modified.

23. Ibid., 295–306.

24. In analyzing Milošević's speech at the Amselfeld in 1989, the late Edit Petro-vić made a point that corroborates what I am saying here. In her words, Milošević "sought to combine history, memory, and continuity, promoting the illusion that the Serbs who fought against the Turks in Kosovo in 1389 are somehow the same as the Serbs fighting for Serbian national survival today" (Edit Petrović, "Ethnonationalism and the Dissolution of Yugoslavia," 170).

25. Marcel Mauss, for example, in his essay "La nation" (1920), placed the emer-gence of the nation in the developmental perspective of a process of elaboration of human societies. In this process, Mauss considered the contractual recognition of popular sovereignty to have become a historical "fact" among European nations. Moreover, as much as their members might consider themselves to be a homogeneous

group, their nation was composed of a mixture of populations. See Marcel Mauss, "La nation," in *Oeuvres*, vol. 3, *Cohésion sociale et division de la sociologie*, 573–625. In regard to Pierre Bourdieu, there is a manifest tension between the Marxist rhetoric of certain of his early works, such as *Outline of a Theory of Practice* or *Distinction: A Social Critique of the Judgment of Taste*, which strongly suggest that aesthetic, political, and sociocultural systems are expressions of ideology and the ideal of democratic pluralism, which, to a certain degree, may claim a validity that is not reducible to the particular interests of ideological sources. This point has been forcefully made by Jeffrey C. Alexander in "The Reality of Reduction: The Failed Synthesis of Pierre Bourdieu," in *Fin de Siècle Social Theory*, 128–217. If in these works Bourdieu's conception of democracy remains ambiguous, later writings favor democratic pluralism, above all in a negative sense, through their quest to unmask the forces in contemporary society, such as the mass media, that have tended to limit and distort the practice of democratic participation. In this context Bourdieu has coordinated a theory of the habitus with the ideal of political democracy, which clearly favors pluralistic participation. He has explicitly rejected Stalinism and Maoism as so many forms of "irresponsible utopianism" and "unrealistic radicality," which deny the realities of the social world. See Pierre Bourdieu, *Pascalian Meditations*, 41. See also his *Language and Symbolic Power*, and *Sur la télévision*, as well as Chad Alan Goldberg, "Struggle and Solidarity."

26. The paradigmatic role of the writings of Maurice Barrès in the genesis of the contemporary political ideology of the extreme right has been identified by Zeev Sternhell in his study *Maurice Barrès et le nationalisme français*; and by Marcel Detienne, *L'identité nationale, une énigme*.

27. Maurice Barrès, *Romans et voyages*, 1:950–51 (*L'appel au soldat*).

28. Maurice Barrès, *La terre et les morts*, 27. Concerning Barrès' essay *La terre et les morts*, see the remarkable analysis of Marcel Detienne, "La dette envers les morts," 49–70.

29. Maurice Barrès, *Scènes et doctrines du nationalisme*, 17 ("Que le nationalisme est l'acceptation d'un déterminisme").

30. Barrès, *La terre et les morts*, 23. Referring to the *Mémoires d'outre-tombe* of Chateaubriand, Barrès wrote in characteristic fashion, "These memories (*souvenirs*), the ardor of which Chateaubriand would seem to ask us to pardon, are propagated throughout, and lend fertility to, the whole of our modern literature. We have in our blood the fever of the first volume of the *Mémoires d'outre-tombe*" (*Scènes et doctrines du nationalisme*, 145).

31. Ibid.

32. Maurice Barrès, *Le bi-centenaire de Jean-Jacques Rousseau*, 18–19.

33. Besides the three volumes of Zeev Sternhell's work, *La France entre nationalisme et fascisme*, in which the first volume on Maurice Barrès introduces an historical investigation of later political currents of the extreme right, see, for example, Peter Davies's interpretation of the relation between Barrès, Maurras, and the contempo-

rary French extreme right in his *The National Front in France*; and Michel Winock, *Nationalisme, antisémitisme et fascisme en France*, 39–46.

34. Jean-Marie Le Pen, *Les Français d'abord*, 82.

35. Jean-Marie Le Pen, "La mémoire et l'espérance," 2. Ideologues of the party in former years, such as Bruno Mégret, a previous member of the European parliament, and Georges-Paul Wagner, have emphasized the role of Barrès as a primary source of their party's notion of the nation and of national roots, even if Mégret has cautioned against overemphasis of Barrès's regionalism in cases where it threatens, as in Corsica, to undermine national unity. See Georges-Paul Wagner, "Il y a un siècle, Barrès et Maurras ont forgé notre langage: 'nationalisme,' 'enracinement,' 'décentralisation,'" 3; and Bruno Mégret, "La France et son peuple," 3.

36. Concerning Le Pen's idea of race as a factor in national homogeneity, see for example his pronouncement in the "FN Brochure," supplement to *National hebdo*, 268 (August 15, 1989), cited by Peter Davies in *The National Front in France*, 81–82. On nuances in the National Front program in regard to nationalist ideology, see Davies, *National Front in France*, 222.

37. Jean-Marie Le Pen, "Entendez le chant du peuple français," 7. See also Maryse Souchard et al., *Le Pen, les mots*, 51–52.

38. Jean-Marie Le Pen, "Le discours de La Trinité: Démarxiser La France," 7–8.

39. Le Pen, *Les Français d'abord*, 156; Jean-Marie Le Pen, "Le discours de Jean-Marie Le Pen au Palais des Congrès de Paris" (23 January 1991), 7.

40. While publicly disavowing her father's biting ethnic slurs and denying their anti-Semitic innuendos, Marine has retained her party's ultranationalist discourse in favor of an authoritarian state and against European financial and political unity, globalization and, above, all multiculturalism, which is for her the ideological counterpart of what she describes as the deracination of the indigenous French population through decades of immigration; see "Jean-Marie Le Pen critiqué au FN pour une nouvelle sortie," *Le Monde*, 8 June 2014; and Marine Le Pen, *Pour que vive la France*.

41. Richard Millet, *Langue fantôme*, 116–17.

42. Maurice Barrès, *Romans et voyages*, 1:1173 (*Leurs figures*).

CHAPTER 5

1. Here I draw on the apt remarks of Niklas Luhmann: "The function of the mass media lies in the final analysis in the direction of the self-observation of the social system. [. . .] What is at issue here is an observation (*Beobachtung*), that produces the conditions of its own possibility and in this sense proceeds autopoetically" (*Die Realität der Massenmedien*, 173).

2. "Writing [. . .] has this strange quality, and is very like painting; for the creatures of painting stand like living beings, but if one asks them a question, they preserve a solemn silence. And so it is with written words; you might think they spoke as if they had intelligence, but if you question them, wishing to know about their sayings,

they always tell you one and the same thing. And every word, when once it is written, is bandied about, alike among those who understand and those who have no interest in it, and it knows not to whom to speak, or not to speak" (Plato, *Phaedrus* 275 d–e).

3. Georg Simmel, *The Philosophy of Money*, 455; translation modified.

4. In his essay "On Some Motifs in Baudelaire," Walter Benjamin aptly characterized the principles of journalistic information as "freshness of news, brevity, comprehensibility, and, above all, lack of connection (*Zusammenhangslosigkeit*) between individual news items" (158–59).

5. The phenomenon of "hypermediation" in the contemporary news media has been described by media theorists in the following terms: "The CNN site is hypermediated—arranging text, graphics, and video in multiple panes and windows and joining them with numerous hyperlinks; yet the web site borrows its sense of immediacy from the televised CNN newscasts. At the same time televised newscasts are coming to resemble web pages in their hypermediacy" (Jay David Bolter and Richard Grusin, *Remediation*, 9).

6. Educational magazines, like educational television, may make an effort to fill in the deeper temporal context in which current events are presented and thus to re-contextualize them. This, however, constitutes the exception and is not characteristic of everyday news broadcasts or Web sites.

7. Reinhart Koselleck, *Vergangene Zukunft: Zur Semantik geschichtlicher Zeiten*, 349–75 ("'Erfahrungsraum' und 'Erwartungshorizont'—Zwei historische Kategorien").

8. François Hartog, *Régimes d'historicité*, 28–29, 119–27.

9. "The present has become the horizon. Without future or past, it generates, from day to day, the past and the future that it requires, day after day, and places a premium on immediacy"; "a present which is massive, invasive, and omnipresent, having no other horizon than itself, daily fashioning the past and future which, day after day, it requires" (ibid., 126, 200).

10. In accord with Pierre Nora's theories in *Les lieux de mémoire*, François Hartog thus concludes: "In France, the *Lieux [de mémoire]* led at once to a recognition of the presence of the national (*du national*) and of its profound transformation. It was not the messianic nation, but a nation-heritage (*une nation-patrimoine*), or once again the nation as a shared culture, the vehicle of the national without nationalism (*le national sans nationalisme*), living yet pacified, in a France which could content itself with the cultivation of its memory as one cultivates a garden: like history in early retirement" (ibid., 160–61).

11. In one of the rare passages in his book that deal with the media, François Hartog indeed approaches this conclusion when he writes, "If time has been a commodity for a long time, its present consumption emphasizes the ephemeral. The media, the extraordinary development of which has accompanied this movement that is, in the proper sense, their *raison d'être*, adopt this same procedure. In the ever more rapid race toward the "live" (*au direct*), they produce, consume, recycle with increas-

ing speed, an ever greater number of words and images and thus compress time: in a minute and a half a topic may be treated that spans thirty years of history" (ibid., 125–26).

12. Ernst Bloch, in his elaboration of a concept of historical time in the 1930s, suggested what might be applied as a complement and corrective to the concept of "presentism," which, in its generality, risks overlooking essential sociopolitical phenomena that do not correspond to its grid of interpretation. Bloch coined the terms "non-simultaneity" (*Ungleichzeitigkeit*), and "simultaneity of the non-simultaneous" (*Gleichzeitigkeit des Ungleichzeitigen*) to interpret a plurality of temporal perspectives that coexist among contemporaneous sociopolitical groups and the vulnerability of certain groups to the power of archaic imagery and symbols that are mobilized in political mythologies. In signaling the existence of a "simultaneity of the non-simultaneous," Bloch sought to account for the persistence over generations, in the context of technologically rationalized societies, of long-standing group aspirations that have been frustrated over the course of centuries and come to the fore in archaic symbols that mobilize violent passions. For our purposes, the *temporal* reference of the concept of "non-simultaneity" is particularly suggestive, for it indicates a source of divergences in the collective modes of sedimentation, stratification, and fragmentation of the symbolic representations of time upon which collective memory draws. See Ernst Bloch, *Erbschaft dieser Zeit*.

13. John B. Thompson, in *The Media and Modernity* (179–206), provides an enlightening analysis of this theme. As Thompson aptly writes, "The mediazation of tradition endowed it with a new life: tradition was increasingly freed from the constraints of face-to-face interaction and took on a range of new traits. Tradition was deritualized; it lost its moorings in the practical contexts of everyday life. But the uprooting of traditions did not starve them of sustenance. On the contrary, it prepared the way for them to be extended and renewed by being re-embedded in new contexts and re-moored to spatial units which exceeded the bounds of face-to-face interaction" (180). The question remains, nevertheless, whether this act of "re-embedding" performed by the media does not place traditions in a very different symbolic framework than that of the face-to-face relations on which tradition was originally based.

14. Jacob Burckhardt, *Erinnerungen aus Rubens*, 232–35.

15. John Ruskin, *Modern Painters*, 2:57.

16. Charles Baudelaire, *Œuvres complètes*, 2:695 ("La modernité").

17. In the section of his essay *Le peintre de la vie moderne* entitled "Le beau, la mode et le bonheur," Baudelaire wrote, "The beautiful is composed of an eternal, invariable element, the quantity of which is extremely difficult to determine, and of a relative, circumstantial element which will be, so to speak, successively or taken together, epoch, mode, morals, passion" (ibid., 685).

18. Aby Warburg, "Heidnisch-antike Weissagung in Wort und Bild zu Luthers Zeiten (1920)," 456.

19. Mason Jackson, *The Illustrated Press*; Martina Baleva, *Bulgarien im Bild*.

20. Helmuth Plessner has characterized this tendency in the following terms: "The greatest possible fidelity to the seen as such, to the experienced thing (*Gegenstand*), obliged the painter to pay attention to the phenomenon as seen in the eye of the looker, instead of, as previously, portraying a thing of which the appearance is a mere medium that our glance must skip over and forget" ("Über die gesellschaftlichen Bedingungen der modernen Malerei (1965)," 272.

21. In commenting on the purpose of art in 1919, Schwitters exclaimed, "The essence of art is not mere beauty (*bloss Schönheit*), the essence of art lies in its liberating quality (*die Eigenschaft, zu befreien*)." See Kurt Schwitters, *Das literarische Werk*, 5:26–33 ("Das Problem der abstrakten Kunst" [July–August, 1919]).

22. Robert Rauschenberg, "Notes on Stoned Moon," 247, cited in Katharina Hoins, *Medien als Material der Kunst*, 66. The exhibition "Art and Press," which, in 2012, displayed Rauschenberg's *Study for Currents no. 27* at the Gropius-Bau in Berlin, focused on the relation between journalism and art since the mid-nineteenth century. It explored the development of artistic reflection on the journalistic format of the mass media, which has lost nothing of its vitality as a topic of contemporary artistic production. Beside Robert Rauschenberg's work, it included a broad selection of more recent expressions of this evocative form by artists such as Melissa Gordon, Damien Hirst, Marine Hugonnier, and Marcus Lüpertz. See Walter Smerling, ed., *Art and Press: Kunst, Wahrheit, Wirklichkeit*.

23. Helmuth Plessner has eloquently stated, in this vein, "Since society in the process of industrialization had to become pluralistic, it imposed through this process the liberation of the artist, who was thereby confined within the aesthetic region of *l'art pour l'art*. Industrial society has to pay the consequences for this development: *le choc pour le choc*" ("Über die gesellschaftlichen Bedingungen der modernen Malerei," 266).

24. On the concept of the Schlüsselbild, see especially Peter Ludes, *Multimedia und Multimoderne*, 61–54; and Tanja Zimmermann, "Semmeln in Rožna dolina."

25. Diane Waldman, *Roy Lichtenstein*, 6–7.

26. Roy Lichtenstein, "An Interview with Roy Lichtenstein," n.p.

27. Roy Lichtenstein, "What Is Pop Art?" 24–25.

28. Ibid.

29. Lichtenstein, "An Interview with Roy Lichtenstein." On the occasion of the 1969 Guggenheim retrospective of Lichtenstein's work, Max Kozloff summed up his contemporary reaction to Lichtenstein's art: "In that distant year (1962), [. . .] there was, too, the fierce disbelief that anything so brazen as these commercial icons could have found their way onto prepared and stretched canvas [. . .] Though each object still conventionally reads as what it is, it tends to lose its symbolic leavening, and lifts off, freely created in its own right" ("Lichtenstein at the Guggenheim," 7, 10).

30. Smirnoff was sued for commercial use of the image and settled out of court in the year 2000. On the bizarre history of the icon, see David Bourdon, *Warhol*; and Trisha Ziff, *Che Guevara*.

31. A broad collection of famous doctored photos drawn from the international press that had an important political impact in the twentieth century was the topic of an exhibition at the Haus der Geschichte in Bonn, Germany in 1997–1998. See Hermann Schäfer, ed., *Bilder, die Lügen*.

32. See the seminal work of Gerhard Paul, *Bildermacht*, 155–98.

33. Roland Barthes has emphasized this quality of the photograph in its capacity to refer the viewer to in the flesh encounters: "Photography's inimitable feature [. . .] is that someone somewhere has seen the referent (even if it is a matter of objects) *in flesh and blood (en chair et en os)*, or again *in person*" (*Camera Lucida—Reflections on Photography*, 79).

34. See the account by David Campbell, "Atrocity, Memory, Photography."

35. Oliviero Toscani, *La Pub est une charogne qui nous sourit*, 92–93.

36. I borrow the suggestive term *remediation* from Jay David Bolter and Richard Grusin to characterize the way in which new media integrate and appropriate to their own ends the techniques of earlier media. According to their description of the process of remediation, "What is new about the new media comes from the particular ways in which they refashion older media and the ways in which older media refashion themselves to answer the challenges of new media" (*Remediation*, 15).

37. Stanley Cavell has aptly characterized the difference between film and video as a distinction between "viewing" and "monitoring." Where film provides a succession of "automatic world projections" television, in his terms, is based on a "current of simultaneous event reception" ("The Fact of Television," 85–86). From the perspective of my analysis, each of these ways of bringing to public visibility highlights nuances in the symbolic modes of spatiotemporal and logical configuration.

38. Much has been written on the role of the informality of the TV setting in creating a sense of proximity and familiarity as an ordinary kind of experience in contrast to the more confined space, separate from the home, that characterizes the movie theater. On this theme, see, for example, Jane Feuer, "The Concept of Live Television," 13–16. The idea that the formality of the television newsroom studio creates a certain distance in regard to the viewer and the role of eye contact in attenuating this distance have been examined by Andrew Ballantyne in his article "Architectonics of 'The Box,'" 129–30. In every case, television does not simply mirror the outside world, but above all reconfigures it in its own specific format. Paul Connerton has expressed this point nicely: "Television is not a set but a setting, for all processes that are communicated, in politics, business, sport and art" (*How Modernity Forgets*, 82).

39. Cézanne's contemporaries in Aix-en-Provence were as indifferent to the quarry as they were to his paintings, and it was put up for sale shortly after World War II. In 1954 part of the quarry was purchased by the American enthusiast of Cézanne's painting, George Bunker, who bequeathed it to the city of Aix upon his death in 1991 on the condition that the city conserve it as a public park dedicated to the memory of Cézanne.

40. In this sense the art historian Max Imdahl wrote that "the work of the media

cannot be to pursue works in original form" (*Gesammelte Schriften*, 3:517 ["Moderne Kunst und Medien"]).

41. Neil Postman provides an insightful analysis of the commercial and show-business aspects of evangelical TV, and he also analyzes the limits of the TV format as a mode of communication for religious messages: "There is no way to consecrate the space in which a television show is experienced. It is an essential condition of any traditional religious service that the space in which it is conducted must be invested with some measure of sacrality. [. . .]. If an audience is not immersed in an aura of mystery and symbolic otherworldliness, then it is unlikely that it will call forth the state of mind required for a nontrivial religious experience" (*Amusing Ourselves to Death*, 118–19).

42. As a recent analyst has written, "The characteristic mixture of news, entertainment, drama, and sports, so typical of journalism, was successfully applied to TV almost from the beginning of the operation of TV services" (Evan Guter, "Anti-Mimesis Live," 144). See also Albert Abramson, *The History of Television, 1880 to 1941*.

43. Niklas Luhmann refers to the triple function of the mass media in terms of "news" (*Nachrichten*), "advertising" (*Werbung*), and "entertainment" (*Unterhaltung*). In the chapter "The Construction of Reality" of his work *Die Realität der Massenmedien*, he adds the following observation: "All closer analyses and above all empirical investigations will indeed have to begin from the sphere that most directly serves to portray reality and is also declared and perceived to do so: the news and reporting services" (120, 141).

44. Barbie Zelizer, *Covering the Body*, 67–73. On this aspect of journalistic reporting of the assassination, Tom Wicker, who covered the president's visit to Dallas that day as a member of the *New York Times* White House staff, noted, "At first no one knew what happened, or how, or where, much less why. Gradually, bits and pieces began to fall together. [. . .] Even now, [. . .] I know no reporter who was there who has a clear and orderly picture of that surrealistic afternoon; it is still a matter of bits and pieces thrown hastily into something like a whole" ("A Reporter Must Trust His Instinct," 81).

45. Zelizer, *Covering the Body*, 129.

46. Ibid., 184–85.

47. Milena Michalski and James Gow, *War, Image, and Legitimacy*, 121–83; Ivan Zveržhanovski, "Watching War Crimes."

48. Romain Lecomte, "Internet et la reconfiguration de l'espace public tunisien," 198–229; Khaled Zouari, "L'impact des TIC dans la révolution tunisienne."

49. Gilad Lotan et al., "The Revolutions Were Tweeted."

50. The suggestion has recently been made that film and video presentations may elicit in those who view them a "prosthetic memory," capable of creating vicarious forms of experience and remembrance in place of lived events. This idea has the merit of identifying possibilities that the mass media afford of vicarious discovery of foreign contexts. The metaphor of "prosthesis," however, should not lead us to believe

that vicarious memories may function in the direct manner of artificial limbs or teeth, and thus to overlook the shift in symbolic modes of configuration that, in regard to the lifeworld, all simulations of experience in mass media format engender. On this theme, see Alison Landsberg, *Prosthetic Memory*.

51. Bolter and Grusin, *Remediation*, 53.

52. Neil Postman and Steve Powers, *How to Watch TV News*, 75–89; Pierre Bourdieu, *Sur la télévision*, 28–29.

53. Pierre Bourdieu concludes his remarks on the influence of television with the following observation: "Television, which is ruled by ratings, contributes to the burden on the consumer who is presumed to be free and enlightened in regard to the constraints imposed by the market, which have nothing to do with the democratic expression of an enlightened and rational collective opinion, of a kind of public reason, as cynical demagogues would lead us to believe" (*Sur la télévision*, 78).

54. Haroun Farocki and Andrei Ujică, *Videograms of a Revolution*. The Romanian revolution of 1989 provided one of the themes explored by French cineaste Chris Marker in his video work of 1990–94, *Zapping Zone, Proposals for an Imaginary Television*, which juxtaposes a series of video presentations of different topics, some of which were centered on political events in Eastern Europe. In one of them, entitled "Détour, Ceaucescu," Marker presented footage of the initial airing on the French television network TF1 of the trial and execution of Ceaucescu and his wife in December 1989. Whereas TF1 had presented this video without commercial interruption, in "Détour Ceaucescu" the depiction of the trial and execution of the dictator and his wife was continually interspersed with advertising for commercial products. Marker's depiction of constant zapping between TV stations created an ironic portrayal of the video format of television news reporting that mixed the dismal scenes of the trial and execution, filmed in black and white, with the trivialities of everyday advertising, presenting in vivid colors women in bathing suits in exotic places, cleaning products, dogs and vacuum cleaners, sports cars and food snacks.

55. Konrad Petrovszky and Ovidiu Tichindeleanu, "Capital, Politics, and Media Technology," 29–63. I would like to thank Dr. Adrian Costache of the University of Cluj for information concerning the events of the Romanian revolution of 1989.

56. Roland Barthes, *Mythologies*, 217 ("Le mythe, aujourd'hui").

57. Ivan Čolović, "Football, Hooligans and War."

58. Ibid.

59. In novelistic form, the complex interrelation between sports and war in the Balkan conflict of the 1990s is poignantly portrayed by Saša Stanišić in *Wie der Soldat das Grammofon Repariert*. In Stanišić's narrative, opposing sides engage in a football match during a pause in the war, only to begin killing one another following the end of the match.

60. Robert Thomas, *Serbia under Milosevic*, 219.

61. Jean-Christophe Buisson, "Ceca, La Madonna des Balkans."

62. Lamar Smith, Congressional hearing before the Committee on the Judiciary, House of Representatives, First Session of the One Hundred and Tenth Congress of the United States on H. R. 2128, *Sunshine in the Courtroom Act of 2007*, Sept. 27, 2007, 8.

63. Joe Chidley, "The Simpson Jury Faces the Race Factor."

64. Interview with Peter Arnella, "The O. J. Verdict." Peter Arenella was the legal consultant to ABC News during the Simpson trial and is a professor of law at the UCLA Law School.

CHAPTER 6

1. In Heidegger's work immediately following *Being and Time*, notably in his 1928 Freiburg course lectures, *Metaphysical Foundations of Logic from Leibniz Onward* (*Metaphysische Anfangsgründe der Logik im Ausgang von Leibniz*) and in *Kant and the Problem of Metaphysics* (*Kant und das Problem der Metaphysik*, 1929), he related the theme of human finitude to that of memory. He thereby assigned to reminiscence in its fundamental sense (*Wiedererinnerung*) the metaphysical task of recalling the finite ground of existence that the Western tradition, in the manifold forms of its quest for permanence and for stable criteria of truth, had continually neglected. The task of reminiscence in this finite perspective was not to retrieve, but above all to break with tradition, engaging the resolute critique initiated in *Being and Time* of all presuppositions concerning self-sustaining historical continuity and the presumption that meaning in history was to be sought in its objective cohesion as an overarching process. Indeed, the only trans-historical unity that Heidegger identified in this early period of his work was that of the forgetfulness of Being itself, which provided a hidden continuity linking together the epochs of history. See Martin Heidegger, *Kant und das Problem der Metaphysik* (1929), 227; and *Metaphysische Anfangsgründe der Logik im Ausgang von Leibniz* (1928), 186.

2. Martin Heidegger, *Sein und Zeit*, 386. It would reach beyond the framework of our present discussion to examine later developments in Heidegger's orientation when, after 1933, in particular in his *Schwarze Hefte*, his discourse was extended to embrace the Nazi ideology and the political mythology that animated its monolithic conception of collective existence. "The Germans," as Heidegger writes in this recently published series of volumes, "are alone capable of poeticizing and saying Being in an original manner." At the same time, they are "threatened by a growing incapacity to remember" (*Unkraft der Erinnerung*); by the danger of choosing not their own being (*Dasein*), but of "relinquishing themselves to planetary machinations" (*Machenschaften*), whose primary characteristic lies in their "absence of memory." The identification of these "machinations" with Jews and what he perceived to be other enemies of the Germans is made abundantly clear in these volumes. Here Heidegger's perspective, nourished as it was by the ideology of the *êthos*, proved still more blind

than in *Sein und Zeit* to the finitude of group existence that the dynamics of collective memory bring to light. See Martin Heidegger, *Überlegungen II–VI*, 27, 276, 296; *Überlegungen, VII–XI*, 10; and *Überlegungen XII–XV*, 55–56, 133, 243, 262.

3. Fernand Braudel, *La méditerranée et le monde méditerranéen*, 1:13. On the theme of historical time in Braudel's work, see Ulrich Raulff, *Der unsichtbare Augenblick*.

4. In criticizing Halbwachs's distinction between collective memory and the historical past in recent years, Peter Burke applied the category of "social memory" both to the remembered and historical past, thus eliminating any fundamental distinction between memory retained by living contemporary generations and the recollection of an historical past gleaned on the basis of documents and indirect testimony. My own argument in this chapter submits this assumption to critical scrutiny. See Peter Burke, "History as Social Memory," 98–99.

5. See David Lowenthal, *The Past Is a Foreign Country*. More recently, Eelco Runia has focused on the phenomenon of discontinuity between past and present, which he aptly characterizes as the past's capacity to "spring surprises on us" (*Moved by the Past*, 81–82).

6. Aleida and Jan Assmann, "Schrift, Tradition und Kultur," 28–29; Jan Assmann, *Cultural Memory and Early Civilization*, 34–41.

7. Assmann, *Cultural Memory*, 39.

8. Jan Assmann, *Religion und kulturelles Gedächtnis*, 38–44.

9. Assmann, *Cultural Memory*, 37–38.

10. In more recent works, Aleida Assmann would seem to acknowledge this point where she refers to symbol and image as a basis for collectively shared cultural remembrance that may be evaluated in terms of rational and moral criteria (*Der lange Schatten der Vergangenheit*, 29–37).

11. Denis Diderot, *Œuvres*, 1067 ("Éloge de Richardson").

12. Jean-Jacques Rousseau, *Émile ou l'éducation*, bk. 4, 310.

13. Schopenhauer noted that if all historical writing lies far from the truth it claims to grasp, the most "interesting" form of historical writing is autobiography because it most closely resembles the novel. See Arthur Schopenhauer, *Die Welt als Wille und Vorstellung*, vol. 2, pt. 2, 519. Nietzsche's pronouncements on this theme in the second of the *Untimely Meditations*, as I noted in the introduction, were particularly influential: "Only when historiography tolerates being transformed into art, and thus becomes a pure artistic creation, can it maintain or perhaps even arouse instincts" (*Unzeitgemässe Betrachtungen I–III*, 292). Theodor Lessing's expression of thoroughgoing historical skepticism in his comparisons of history to the work of art may be found in *Die Geschichte als Sinngebung des Sinnlosen*, 104–110.

14. "Le fait n'a jamais qu'une existence linguistique" or, as Barthes writes, "One understands that from that point onward, the notion of an historical 'fact' would often, here and there, arouse a certain suspicion (*méfiance*). Nietzsche had already said: 'There are no facts in themselves. It is always necessary to begin by making sense (*introduire un sens*) in order that there might be a fact.' From the moment where lan-

guage intervenes (and when does it not intervene?), the fact can only be defined in a tautological manner" (Roland Barthes, "Le discours de l'histoire," in *Le bruissement de la langue*,163). See also Barthes's comparison of Nietzsche's interpretation of facts with the historiographical practice of Michelet in his essay, "Aujourd'hui, Michelet," in *Le bruissement de la langue*, 243 ("It's Michelet who is right. Here he is, quite paradoxically, standing alongside Nietzsche.").

15. Barthes, "Le discours de l'histoire," 163.

16. Ibid., 174.

17. Roland Barthes, "L'effet du reel," in *Le bruissement de la langue*, 179–87.

18. The parallel to the Cartesian theory of the imagination in Barthes and in structuralist and poststructuralist theory is striking. Suffice it to note in this context the counterconception of the imagination presented by Goethe in a comment to Eckermann, to which I alluded in an earlier chapter, where Goethe underlines the essential role of the imagination in the identification of reality, his notion of an "imagination for the truth of the real" ("*Phantasie für die Wahrheit des Realen*"); see Goethe, *Eckermann Gespräche mit Goethe*, 154. On the concept of imagination in Descartes, see Dennis L. Sepper, *Descartes's Imagination*.

19. Hayden White, *The Content of the Form*, 35–37 ("The Question of Narrative in Contemporary Historical Theory").

20. Ibid., ii.

21. In his essay, "The Historical Text as Literary Artifact" (*Tropics of Discourse*, 83–84), Hayden White refers to Collingwood's concept of the use of "constructive imagination" in the representation of historical narratives, capable of distinguishing the most plausible story among different possibilities. As he notes, Collingwood's constructive imagination functions as an *a priori* faculty through which, on the model of Kant's transcendental schematism, particular factual instances may be apprehended through general forms of explanation. Where White is critical of this abstract and essentially ahistorical model of the imagination, his own conception of it limits it to the function of organizing historical narratives in terms of rhetorical tropes. In confining the role of imagination to this essentially literary task, his theory reveals an unmistakable resemblance to that of Roland Barthes's conception of it as a capacity for producing essentially fictive narratives.

22. Ibid., 82, 87, 89, 99. For critical analysis of Hayden White's theories, see Lionel Gossman, *Towards a Rational Historiography*; and *Between History and Literature*, 285–324; see also Luiz Costa Lima, *Mimesis*, 170–78; and Jorn Rüsen, *Lebendige Geschichte*, 3:22.

23. In "The Historical Text as Literary Artifact," Hayden White makes the suggestive comment that the philosophy of language might help us "understand what is fictive in all putatively realistic representations of the world and what is realistic in all manifestly fictive ones" (*Tropics of Discourse*, 88). I fully concur with Paul Ricœur's remark that White "does not really show us what is realistic in all fiction, [since] only the fictive side of the purportedly realistic representation of the world is stressed"

(*The Reality of the Historical Past*, 51). There seems to be an ambiguity in White's use of the term *realistic*, which may refer to an account of "reality" or to "realism" as a literary genre.

24. This point has been developed by Erich Auerbach in *Mimesis*, 441.

25. On the theme of memory in Scott's novels, see Catherine Jones, *Literary Memory*, and Ann Rigney, *The Afterlives of Walter Scott*.

26. Walter Scott, *Biographical Memoirs*, 1:32–33 ("Samuel Richardson").

27. Ibid., 49–50; Walter Scott, *Biographical Memoirs*, 2:12 ("Henry Mackenzie").

28. Scott, *Biographical Memoirs*, 1:49–50.

29. Scott, *Biographical Memoirs*, 2:9.

30. Walter Scott, *Biographical Memoirs*, 1:332–33 ("Clara Reeve").

31. Walter Scott, "General Preface to the Waverly Novels" (1829), in *Waverly; or, 'Tis Sixty Years Since*, 353.

32. Scott, *Waverly*, 263.

33. Hume, *Treatise of Human Nature*, 171–73.

34. Walter Scott, "Dedicatory Epistle to the Rev. Dr. Dryasdust, F.A.S.," in *Ivanhoe*, 11.

35. Scott, *Biographical Memoirs*, 1:16n.

36. John Scott, *Journal of a Tour to Waterloo and Paris in Company with Walter Scott in 1815*, 27–28, 85.

37. Sir Joshua Reynolds, *Discourses Delivered to Students of the Royal Academy* (1780), in *Works*, 1:84–87 and 2:142–43; "Journey to Flanders and Holland in the year 1781," 314; "Annotations on Du Fresnoy's Poem," 110.

38. On this aspect of the theory of historical painting in France, see Stefan Germer, *Historizität und Autonomie*, 11–15.

39. Walter Scott, *Ivanhoe*, 11.

40. "It is ridiculous enough for me," as he wrote in his *Journal*, "in a state of insolvency for the present, to be battling about gold and paper currency. It is something like the humorous touch in Hogarth's 'Distressed poet,' where the poor starveling of the muses is engaged, when in the abyss of poverty, in writing an Essay on the payment of the National Debt" (Walter Scott, *The Journal of Walter Scott*, 1:140).

41. Walter Scott, *The Antiquary*, 3 ("Advertisement").

42. Walter Scott, "General Preface," in *Waverly*, 354.

43. Scott, *Antiquary*, 3. Ann Rigney has perceptively noted in this regard that "the subtitle to *Waverly*, the first novel–'tis sixty years since'—had already indicated Scott's preoccupation with generational change, and with the fascinating transition from first-hand testimony to mediated memory" (*The Afterlives of Walter Scott*, 21).

44. Scott, *Biographical Memoirs*, 1:333–34 ("Clara Reeve").

45. Walter Scott, *Waverly*, 340.

46. Ibid., 341. On the question of the role of the eyewitness in Scott's romances, see Wolfgang Iser, *Der Implizite Leser*, 148.

47. Scott, *Waverly*, 340.

48. Johann Wolfgang von Goethe, who was a particularly astute judge of Scott's accomplishments, voiced his opinion concerning the unique quality of this work in a comment to Eckermann: "After reading *Waverly*, you will understand why Walter Scott still designates himself the author of that work; for there he showed what he could do, and he has never since written anything to surpass, or even equal, that first published novel" (*Conversations with Eckermann and Soret*, reprinted in John O. Hayden, ed., *Walter Scott: The Critical Heritage*, 308).

49. Scott, *Waverly*, 340.

50. Walter Scott, *Ivanhoe*, 12; Walter Scott, *Biographical Memoirs*, 1:333–34 ("Clara Reeve").

51. Augustin Thierry, "Lettre V," in *Lettres sur l'histoire de France*, 5:61–62.

52. Leopold von Ranke, "Diktat vom November 1885," 61; Leonard Krieger, *Ranke*, 98.

53. Hippolyte Taine, *Histoire de la littérature anglaise*, 4:277.

54. Scott, *Ivanhoe*, 10–11.

55. Walter Scott, *Life of Napoleon Buonaparte*, 1:2.

56. Scott, *Journal of Sir Walter Scott*, 2:485–86.

57. Victor Hugo, *Notre-Dame de Paris*, 365, 491.

58. Ibid., 53–54.

59. Ibid., 193; English translation, *The Hunchback of Notre Dame*, 108.

60. Hippolyte Taine, *Les Origines de la France contemporaine*, 1:259.

61. Théophile Gautier, *Les beaux-arts et l'Europe*, 1:145.

62. Hippolyte Taine, *La philosophie de l'art*, 517.

63. Marcel Proust, *Contre Sainte-Beuve*, 555 ("Reynaldo Hahn").

64. Marcel Proust, "Preface," xxiii–xix; see also 147–48; "Après la Guerre," 583.

65. Marcel Proust, *Le Côté des Guermantes*, 420.

66. Marcel Proust, Letter to Henri de Régnier, 14 April 1920, in *Correspondance*, 19:214–15. In his book on Manet, published in 1924, Proust's friend, the painter and critic Jacques-Émile Blanche, summed up in this manner the change in attitude toward the *Olympia* of Manet: "Today one of the pearls of the Louvre, [. . .] the *Olympia*, has begun to lose the 'disturbing' connotations that earned it, sixty years ago, the insults of decent people and the devotion of certain 'unwholesome spirits'" (*Manet*, 34).

67. "However, the eldest would have been able to say that during their lives they had seen, the more the years removed them from the event, the unbridgeable distance diminish" (Proust, *Le Côté des Guermantes*, 420).

68. Ibid., 420.

69. Proust's depiction of Swann is at least partly drawn from real-life situations, and notably from the difficulties encountered by Jewish art historian and patron Charles Ephrussi during the Dreyfus affair. On the theme of Charles Ephrussi and contemporary painting in Proust's novel, see Kazuyoshi Yoshikawa, "Elstir," 89–94.

70. Proust, *Le Côté des Guermantes*, 400–401. The position of the duc de Guer-

mantes in this context is complex. After first espousing an anti-Dreyfusard position corresponding to that of his milieu, the acquaintance with three young pro-Dreyfus women at a spa at a later point in the novel leads him to change his mind, which partly accounts for his failure to be elected president of the aristocratic Jockey Club.

71. Ibid., 682.

72. Proust, *Correspondance*, 19:214–15.

73. Proust, *Contre Sainte-Beuve*, 531–32 ("Les années créatrices").

74. In this regard, Hannah Arendt's admonition that the threat of totalitarianism has not disappeared with the collapse of previous totalitarian regimes, since it derives from the condition of mass sociopolitical existence, takes on a particular significance in our contemporary period. Totalitarian solutions to problems of overpopulation, of economically superfluous and socially rootless human masses, "may well survive the fall of totalitarian regimes in the form of strong temptations which will come up whenever it seems impossible to alleviate political, social, or economic misery in a manner worthy of man" (*The Origins of Totalitarianism*, 459).

75. Ricœur, *Memory, History, Forgetting*, 21, 494–97.

76. W. G. Sebald, *Austerlitz*, 191–92.

77. Ibid., 192.

78. Ibid., 177.

79. Ibid., 197.

Abramson, Albert. *The History of Television, 1880 to 1941.* Jefferson, NC: Mc-
    Farland, 1987.
Alexander, Jeffrey C. *The Civil Sphere.* Oxford: Oxford University Press, 2006.
———. *Fin de Siècle Social Theory: Relativism, Reduction, and the Problem of Rea-
    son.* London: Verso, 1995.
Anderson, Benedict. *Imagined Communities.* London: Verso, 1991.
Andrić, Ivo. *The Bridge on the Drina.* Translated by Lovett F. Edwards. New York:
    New American Library, 1959.
Ankersmit, Frank. *Sublime Historical Experience: Cultural Memory in the Present.*
    Stanford, CA: Stanford University Press, 2005.
Arendt, Hannah. *Between Past and Future: Eight Exercises in Political Thought.*
    Enlarged edition. Harmondsworth: Penguin, 1987.
———. *The Origins of Totalitarianism.* San Diego: Harcourt, Brace, Jovanovich,
    1973.
Aristotle. *De Anima.* Translated by R. D. Hicks. Cambridge: Cambridge University
    Press, 1907.
———. *Politics.* Translated by H. Rackham. Loeb Classical Library. London:
    William Heinemann; Cambridge, MA: Harvard University Press, 1959.
Arnella, Peter. Interview, "The O. J. Verdict," 1 April 2005, *Frontline*, PBS. Online at
    http://www.pbs.org/wgbh/pages/frontline/oj/interviews/arenella.html (accessed
    Sept. 27, 2015).
Assmann, Aleida. *Der lange Schatten der Vergangenheit: Erinnerungskultur und
    Geschichtspolitik.* Munich: Beck, 2006.
———. *Erinnerungsräume: Formen und Wandlungen des kulturellen Gedächtnisses.*
    Munich: Beck, 1999.
Assmann, Aleida, and Jan Assmann. "Schrift, Tradition und Kultur." In *Zwischen*

    Festtag und Alltag: Zehn Beiträge zu Thema 'Mündlichkeit und Schriftlichkeit,' edited by Wolfgang Raible, 42–56. Tübingen: Narr, 1988.

Assmann, Jan. *Cultural Memory and Early Civilization: Writing, Remembrance, and Political Imagination.* Cambridge, UK: Cambridge University Press, 2011.

———. *Religion und kulturelles Gedächtnis: Zehn Studien.* Munich: Beck, 2000.

Auerbach, Erich. *Mimesis: Dargestellte Wirklichkeit in der abendländischen Literatur.* Bern/Munich: Francke, 1964.

Augustine of Hippo. *Confessions.* Translated by William Watts. 2 vols. Loeb Classical Library. Cambridge, MA: Harvard University Press, 1988.

———. *La Trinité/De Trinitate.* In *Oeuvres*, vols. 15–16. Translated by P. Agaësse, SJ. Paris: Études Augustiniennes, 1991.

Aulard, François Victor Alphonse. *Le culte de la raison et le culte de l'Être suprême (1793–1794): Essai historique.* Paris: Felix Alcan, 1892.

———. *Histoire politique de la Révolution Française: Origines et développement de la Démocratie et de la République (1789–1804).* Paris: Armand Colin, 1921.

Baczko, Bronislaw. "Le calendrier républicain." In *Les lieux de mémoire*, edited by Pierre Nora, 1:67–196. Paris: Gallimard, 1984.

Ballantyne, Andrew. "Architectonics of 'The Box': Television's Spatiality." In *Television: Aesthetic Reflections*, edited by Ruth Lorand, 127–38. New York: Peter Lang, 2002.

Balent, Magali. "La 'vision du monde' du Front national: Quel devenir après le départ de Jean-Marie Le Pen?" *Publications de Sciences Po/Cevipof* (January 2011): 35 (Note de recherche).

Baleva, Martina. *Bulgarien im Bild: Die Erfindung von Nationen auf dem Balkan in der Kunst des 19. Jahrhunderts.* Köln/Weimar/Wien: Böhlau, 2012.

Barash, Jeffrey Andrew, ed. *The Symbolic Construction of Reality: The Legacy of Ernst Cassirer.* Chicago: University of Chicago Press, 2008.

———. "Virtuelle Erfahrung, kollektive Erinnerung und die Gestaltung der Öffentlichkeit im Aktualitätsfeld der Massenmedien: Das Beispiel des ehemaligen Jugoslawien." In *Traumata der Transition*, edited by Boris Previšić Mongelli and Svjetlan Lacko Vidulic, 117–32. Tübingen: Francke Verlag, 2015.

———. "Was ist ein Symbol? Bemerkungen über Paul Ricœurs kritische Stellungnahme zum Symbolbegriff bei Ernst Cassirer." In *Internationales Jahrbuch für Hermeneutik*, edited by G. Figal, 6. Tübingen: Mohr/Siebeck, 2007.

Barrès, Maurice. *La terre et les morts (Sur quelles réalités fonder la conscience française).* Paris: Bureau de la patrie française, 1899.

———. *Le bi-centenaire de Jean-Jacques Rousseau.* Paris: Éditions de l'indépendance, 1912.

———. *Romans et voyages.* 2 vols. Paris: Robert Laffont, 1994.

———. *Scènes et doctrines du nationalisme.* Paris: Félix Juven, 1902.

Barthes, Roland. *Le bruissement de la langue: Essais critiques.* Vol. 4. Paris: Seuil, 1984.

———. *Camera Lucida: Reflections on Photography*. Translated by Richard Howard. New York: Hill and Wang, 1981.

———. *Mythologies*. Paris: Seuil, 1957.

———. *Système de la mode*. Paris: Seuil, 1967.

Baudelaire, Charles. *Œuvres complètes*. 2 vols. Paris: Gallimard/Pléiade, 1976.

Benjamin, Walter. *Illuminations: Essays and Reflections*. Edited by Hannah Arendt; translated by Harry Zohn. New York: Schocken, 1969.

———. "On Some Motifs in Baudelaire." In *Illuminations*, 155–200.

———. "The Storyteller." In *Illuminations*, 83–110.

———. "The Work of Art in the Age of Mechanical Reproduction." In *Illuminations*, 217–52.

Bergson, Henri. *Matière et Mémoire*. Paris: Presses Universitaires de France, 1941.

Bernecker, Sven. *Memory: A Philosophical Study*. Oxford: Oxford University Press, 2009.

Bernstein, Richard J. *Freud and the Legacy of Moses*. Cambridge: Cambridge University Press, 1998.

Blanche, Jacques-Émile. *Manet*. Paris: Rieder, 1924.

———. *Propos de peintre*. Paris: Émile Paul Frères, 1919.

Bloch, Ernst. *Erbschaft dieser Zeit*. Frankfurt am Main: Suhrkamp, 1985.

Blumenberg, Hans. *Arbeit am Mythos*. Frankfurt am Main: Suhrkamp, 1979.

Bolter, Jay David, and Richard Grusin. *Remediation: Understanding New Media*. Cambridge, MA: MIT Press, 2000.

Bourdieu, Pierre. *Distinction: A Social Critique of the Judgment of Taste*. Translated by Richard Nice. London and New York: Routledge. 1984.

———. *Language and Symbolic Power*. Translated by Gino Raymond and Matthew Adamson. Cambridge, MA: Harvard University Press, 1999.

———. *Outline of a Theory of Practice*. Translated by Richard Nice. Cambridge: Cambridge University Press, 1977.

———. *Pascalian Meditations*. Translated by Richard Nice. Stanford, CA: Stanford University Press, 2000.

———. *Sur la télévision suivi de l'empire du journalisme*. Paris: Raisons d'Agir, 1998.

Bourdon, David. *Warhol*. New York: Abrams, 1995.

Braga, Joaquim. *Die symbolische Prägnanz des Bildes: Zu einer Kritik des Bildbegriffs nach der Philosophie Ernst Cassirers*. Freiburg: Centaurus, 2012.

Braudel, Fernand. *La méditerranée et le monde méditerranéen à l'époque de Philippe II*. 3 vols. Paris: Armand Colin, 1990.

Buisson, Jean-Christophe. "Ceca, La Madonna des Balkans." *Figaro Magazine*, 1 March 2003): 50–54.

Burckhardt, Jacob. *Erinnerungen aus Rubens*. Basel: Lendorff, 1898.

Burke, Peter. "History as Social Memory." In *Memory: History, Culture and the Mind*, edited by Thomas Butler, 97–113. Oxford: Blackwell, 1989.

Butler, Samuel. *Unconscious Memory*. London: Fifield, 1910. Orig. pub. 1880.

Campbell, David. "Atrocity, Memory, Photography: Imaging the Concentration Camps of Bosnia—The Case of ITN versus Living Marxism." Part 1. *Journal of Human Rights* 1, no. 1:1–33. Part 2. *Journal of Human Rights* 1, no. 2:143–72.

Casey, Edward S. *Getting Back into Place: Toward a Renewed Understanding of the Place-World*. Bloomington: Indiana University Press, 1993.

———. *Remembering: A Phenomenological Study*. Bloomington: Indiana University Press, 1987.

Cassirer, Ernst. *An Essay on Man: An Introduction to a Philosophy of Human Culture*. New Haven: Yale University Press, 1992.

———. *Philosophie der symbolischen Formen*. 3 vols. Darmstadt: Wissenschaftliche Buchgesellschaft, 1994.

———. *Zur Logik der Kulturwissenschaften*. Darmstadt: Wissenschaftliche Buchgesellschaft, 1961.

Catroga, Fernando. *Memória, história e historiografia*. Coimbra: Quarteto, 2001.

Cavell, Stanley. "The Fact of Television." In "Print Culture and Video Culture," edited by Stephen R. Graubard. Special issue, *Daedalus* 111, no. 4. (1982): 75–96.

———. *The World Viewed: Reflections on the Ontology of Film*. Cambridge, MA: Harvard University Press, 1979.

Chateaubriand, François-René de. *Mémoires d'outre-tombe*. 2 vols. Paris: Gallimard/ Pléiade, 1951.

———. *Mémoires d'outre-tombe*. Vol. 1, edited by Jean-Claude Berchet. Paris: Garnier, 1989.

Chidley, Joe. "The Simpson Jury Faces the Race Factor." *Maclean's* 108, no. 41:69–70.

Coady, C. A. J. *Testimony: A Philosophical Study*. Oxford: Clarendon Press, 1992.

Čolović, Ivan. "Football, Hooligans and War." In *The Politics of the Symbol in Serbia*, 259–86. London: Hurst and Company, 2002.

Compagnon, Antoine. *Proust entre deux siècles*. Paris: Seuil, 1989.

Connerton, Paul. *How Modernity Forgets*. Cambridge: Cambridge University Press, 2009.

———. *How Societies Remember*. Cambridge: Cambridge University Press, 1989.

Costa Lima, Luiz. *Mimesis: Herausforderung an das Denken*. Berlin: Kadmos, 2012.

Croce, Benedetto. *Aesthetic as a Science of Expression and General Linguistic*. Translated by D. Ainslie. London: Macmillan, 1929. Orig. pub. 1902.

———. *Theory and History of Historiography*. Translated by Douglas Ainslie. Colchester: Spottiswoode, Ballantyne, 1921. Orig. pub. 1917.

Davidson, Donald. *Essays on Actions and Events*. Oxford: Clarendon Press, 1980.

Davies, Peter. *The National Front in France: Ideology, Discourse and Power*. London: Routledge, 1999.

Defoe, Daniel. *The Life and Strange Surprizing Adventures of Robinson Crusoe, of York, Mariner*. London: Oxford University Press, 1972.

Detienne, Marcel. "La dette envers les morts." In *L'identité nationale, une énigme*, 49–70. Paris: Gallimard, 2010.

Diderot, Denis. *Œuvres*. Paris: Gallimard/Pléiade, 1951.

Dilthey, Wilhelm. *Der Aufbau der geschichtlichen Welt in den Geisteswissenschaften*. In *Gesammelte Schriften*. Vol. 7. Stuttgart: Teubner, 1973.

Droysen, Johann Gustav. *Historik: Vorlesungen über Enzyklopädie und Methodologie der Geschichte*. Edited by Rudolf Hübner. Munich: Oldenbourg, 1977.

Dulong, Renaud. *Le témoin oculaire: Les conditions sociales de l'attestation personnelle*. Paris: Éditions de l'École des Hautes Etudes en Sciences Sociales, 1998.

Durkheim, Émile. *L'évolution pédagogique en France des origines à la Renaissance*. Introduction by Maurice Halbwachs. Paris, Felix Alcan, 1938.

Edelman, Gerard M. *The Remembered Present: A Biological Theory of Consciousness*. New York: Basic Books, 1989.

Elias, Norbert. *Über den Prozess der Zivilisation*. 2 vols. Frankfurt am Main: Suhrkamp, 2010.

Emden, Christian J. *Friedrich Nietzsche and the Politics of History*. Cambridge: Cambridge University Press, 2008.

Fabre d'Eglantine, Philippe François Nazaire. *L'Evangile des Républicains précédé du Rapport fait par le citoyen Fabre d'Eglantine, sur le nouveau Calendrier décrété par la Convention Nationale*. Paris: Lallemand, An deuxième de la République Française.

Farocki, Haroun, and Ujică Andrei. *Videograms of a Revolution*. Documentary film. Bremen: Bremer Institut Film und Fernsehen, Facets Video DVD, 1992.

Fassin, Didier. *When Bodies Remember: Experiences and Politics of AIDS in South Africa*. Translated by Amy Jacobs and Gabrielle Varro. Berkeley: University of California Press, 2007.

Feuer, Jane. "The Concept of Live Television: Ontology as Ideology." In *Regarding Television: Critical Approaches—An Anthology*, edited by Ann E. Kaplan, 12–21. Frederick, MD: University Publications of America, 1983.

Freud, Sigmund. *Beyond the Pleasure Principle*. In Freud, *Complete Psychological Works*, 18 (1955):7–64.

———. *The Future of an Illusion*. In Freud, *Complete Psychological Works*, 21 (1961): 5–58.

———. "Group Psychology and the Analysis of the Ego." In Freud, *Complete Psychological Works*, 18 (1955): 65–144.

———. *The Interpretation of Dreams*, pt. 1. In Freud, *Complete Psychological Works*, 4 (1953): xi–310.

———. *Moses and Monotheism*. In Freud, *Complete Psychological Works*, 23 (1964): 6–208.

———. "On Narcissism: An Introduction" (1914). In Freud, *Complete Psychological Works*, 14 (1957): 72–102.

———. "Remembering, Repeating, Working Through" In *Complete Psychological Works*, 12 (1958): 145–56.

———. "Screen Memories." In *Complete Psychological Works*3 (1962): 300–321.

———. *The Standard Edition of the Complete Psychological Works of Sigmund Freud.* Translated by James Strachey. 24 vols. London: The Hogarth Press and the Institute of Psychoanalysis, 1953–74.

———. "The Unconscious" (1915). In Freud, *Complete Psychological Works*, 14 (1957): 159–215. (Appendix A, "Freud and Ewald Hering").

Friguglietti, James. "The Social and Religious Consequences of the French Revolutionary Calendar." PhD diss., Harvard University, 1966.

Gautier, Théophile. *Les beaux-arts et l'Europe.* 2 vols. Paris: Lévy Frères, 1855.

Geary, Patrick, J. *Phantoms of Remembrance: Memory and Oblivion at the End of the First Millennium.* Princeton, NJ: Princeton University Press, 1994.

Gensburger, Sarah, and Marie-Claire Lavabre. "Entre 'devoir de mémoire' et 'abus de mémoire': La sociologie de la mémoire collective comme tierce position." In *L'histoire entre mémoire et épistémologie: Autour de Paul Ricœur*, edited by Bertrand Müller, 75–98. Lausanne: Payot/Lausanne, 2005.

Gerhardt, Volker. *Öffentlichkeit: Die politische Form des Bewusstseins.* Munich: Beck, 2012.

Germer, Stefan. *Historizität und Autonomie: Studien zu Wandbildern in Frankreich des 19. Jahrhunderts.* Hildesheim: Olms, 1988.

Goethe, Johann Wolfgang von. *Conversations with Eckermann and Soret.* Translated by John Oxenford. New York: M. W. Dunne, 1901.

———. *Eckermann Gespräche mit Goethe in den letzten Jahren seines Lebens.* Frankfurt am Main: Insel, 1987.

Goldberg, Chad Alan. "Struggle and Solidarity: Civic Republican Elements in Pierre Bourdieu's Political Sociology." *Theory and Society* 42, no. 4: 369–94.

Goodman, Nelson. "Routes of Reference," *Critical Inquiry* 1, no. 1: 121–32.

———. *Ways of World-Making.* Indianapolis, IN: Hackett, 1978.

Gossmann, Lionel. *Between History and Literature.* Cambridge, MA: Harvard University Press, 1990.

———. *Towards a Rational Historiography.* Philadelphia, PA: American Philosophical Society, 1989.

Guter, Evan. "Anti-Mimesis Live." In *Television: Aesthetic Reflections*, edited by Ruth Lorand, 139–60. New York: Peter Lang, 2002.

Halbwachs, Maurice. *Les cadres sociaux de la mémoire.* Paris: Albin Michel, 1994.

———. *La mémoire collective.* Paris: Albin Michel, 1997.

———. *The Psychology of Social Class.* Translated by Claire Delavenay. Glencoe, IL: Free Press, 1958. Orig. pub. 1938.

Hansen, Drew D. *The Dream: Martin Luther King, Jr., and the Speech that Inspired a Nation.* New York: Harper/Collins, 2003.

Harari, Yuval Noah. "Scholars, Eyewitnesses, and Flesh-Witnesses of War: A Tense

Relationship." In "Eyewitness Narratives," edited by Leona Toker. Special issue, *Partial Answers* 7, no. 2 (2009): 213–28.

Hartog, François. *Régimes d'historicité: Présentisme et expériences du temps*. Paris:
Seuil, 2003.

Hayden, John O., ed. *Walter Scott: The Critical Heritage*. London: Routledge,
1970.

Hegel, G. W. F. *Phänomenologie des Geistes*. Vol. 3 of *Werke*. Frankfurt am Main:
Suhrkamp, 1970.

———. *Vorlesungen über die Ästhetik*. 3 vols. Vols. 13, 14, and 15 of *Werke*. Frankfurt
am Main: Suhrkamp, 1986.

———. *Vorlesungen über die Geschichte der Philosophie*. 3 vols. Vols. 18, 19, and 20 of
Werke. Frankfurt am Main: Suhrkamp, 1986.

Heidegger, Martin. "Einleitung in die Phänomenologie der Religion" (1920–21). In
Phänomenologie des religiösen Lebens, vol. 60 of *Gesamtausgabe*. Frankfurt am
Main: Klostermann, 1995.

———. *Kant und das Problem der Metaphysik* (1929). Vol. 3 of *Gesamtausgabe*.
Frankfurt am Main: Klostermann, 2010.

———. *Metaphysische Anfangsgründe der Logik im Ausgang vom Leibniz* (1928).
Vol. 26 of *Gesamtausgabe*. Frankfurt am Main: Klostermann, 1978.

———. *Sein und Zeit*. Tübingen: Niemeyer, 1972. Orig. pub. 1927.

———. *Überlegungen II–VI (Schwarze Hefte 1931–1938)*. Vol. 94 of *Gesamtausgabe*.
Frankfurt am Main: Klostermann, 2014.

———. *Überlegungen, VII—XI (Schwarze Hefte 1938/39)*. Vol. 95 of *Gesamtausgabe*.
Frankfurt am Main: Klostermann, 2014.

———. *Überlegungen XII–XV (Schwarze Hefte 1939–1941)*. Vol. 96 of *Gesamtausgabe*.
Frankfurt am Main: Klostermann, 2014.

Held, Klaus. *Lebendige Gegenwart: Die Frage nach der Seinsweise des transzendenta-
len Ich bei Edmund Husserl, entwickelt am Leitfaden der Zeitproblematik*. Den
Haag: Martinus Nijhoff, 1966.

Hering, Ewald. *Über das Gedächtnis als eine allgemeine Funktion der organischen
Materie* (1870). Leipzig: Akademische Verlagsgesellschaft, 1921.

Hoins, Katharina. *Medien als Material der Kunst*. Berlin: Reimer, 2015.

Hugo, Victor. *Notre-Dame de Paris*. Paris: Livre de Poche, 1998; anonymous English
translation, *The Hunchback of Notre Dame*. New York: Alfred A. Knopf/Every-
man's Library, 2012.

Hume, David. *A Treatise of Human Nature*. Edited by Ernest C. Mossner. Harmondsworth: Penguin, 1969.

Husserl, Edmund. *Die Bernauer Manuskripte über das Zeitbewusstsein, (1917/18)*. In
Husserliana, vol. 33, edited by Rudolf Bernet and Dieter Lohmar. Dordrecht:
Kluwer, 2001.

———. *Cartesian Meditations: An Introduction to Phenomenology*. Translated by
Dorian Cairns. The Hague: Martinus Nijhoff, 1977.

———. *Erfahrung und Urteil: Untersuchungen zur Genealogie der Logik.* Hamburg: Meiner, 1985.

———. *Prolegomena zur reinen Logik: Logische Untersuchungen.* Vol. 2 of *Werke.* Meiner: Hamburg, 1992.

———. *Zur Phänomenologie der Intersubjektivität: Texte aus dem Nachlaß.* Part 2, 1921–28. In *Husserliana,* vol. 14, edited by Iso Kern. Den Haag: Martinus Nijhoff, 1973.

Hutton, Patrick, H. *History as an Art of Memory.* Hanover, NH: University Press of New England, 1993.

Huyssen, Andreas. "Present Pasts: Media, Politics, Amnesia." *Public Culture* 12, no. 1 (2000): 21–38.

———. *Twilight Memories: Marking Time in a Culture of Amnesia.* New York: Routledge, 1995.

Imdahl, Max. *Gesammelte Schriften.* Vol. 3. *Reflexion, Theorie, Methode.* Edited by Gottfried Boehm. Frankfurt am Main: Suhrkamp, 1996.

Iser, Wolfgang. *Der Implizite Leser.* Munich: Fink, 1972.

Jackson, Mason. *The Illustrated Press: Its Origin and Progress.* London: Hurst and Blackett, 1885.

Jones, Catherine. *Literary Memory: Scott's Waverly Novels and the Psychology of Narrative.* Lewisburg, PA: Bucknell University Press, 2003.

Kannsteiner, Wulf. "Finding Meaning in Memory: A Methodological Critique of Collective Memory Studies." *History and Theory* 41 (May 2002): 179–97.

Kearney, Richard. *On Stories.* London: Routledge, 2002.

———. *Poetics of Imagining: From Husserl to Lyotard.* London: Harper Collins Academic, 1991.

Kemp, Martin. *Christ to Coke: How Image Becomes Icon.* Oxford: Oxford University Press, 2011.

King, Martin Luther, Jr. *Autobiography.* Edited by Clayborne Carsen. New York: Warner Books, 2001.

Klein, Kerwin Lee. "On the Emergence of Memory in Historical Discourse." *Representations* 69 (Winter 2000): 127–50.

Koselleck, Reinhart. "Anmerkungen zum Revolutionskalender und zur 'neuen Zeit.'" In *Die Französische Revolution als Bruch des gesellschaftlichen Bewusstseins,* edited by Reinhart Koselleck and Rolf Reichart, 61–64. Munich: Oldenbourg, 1988.

———. "Fiktion und geschichtliche Wirklichkeit." *Zeitschrift für Ideengeschichte: Die Rückkehr der Wahrheit* 1, no. 3 (2007): 39–54.

———. *Vergangene Zukunft: Zur Semantik geschichtlicher Zeiten.* Frankfurt am Main: Suhrkamp, 1979.

Kozloff, Max. "Lichtenstein at the Guggenheim." *Artforum* 8, no. 3 (1969); reprinted in Graham Bader, ed., *Roy Lichtenstein,* 7–16. Cambridge, MA: October Files/ MIT Press, 2009.

Krell, David Farrell. *Of Memory, Reminiscence, and Writing: On the Verge.* Bloomington: University of Indiana Press, 1990.

Krieger, Leonard. *Ranke: The Meaning of History.* Chicago: University of Chicago Press, 1977.

Landsberg, Alison. *Prosthetic Memory: The Transformation of American Remembrance in the Age of Mass Culture.* New York: Columbia University Press, 2004.

Lecomte, Romain. "Internet et la reconfiguration de l'espace public tunisien: Le rôle de la diaspora." *Tic et société* 3, no. 1 (2009): 198–229.

Léger, Fernand. "Les réalisations picturales actuelles" (Contemporary achievements in painting). In *Fonctions de la peinture*, 20–29. Paris: Gonthier, 1965.

Leibniz, G. W. *Nouveaux essais sur l'entendement humain.* Vol. 5 of *Die philosophischen Schriften*, edited by C. J. Gerhardt. Hildesheim: Olms, 1978.

Le Pen, Jean-Marie. "Entendez le chant du peuple français," *Présent*, 5 September 1996, 7.

———. "La mémoire et l'espérance." *La Lettre de Jean-Marie Le Pen*, no. 146 (November 1991), 1–2.

———. "Le discours de Jean-Marie Le Pen au Palais des Congrès de Paris" (23 January 1991). *Présent*, no. 2249 (28–29 January 1991): 7.

———. "Le discours de La Trinité: Démarxiser La France." *Présent*, no. 2396 (30 August, 1991): 7–8.

———. *Les Français d'abord.* Mesnil-sur-l'Estrée: Carrère-Michel Lafon, 1984.

Le Pen, Marine. *Pour que vive la France.* Paris: Grancher, 2012.

Lessing, Theodor. *Die Geschichte als Sinngebung des Sinnlosen.* Hamburg: Rütten und Loening Verlag, 1962.

Lichtenstein, Roy. "An Interview with Roy Lichtenstein." In *Roy Lichtenstein: Graphic Work, 1970–1980.* Whitney Museum of Art Downtown Branch, Catalogue, 1981, unpaginated.

———. "What Is Pop Art? Answers from Eight Painters, Part 1: Jim Dine, Robert Indiana, Roy Lichtenstein, Andy Warhol." Interview with G. R. Swenson, *ARTnews* 62, no. 7 (1963): 24–25.

Liu, Sarah. "The Illiterate Reader: Aphasia after Auschwitz." In "Eyewitness Narratives," edited by Leona Toker. Special issue, *Partial Answers* 7, no. 2 (2009): 319–42.

Locke, John. *An Essay Concerning Human Understanding.* Harmondsworth: Penguin, 1997.

Lotan, Gilad, Erhardt Graeff, Mike Ananny, Devin Gaffney, Ian Pearce, and Danah Boyd. "The Revolutions Were Tweeted: Information Flows During the 2011 Tunisian and Egyptian Revolutions." *International Journal of Communications* 5 (2011): 1375–1405.

Lowenthal, David. *The Past Is a Foreign Country.* Cambridge: Cambridge University Press, 1985.

Ludes, Peter. *Multimedia und Multimoderne. Schlüsselbilder: Fernsehen und World*

Wide Web—Medienzivilisierung in der europäischen Währungsunion. Wiesbaden: Westdeutscher Verlag, 2001.

Luhmann, Niklas. *Die Realität der Massenmedien*. Wiesbaden: Vs Verlag, 2004.

Macchiavelli, Niccolò. *The Prince*. Edited by Quentin Skinner and Russell Price. Cambridge: Cambridge University Press, 1988.

Manzoni, Alessandro. *The Betrothed*. Translated by Bruce Penman. Harmondsworth: Penguin, 1984.

Margalit, Avishai. *The Ethics of Memory*. Cambridge, MA: Harvard University Press, 2002.

Marker, Chris. "Détour, Ceaucescu." In *Zapping Zone, Proposals for an Imaginary Television*. 1990–94. Chris Marker Archive, Musée national d'art moderne, Centre Georges Pompidou Paris, inventory number, AM-1990 160.

Matsuda, Matt K. *The Memory of the Modern*. New York, Oxford: Oxford University Press, 1996.

Mauss, Marcel. "Les techniques du corps" (1934). In *Sociologie et Anthropologie*, 365–86. Paris: Presses Universitaires de France, 1983.

——. *Oeuvres*. 3 vols. Paris: Editions de minuit, 1968–1969.

Mégret, Bruno. "La France et son peuple." *La Lettre de Jean-Marie Le Pen*, no. 127 (15 December 1990), 3.

Mendels, Doron. *Memory in Jewish, Pagan and Christian Societies of the Graeco-Roman World*. London/New York: Continuum and T and T Clark International, 2004.

——, ed. *On Memory: An Interdisciplinary Approach*. Frankfurt am Main: Peter Lang, 2007.

Michalski, Milena, and James Gow. *War, Image, and Legitimacy: Viewing Contemporary Conflict*. Oxon: Routledge, 2007.

Michelet, Jules. *Histoire de la Révolution Française*. 9 vols. Paris: Abel Pilon, 1883.

Millet, Richard. *Langue fantôme: Essai sur la paupérisation de la littérature suivi de Éloge littéraire de d'Anders Breivik*. Paris: Pierre-Guillaume de Roux, 2012.

Mondrian, Piet. "La nouvelle plastique dans la peinture." *De Stijl* 1 (October 1917); republished in Michel Seuphor, *Dictionnaire de la peinture abstraite*. Paris: F. Hazan, 1957.

Moore, Gregory. *Nietzsche, Biology, and Metaphor*. Cambridge: Cambridge University Press, 2002.

Nietzsche, Friedrich. *Aus dem Nachlass der Achzigerjahre: Briefe (1861–89)*. Edited by Karl Schlechta. Vol. 4 of *Werke*. Frankfurt am Main: Ullstein 1979.

——. *Die Geburt der Tragödie*. Vol. 3 of *Kritische Gesamtausgabe*, edited by Giorgio Colli and Mazzino Montinari, pt. 1. Berlin: Walter de Gruyter, 1972.

——. *Jenseits von Gut und Böse*. Vol. 6 of *Kritische Gesamtausgabe*, edited by Giorgio Colli and Mazzino Montinari, pt. 2. Berlin: Walter de Gruyter, 1968.

——. *Nachgelassene Fragmente: Frühjahr—Herbst 1884*. Vol. 7 of *Kritische Gesamt-*

ausgabe, edited by Giorgio Colli and Mazzino Montenari, pt. 2. Berlin: Walter de Gruyter, 1974.

———. *Unzeitgemässe Betrachtungen I–III.* Vol. 3 of *Kritische Gesamtausgabe*, edited by Giorgio Colli and Mazzino Montinari, pt. 1. Berlin: Walter de Gruyter, 1972.

———. *Vom Nutzen und Nachteil der Historie für das Leben.* In *Unzeitgemässe Betrachtungen* II. Vol. 3 of *Kritische Gesamtausgabe*, edited by Giorgio Colli and Mazzino Montenari, pt. 1, 292. Berlin: Walter de Gruyter, 1972.

———. *Zur Genealogie der Moral, 1886–1887.* Vol. 6 of *Kritische Gesamtausgabe*, edited by Giorgio Colli and Mazzino Montinari, pt. 2. Berlin: Walter de Gruyter, 1968.

Nora, Pierre. "L'avènement mondial de la mémoire." *Transit*, no. 22 (19 April 2002): 1–8.

———. "Entre mémoire et histoire: La problématique des lieux." Introduction to *Les lieux de mémoire*, vol. 1, *La République*. Paris: Gallimard, 1984, xv–xlii.

———. "Introduction." In *Les lieux de mémoire*. Vol. 3, *Les Traditions*, pt. 2. Paris: Gallimard, 1992.

———. "Liberté pour l'histoire!" *Le Monde*, 10 October 2008.

———. "Malaise dans l'identité historique." In *Liberté pour l'histoire*, by Pierre Nora and Françoise Chandernagor, 11–24. Paris: Editions du CNRS, 2008.

Nuzzo, Angelica. *Memory, History, Justice in Hegel.* Basingstoke, Hampshire, UK: Palgrave-Macmillan, 2012.

Olick, Jeffrey K. "Collective Memory: The Two Cultures." *Sociological Theory* 17, no. 3 (1999): 333–48.

Olick, Jeffrey K., Vered Vinitzky-Seroussi, and Daniel Levy. *The Collective Memory Reader.* Oxford: Oxford University Press, 2011.

Panofsky, Erwin. *Gothic Architecture and Scholasticism.* Latrobe, PA: Archabbey Press, 1951.

Paul, Gerhard. *Bildermacht: Studien zur Visual History des 20. und 21. Jahrhunderts.* Göttingen: Wallstein, 2013.

Petit, Philip. *The Common Mind: An Essay on Psychology, Society, and Politics.* Oxford: Oxford University Press, 1996.

Petrović, Edit. "Ethnonationalism and the Dissolution of Yugoslavia." In *Neighbors at War: Anthropological Perspectives on Yugoslav Ethnicity, Culture, and History*, edited by Joel Martin Halpern and David A. Kideckel, 164–86. State College, PA: Penn State University Press, 2000.

Petrovszky, Konrad, and Ovidiu Tichindeleanu. "Capital, Politics, and Media Technology: Making sense of the Romanian Revolution" In *Romanian Revolution Televised: Contributions to the Cultural History of Media.* Cluj, Romania: Idea Design and Print, 2011.

Plato. *Phaedo.* Translated by Harold N. Fowler. In *Euthyphro, Apology, Crito, Phaedo, Phaedrus.* Vol. 1 of *Works.* Cambridge, MA: Harvard University Press; London: W. Heinemann/Loeb Classical Library, 1977.

Plato. *Phaedrus*. Translated by Harold N. Fowler. In *Euthyphro, Apology, Crito, Phaedo, Phaedrus*. Vol. 1 of *Works*. Cambridge, MA: Harvard University Press; London: Heinemann/Loeb Classical Library, 1977.

Plessner, Helmuth. "Grenzen der Gemeinschaft: Eine Kritik des sozialen Radikalismus (1924)." In *Gesammelte Schriften*. Vol. 5. *Macht und menschliche Natur*. Frankfurt am Main: Suhrkamp, 1981, 11–133.

———. "Über die gesellschaftlichen Bedingungen der modernen Malerei (1965): Ernst Bloch zum achtzigsten Geburtstag." In *Gesammelte Schriften*. Vol. 10. *Schriften zur Soziologie und Sozialphilosophie*. 265–84. Frankfurt am Main: Suhrkamp, 1981.

Postman, Neil. *Amusing Ourselves to Death: Public Discourse in the Age of Show Business*. New York: Penguin, 2006.

Postman, Neil, and Steve Powers. *How to Watch TV News*. London: Penguin, 2008.

Proust, Marcel. "Après la Guerre." In *Contre Sainte-Beuve précédé de Pastiches et mélanges et suivi de Essais et articles*. Paris: Gallimard/Pléiade, 1971.

———. *Correspondance*. 21 vols. Edited by Philip Kolb. Paris: Plon, 1970–1991.

———. "Preface." In *Propos de peintre*, by Jacques-Émile Blanche. Paris: Émile Paul Frères, 1919.

———. *Du côté de chez Swann. À l'ombre des jeunes filles en fleurs*. In *À la recherche du temps perdu*. Vol. 1. Paris: Gallimard/Pléiade, 1954.

———. *Le Côté de Guermantes. Sodomme et Gomorrhe*. In *À la recherche du temps perdu*. Vol. 2. Paris: Gallimard/Pléiade, 1954.

———. *La Prisonnière. La Fugitive. Le Temps retrouvé*. In *À la recherche du temps perdu*. Vol. 3. Paris: Gallimard/Pléiade, 1954.

Quine, Wilfred. *Quiddities*. Cambridge, MA: Belknap Press, 1987.

Ranke, Leopold von. "Diktat vom November 1885." In *Sämtliche Werke*, vols. 53/54, edited by A. Dove, 61. Leipzig: Dunker und Humblot, 1890.

Raulff, Ulrich. *Der unsichtbare Augenblick: Zeitkonzepte in der Geschichte*. Göttingen: Wallstein, 1999.

Rauschenberg, Robert. "Notes on Stoned Moon Lithographic Project (28 October 1969)." *Studio International* (London) 178, no. 917 (1969): 246–47.

Renan, Ernest. *L'avenir de la science: Pensées de 1848*Paris: Calmann-Lévy, 1905.

———. *Qu'est-ce qu'une nation? et autres essais politiques*. Paris: Agora, 1992.

Reynolds, Sir Joshua. *Discourses Delivered to Students of the Royal Academy* (1780). 3 vols. In *Works*, vols. 1 and 2, 1–218.

———. "Annotations on Du Fresnoy's Poem." In *Works*, 3:93–196.

———. "Journey to Flanders and Holland in the year 1781." In *Works*, 2:245–427.

———. The *Works of Sir Joshua Reynolds, Knight; Late President of the Royal Academy*. 3 vols. London: T. Cadell Jr. and W. Davies, 1801.

Ricœur, Paul. "L'écriture de l'histoire et la representation du passé." *Le Monde*, 14 June 2000.

——. *Freud and Philosophy: An Essay on Interpretation*. Translated by Denis Savage. New Haven, CT: Yale University Press, 1970.

——. *Memory, History, Forgetting*. Translated by Kathleen Blamey and David Pellauer. Chicago: University of Chicago Press. 2004.

——. *Oneself as Another*. Translated by Kathleen Blamey. Chicago: University of Chicago Press, 1992.

——. *The Reality of the Historical Past*. Milwaukee, WI: Marquette University Press, 1984.

——. *Time and Narrative*. 3 vols. Translated by Kathleen Blamey and David Pellauer. Chicago: University of Chicago Press, 1984–88.

Rigney, Ann. *The Afterlives of Walter Scott: Memory on the Move*. Oxford: Oxford University Press, 2012.

Rochlitz, Rainer. *Le Vif de la critique*. Vol. 3 of *Philosophie contemporaine*. Brussels: La Lettre volée, 2010.

——. "La mémoire privatisée," *Le Monde*, 26 June 2000.

Rousseau, Jean-Jacques. *Émile ou l'éducation*. Paris: Garnier/Flammarion, 1966.

Runia, Eelco. *Moved by the Past: Discontinuity and Historical Mutation*. New York: Columbia University Press, 2014.

Rüsen, Jorn. *Lebendige Geschichte: Grundzüge einer Historik*. Vol. 3. Göttingen: Vandenhoeck und Ruprecht, 1989.

Ruskin, John. *Modern Painters*. 5 vols. Vols. 3–7 of *The Complete Works of John Ruskin*, edited by E. T. Cook and Alexander Wedderburn. London: George Allen, 1903–5.

Schäfer, Hermann, ed. *Bilder, die Lügen*. Bonn: Bouvier, 1998.

Schopenhauer, Arthur. *Die Welt als Wille und Vorstellung*. Zürich, Diogenes, 1977.

Schwitters, Kurt. *Das literarische Werk*. 5 vols. Edited by Friedhelm Lach. Cologne: Dumont/Schauberg, 1998.

Scott, John. *Journal of a Tour to Waterloo and Paris in Company with Walter Scott in 1815*. London: Saunders and Otley, 1842.

Scott, Walter. *The Antiquary*. Edited by David Hewitt. Vol. 3 of *Edinburgh Edition of the Waverly Novels*. Edinburgh: Edinburgh University Press; New York: Columbia University Press, 1995.

——. *Biographical Memoirs*. 2 vols. Vols. 3 and 4 of *The Miscellaneous Prose Works of Walter Scott*. Edinburgh: Cadell, 1834.

——. *Ivanhoe*. Edited by Graham Tulloch. Vol. 8 of *Edinburgh Edition of the Waverly Novels*. Edinburgh: Edinburgh University Press; New York: Columbia University Press, 1998.

——. *The Journal of Walter Scott from the Original Manuscript*. 2 vols. New York: Harper Brothers, 1890.

——. *Life of Napoleon Buonaparte with a Preliminary View of the French Revolution*. 8 vols. Vols. 8–15 of *The Miscellaneous Prose Works of Sir Walter Scott*. Edinburgh: Cadell, 1834.

———. *Old Mortality*. Harmondsworth: Penguin, 1995.

———. *Waverly; or, 'Tis Sixty Years Since*. Edited by Claire Lamont. Oxford: Oxford University Press.

Sebald, W. G. *Austerlitz*. Translated by Anthea Bell. Harmondsworth: Penguin, 2001.

Sepper, Dennis L. *Descartes's Imagination: Proportion, Images, and the Activity of Thinking*. Berkeley: University of California Press, 1996.

Seuphor, Michel. *Dictionnaire de la peinture abstraite*. Paris: F. Hazan, 1957.

Sévigné, Marie de Rabutin-Chantal, Marquise de. *Correspondance*. 3 vols. Edited by Roger Duchêne. Paris: Gallimard/Pléiade, 1972.

Simmel, Georg. *The Philosophy of Money*. Translated by Tom Bottomore and David Frisby. London: Routledge and Kegan Paul, 1978.

Smerling, Walter, ed. *Art and Press: Kunst, Wahrheit, Wirklichkeit*. Bonn: Weinand/ Stiftung für Kunst und Kultur, 2012.

Smith, Lamar. Statement at the Congressional Hearing before the Committee on the Judiciary House of Representatives, First Session of the One Hundred and Tenth Congress of the United States on H. R. 2128, *Sunshine in the Courtroom Act of 2007*, document serial number 110–160, Sept. 27th, 2007. Washington: U.S. Government Printing Office, 2009.

Sorabji, Richard. *Aristotle on Memory*. London: Duckworth, 2004.

Souchard, Maryse, Stéphane Wahnich, Isabelle Cuminal, and Virginie Wathier. *Le Pen, les mots: Analyse d'un discours d'extrême droite*. Paris: La Découverte, 1998.

Stanišić, Saša. *Wie der Soldat das Grammofon Repariert*. Munich: Luchterhand, 2006.

Sternhell, Zeev. *Maurice Barrès et le nationalisme français*. Vol. 1 of *La France entre nationalisme et fascisme*. 3 vols. Paris: Fayard, 2000.

Taine, Hippolyte. *Essais de critique et d'histoire*. Paris: Hachette, 1892.

———. *Histoire de la littérature anglaise*. 5 vols. Paris: Hachette, 1864.

———. *L'Ancien régime*. Vol. 1 of *Les Origines de la France contemporaine*. Paris: Hachette , 1891.

———. *Le gouvernement révolutionnaire*. Vol. 3 of *La Révolution*. In *Les Origines de la France contemporaine*, part 2. Paris: Hachette, 1892.

———. *La philosophie de l'art*. Paris: Fayard, 1985.

Taubira, Christiane. "Mémoire, histoire et droit." *Le Monde*, 16 October 2008.

Terdiman, Richard. *Present Past: Modernity and the Memory Crisis*. Ithaca, NY: Cornell University Press, 1993.

Thierry, Augustin. *Lettres sur l'histoire de France*. Vol. 5 of *Oeuvres Complètes*. Paris: Furne, 1846.

Thomas, Robert. *Serbia under Milosevic: Politics in the 1990s*. London: Hurst, 1999.

Thompson, John B. *The Media and Modernity A Social Theory of the Media*. Cambridge: Polity Press, 1995.

Tocqueville, Alexis de. *De la démocratie en Amérique*. 2 vols. Paris: Gallimard/Folio, 1961.

Todorov, Tzvetan. *Les abus de la mémoire*. Paris: Arléa, 1995.

Toscani, Oliviero. *La Pub est une charogne qui nous sourit*. Paris: Hoëbeke, 1995.

Valéry, Paul. "La conquête de l'ubiquité." In *Pièces sur l'art*. Vol. 2 of *Oeuvres*, 1283–87. Paris: Gallimard/Pléiade, 1960.

Verene, Donald Phillip. *Hegel's Recollection: A Study of Images in the Phenomenology of Spirit*. Albany: SUNY Press, 1985.

———. *Philosophy and the Return to Self-Knowledge*. New Haven, CT: Yale University Press, 1997.

Wagner, Georges-Paul. "Il y a un siècle, Barrès et Maurras ont forgé notre langage: 'Nationalisme,' 'enracinement,' 'décentralisation.'" *Présent*, no. 2398 (2–3 September 1991).

Waldman, Diane. *Roy Lichtenstein*. New York: Solomon Guggenheim Museum, 1993.

Warburg, Aby. "Heidnisch-antike Weissagung in Wort und Bild zu Luthers Zeiten (1920)." In *Werke*, 424–94. Frankfurt am Main: Suhrkamp, 2010.

White, Hayden. *The Content of the Form: Narrative Discourse and Historical Representation*. Baltimore, MD: Johns Hopkins University Press, 1987.

———. *Metahistory: The Historical Imagination in 19th-Century Europe*. Baltimore, MD: Johns Hopkins University Press, 1975.

———. *Tropics of Discourse: Essays in Cultural Criticism*. Baltimore, MD: Johns Hopkins University Press, 1986.

Wicker, Tom. "A Reporter Must Trust His Instinct." *Saturday Review*, 11 January 1964, 81–82, 86.

Winock, Michel. *Nationalisme, antisémitisme et fascisme en France*. Paris: Seuil, 1990.

Winter, Jay. *Remembering War: The Great War between Memory and History in the Twentieth Century*. New Haven, CT: Yale University Press, 2006.

Yoshikawa, Kazuyoshi. "Elstir: Ses aperges et son chapeau haut-de-forme." In *Proust et ses peintres*, edited by Sophie Bertho, 87–94. Amsterdam/Atlanta, GA: Rodopi, 2000.

Young, James. *The Texture of Memory: Holocaust Memorials and Meaning*. New Haven, CT: Yale University Press. 1993.

Zerubavel, Eviatar. *Hidden Rhythms: Schedules and Calendars in Social Life*. Berkeley: University of California Press, 1981.

Zerubavel, Yael. *Recovered Roots: Collective Memory and the Making of Israeli National Tradition*. Chicago: University of Chicago Press, 1995.

Zelizer, Barbie. *Covering the Body: The Kennedy Assassination, the Media, and the Shaping of Collective Memory*. Chicago: University of Chicago Press, 1993.

Ziff, Trisha. *Che Guevara: Revolutionary and Icon*. New York: Abrams Image, 2006.

Zimmermann, Tanja. "Semmeln in Rožna dolina: Eine Erinnerung aus Ljubljana und die Kriegsbilder aus Bosnien." In *Traumata der Transition: Erfahrung und Reflexion des jugoslawischen Zerfalls*, edited by Boris Previšić and Svjetlan Lacko Vidulić, 91–116. Tübingen: Narr/Francke/Attempto Verlag, 2015.

Zouari, Khaled. "Le rôle et l'impact des TIC dans la révolution tunisienne." *Hermès, La Revue* 2, no. 66 (2013): 239–45.

Zveržhanovski, Ivan. "Watching War Crimes: The Srebrenica Video and the Serbian Attitudes to the 1995 Srebrenica Massacre." *Southeast European and Black Sea Studies* 7, no. 3 (2007): 417–30.

INDEX

Abramson, Albert, 235n42

Adams, Ansel, 140

Adams, Eddie, 141

aesthetic sense, 125, 149

Alexander, Jeffrey C., 228–29n25

Ali, Mohammed, 137

Alighieri, Dante, 35

Amselfeld (site of battle of Kosovo), 104, 228n24

Anderson, Benedict, 44

Andrić, Ivo, 103–4; *The Bridge on the Drina*, 103–4

Ankersmit, Frank, 226n20

Antietam, Battle of, 130

aphasia, 43

apperception, analogical, 73–74

Arendt, Hannah, 225n12, 242n74

Aristotle, 1, 4–6, 8, 26, 28, 46, 94–97, 105, 219n6, 223n11

Arkan. *See* Ražnatović, Željko

Arnella, Peter, 166, 237n64

Arp, Jean, 131

Art and Press (art exhibition), 233n22

arts, visual, 124–25, 127–28, 130–31, 133–36, 144, 148–49, 185–87, 196–201, 233nn20–23, 233n29, 234n39, 241n69

Assmann, Aleida, 173–74, 226n18, 238n10

Assmann, Jan, 173–75, 219n1

Atget, Eugène, 140

Auerbach, Erich, 240n24

Augustine of Hippo, Saint, 219

Aulard, François Victor Alphonse, 99

Austro-Hungarian Empire, 104

Avant-Garde, Russian, 131

Baczko, Bronislaw, 228n12

Badinter, Robert, 164–65

Balkan wars of the 1990s, 104–5, 154, 162–64, 236n59

Ballantyne, Andrew, 234n38

Balzac, Honoré de, 34

Barbie, Klaus, 164–65

Barrès, Maurice, 106–8, 112, 229n26, 229n28, 229n30, 229–30n33, 230n35; *L'appel au soldat*, 106, 112; *Leurs figures*, 112

Barry, Jeanne Bécu, comtesse du, 194

Barthes, Roland, 160, 176, 178–82, 224n3, 234n33, 238–39n14, 239n18, 239n21

Baudelaire, Charles, 127–28, 232n17

Beatles (rock group), 133–34

Ben Ali, Zine el-Abidine, 154

Benetton (clothing manufacturer), 144

Benjamin, Walter, 2, 29–31, 65, 80–81, 96, 129, 222n57, 231n4